THE author of this commentary has tried to base his interpretation—or rather the different possible interpretations suggested by him—on a careful analysis of the general structure of the *Tractatus*, of the terminology used in it and of the interrelations between its different statements. He claims that the result shows that a great many of the things said by adherents or adversaries of, for instance, Wittgenstein's picture theory of language are founded on misunderstandings.

The book, however, not only gives an analysis of what the author regards as Wittgenstein's main lines of thought, but also examines critically the theories and ideas involved. The book should, therefore, be of interest to everyone interested in the relation between language and reality whether or not he is also interested to know which are the particular views taken by the young Wittgenstein.

# WITTGENSTEIN'S TRACTATUS

# WITTGENSTEIN'S TRACTATUS

## A CRITICAL EXPOSITION OF ITS MAIN LINES OF THOUGHT

By

### ERIK STENIUS

*Professor of Philosophy at Abo Academy, Finland*

CORNELL UNIVERSITY PRESS
ITHACA, NEW YORK,
1960

# CONTENTS

CHAPTER                                                             PAGE

## I. THE STRUCTURE OF THE TRACTATUS . 1

1. The Formulated Principle of the Numbering . . 3
2. The Main Line of Thought of the Tractatus . . 5
3. Comments and Preambles . . . . . 7
4. The Sentence as a 'Picture' and as a 'Truth-function' . 10
5. The Preparation for the Necessity of Silence . . 12
6. The Comments on the Comments . . . . 14

## II. THE WORLD AS A FACT . . . . 18

1. Can the World Meaningfully be said to be the Totality of Facts? . . . . . . . . . 18
2. Categories . . . . . . . . 20
3. Enigmatic 'Things' . . . . . . 23
4. The Structure of the Field of Perception . . . 23
5. The Organization of the 'World Field' . . . 26

## III. THE CONCEPT OF A *SACHVERHALT* . 29

1. All *Sachverhalte* are not *Tatsachen* . . . 29
2. *Sachverhalte* are 'Atomic' . . . . . 32
3. *Sachverhalte* are Independent of One Another . . 33
4. *Sachlage* and *Tatsache* . . . . . . 34
5. Summary . . . . . . . . 36

## IV. LOGICAL SPACE . . . . . . 38

1. A Model of a 'Logical Structure' of the World . . 38
2. 'Logical Space' . . . . . . . 42
3. Yes-and-no Dimensions . . . . . 44

v

4. Is Every Logical Space Reducible to a Yes-and-no Space? . . . . . . . . 46

5. The Logical Structure of the World in a Yes-and-no Space . . . . . . . . 47

6. *Welt* and *Wirklichkeit* . . . . . . 50

7. The Logical Space as a Space of 'Possible Worlds' . 52

8. Logical Position . . . . . . . 54

9. Hume's Thesis . . . . . . . 58


V. THE CONCEPT OF SUBSTANCE . . . 61

1. 'Things': Individual Objects and Predicates . . 61

2. The Simpleness of 'Things' . . . . . 63

3. The 'Things' as the Substance of the World . . 66

4. The Independence and Non-independence of 'Things' . 66

5. The Logical Form and the Categories . . . 69

6. Logically Homogeneous Spaces with Many-valued Dimensions . . . . . . . 72

7. Logically Unhomogeneous Spaces . . . 77

8. Logical Form and Internal Qualities . . . 79

9. The Substance as What is Persistent in Time . . 81

10. Framework Questions and Questions about What is the Case . . . . . . . . 84


VI. THE CONCEPT OF A PICTURE . . . 88

1. Representations of Facts . . . . . 88

2. The Concept of an Articulate Field . . . 89

3. The Concept of 'Isomorphism' . . . . 91

4. Isomorphic Representations . . . . . 94

5. The Concept of a Picture in the Tractatus . . 96

6. What a Picture Represents and What It Depicts or Presents . . . . . . . . 98

7. The Form of Representation . . . . 99

8. Adequate and Inadequate Pictures . . . 102

9. Naturalistic Pictures . . . . . . 108

10. 'Content', 'Structure' and 'Form' . . . . 108

11. Fictitious Pictures . . . . . . 109

CHAPTER                                                         PAGE

    12. Keys and Clues . . . . . . . . 111
    13. Picture and Thought . . . . . . 112

VII.  THE SENTENCE AS A PICTURE . . . 117

    1. The 'Name Theory' of Linguistic Meaning . . 118
    2. The Concept of a 'Name' . . . . . 120
    3. The Problem of Sentence Meaning . . . 126
    4. The Analogy between a Sentence and a Picture . 128
    5. The False and the True Key of Interpretation . . 130
    6. The Sentence-token as a Fact . . . . . 133
    7. What Names Are . . . . . . 135
    8. The Problem of the False Sentence . . . 140
    9. Fictitious Sentences . . . . . . 141
    10. Summary . . . . . . . . 142

VIII.  THE DESCRIPTIVE CONTENT OF COM-
POUND SENTENCES . . . . . 143

    1. How do Logical Connectives Signify? . . . 144
    2. Complete Descriptions and Pictures . . . 146
    3. The Descriptive Content of Compound Sentences . 151
    4. Quantification . . . . . . . 153
    5. Identity . . . . . . . . 154
    6. The General Form of a Sentence . . . . 155

IX.  DESCRIPTIVE CONTENT AND MOOD . . 157

    1. Sentence-radical and Modal Component . . . 159
    2. Modal Operators . . . . . . 162
    3. The Sentence-radical as a Picture . . . . 164
    4. The Concept of Truth in the Semantics of Sentence-
radicals . . . . . . . . 165
    5. The Semantics of Moods . . . . . 167
    6. The Assertion Sign . . . . . . 170
    7. Sense and Direction . . . . . . 170
    8. The Fundamental Role of Modal Games in Teaching
the Use of Language . . . . . . 173
    9. Summary . . . . . . . . 175

  X. INTERNAL STRUCTURE OF LANGUAGE
     AND REALITY      .   .   .   .   .   .   . 177

        1. The 'Ontological Picture Theory' of Language   . 177
        2. What can be 'Shown' and What can be 'Said'   . . 178
        3. Corresponding Statements on Language and Reality  . 182
        4. Logical Syntax   .   .   .   .   .   .   . 186
        5. Logical Rules   .   .   .   .   .   .   . 197
        6. Elementary Sentences   .   .   .   .   .   . 203
        7. Variables and the Theory of Types   .   .   . 206
        8. Philosophy as an Activity   .   .   .   .   . 207
        9. The Logical Mood   .   .   .   .   .   . 209
       10. Syntactical Metaphors   .   .   .   .   .   . 211
       11. Semantics and Metaphysics   .   .   .   .   . 213

  XI. WITTGENSTEIN AS A KANTIAN PHILO-
      SOPHER   .   .   .   .   .   .   .   . 214

        1. Kantian Philosophy   .   .   .   .   .   . 215
        2. Wittgenstein's Transcendental Deductions   .   . 218
        3. Transcendental Lingualism   .   .   .   .   . 220
        4. Nonsense   .   .   .   .   .   .   .   . 222

  INDEX

        (i) General   .   .   .   .   .   .   .   . 231
       (ii) Passages from Wittgenstein's Writings   .   .   . 240

# PREFACE

I have called my book a critical exposition of the main lines of thought in Wittgenstein's *Tractatus Logico-Philosophicus*. This description stands in need of some explanation.

I think the *Tractatus* is a book from which a very great deal can be learnt. That does not mean that I agree with all that it contains. From my personal point of view the statements in it might—roughly speaking—be divided into four groups. First, there are statements which I believe I understand and which I think are clarifying, stimulating and important. These, of course, form what I find the best part of the book. Secondly come statements which I believe I understand and with some certainty think are essentially false or misleading. Hence I value them next to the statements in the first group. Thirdly, there are those which I do not understand and the value of which I am therefore unable to estimate. And fourthly, there are a number which seem on the one hand to be understandable, but on the other to be so in such a way as to give an indeterminate and obscure impression, hence they become impossible either to accept or reject. Statements of this kind strike me as worse than false statements, because while false statements may be corrected and their correction leads to insight, indeterminate ones are simply unfruitful. My presentation of the *Tractatus* will mainly be restricted to the first and second of these groups. I hope nothing essential has been left out as a consequence of this.

There are some further limitations. In my exposition I have concentrated on the semantical and metaphysical aspects of Wittgenstein's theory. What he says on formal logic and the principles of Mathematics has in part been assimilated into the general view of present-day analytical philosophers; for the rest its interest seems to me to be merely peripheral. I have therefore omitted a detailed analysis of this part of his views and of his controversies with Russell on these questions.

My exposition is not historical. I have tried to analyse the inner structure of the philosophy of the *Tractatus* rather than its relation to the views of other philosophers. I have also made only occasional references to Wittgenstein's earlier notebooks. In the main I think the content of these notebooks corroborates the relevance of my interpretations of the *Tractatus*, but I have not attempted to analyse Wittgenstein's mental development.

Wittgenstein suggests in his Preface that the *Tractatus* will only by understood by those who have themselves already thought the thoughts expressed in it, or at least similar thoughts. The chances of having thought thoughts similar to Wittgenstein's are now much greater than they were forty years ago, when the *Tractatus* was written. Of course it does not follow that when one believes one has understood him one has always understood him rightly. But in many cases it is not essential for my purpose to discuss exactly what Wittgenstein meant when he wrote this or that statement. In attempting a commentary on the contents of the *Tractatus*, I am trying to fill in the spaces of meaning left out between his aphorisms by using as much philosophical imagination as I can supply and as I find appropriate for the task. I may well give a better idea of Wittgenstein's thought if I indicate a line of thought which has strong similarities to his and which I can appreciate, than if I try in an external fashion to formulate exactly something that I might conclude he meant, but with which I have less intellectual sympathy. Otherwise it would be easy to be forced into detailed discussions of a kind which conceal rather than clarify the main chain of ideas and the reasons why they are interesting.

For reasons which will become apparent to the reader I have, in most places, quoted the *Tractatus* in German. In general, however, all quoted passages are paraphrased in English in the text. The English can easily be looked up in the parallel text published by Routledge and Kegan Paul, though the translation is not always satisfactory. The correct translation of many difficult points will be discussed in my book.

Miss Diana Colman has translated some of the chapters from a Swedish manuscript. In the preparation of the rest I have had valuable linguistic assistance from Mr. Chad Walsh, who was Visiting Professor at Abo Academy while I was writing my book. Miss G. E. M. Anscombe has revised the English of the whole book.

My argument has gained much by the detailed criticisms of Professor G. H. von Wright, who has read the book chapter by chapter. I have also profited from my discussions of different points with Miss G. E. M. Anscombe and Mr. P. Geach at Oxford, and from a discussion of semantical questions by letter with Dr. H. Johansen of Copenhagen.

To all these and many others who have kindly assisted me in my work I express my hearty thanks.

I have received financial aid from various sources. In particular I want to express my gratitude to the British Council, whose financial support and helpfulness I enjoyed during a two months' stay at Oxford.

Finally I want to thank my wife for her help with many technical details and my whole family for their patience with the well-known strains which accompany intense research.

Abo, Finland.

*December*, 1958.

# THE STRUCTURE OF THE TRACTATUS

Wittgenstein's Tractatus has, despite its limited scope, undoubtedly been one of the most influential works in modern philosophy. The kind of influence it has had, however, is not so easy to characterize. The TRACTATUS LOGICO-PHILOSOPHICUS is a remarkable book both in arrangement and form: a collection of statements, mostly formulated as aphorisms, whose connection with each other is only indicated by enumerating them with the help of decimal points. They begin with aphorism number 1: *Die Welt ist alles, was der Fall ist*—the world is everything that is the case—and finish with the apparently trivial remark of number 7: *Wovon man nicht sprechen kann, darüber muss man schweigen*—whereof one cannot speak, thereon one must be silent.

Part of the influence of the Tractatus can be traced to this disconnected form. On the one hand the statements in the Tractatus are extremely quotable. Their aphoristic form makes it easy to extract a single statement from its context and regard it as a striking formulation even of views which differ essentially from Wittgenstein's own. On the other hand one has at the same time a feeling that behind what is immediately understandable in any of the statements there lies much more that would be worth understanding. The Tractatus, in fact, is an extremely difficult work. Of this the author himself was conscious when he had completed it. 'This book will perhaps only be understood by those who have themselves already thought the thoughts which are expressed in it—or similar thoughts. It is therefore not a text-book. Its object would be attained if it afforded pleasure to someone who read it with understanding,' Wittgenstein says himself in the preface. And if one really wants to understand the Tractatus one must realize that, despite its seemingly disconnected form, Wittgenstein's treatise is a coherent whole and not a collection of unrelated sayings on different logical and philosophical subjects.

There is one thing to be noted here. Anyone who attends closely to the statements in the Tractatus very soon feels that a 'philosopher' in the traditional meaning of the word is concealed behind the technical expert devoted to detailed questions concerning the logical structure of science. Although Wittgenstein strives to show that all 'metaphysics', and thus all philosophical systems, consist of nonsense, yet Wittgenstein himself can be said to be the constructor of a philosophical system which tries to summarize all the different sides of man's relations to the world under a common angle of approach. One can even assert that Wittgenstein is himself conscious of this: he is at least consistent enough to include his own work when he condemns philosophy as a collection of nonsensicalities. *Meine Sätze erläutern dadurch,* he says in number 6.54, *dass sie der, welcher mich versteht, am Ende als unsinnig erkennt, wenn er durch sie — auf ihnen — über sie hinausgestiegen ist.* Perhaps one could translate this as follows: 'My statements are illuminating in this way: in that he who understands me finally realizes that they are nonsensical when he has used them as steps by means of which he has climbed beyond them.' This means that in reality the 'condemnation' of philosophy as 'nonsense' is no true condemnation at all. It is true that philosophical propositions are nonsensical, 'meaningless', in the sense that they have no clear content, but this does not mean that philosophizing as a mental activity is 'meaningless' in the sense of 'aimless'. Though anyone who has understood Wittgenstein's propositions in the Tractatus should at the same time have understood that they are nonsensical, he will not have read them in vain. The formulated propositions must be 'surmounted'. They form a 'ladder' which one must 'throw away' once one has gone up it—only then does one 'see the world aright' (6.54).[1] One must do so because the Wittgensteinian 'system' is really inexpressible and 'whereof one cannot speak, thereon one must be silent'.

That is the philosophical profundity which lies beneath the apparent triviality of Wittgenstein's last aphorism. It is at the same time a kind of summary of Wittgenstein's book—its result. 'Its whole meaning,' Wittgenstein says in the preface, 'could be summed up somewhat as follows: What can be said at all can be

---

[1] The simile of the 'ladder' which must be thrown away Wittgenstein seems to have, consciously or unconsciously, borrowed from Fritz Mauthner (cf. 4.0031). See concerning this matter Weiler: 'Mauthner'. (For the full title etc. of articles or books referred to in the footnotes, see References, p. 227.)

said clearly; and whereof one cannot speak, thereon one must be silent.'

The fact that, however small the details are with which they are sometimes concerned, Wittgenstein's statements fit into a personal philosophical system is certainly one of the sources of their suggestive power. There are two kinds of philosophical works of any value, those in which the author's thoughts form only a small part of all that he has written down and those in which all that is written down forms only a small part of the author's thoughts. The Tractatus definitely belongs to the latter group. There is a space of meaning around Wittgenstein's statements; they contain much more than one might suppose at first sight.

The fact that Wittgenstein's philosophy in the Tractatus forms a philosophical system goes together with the fact that as a *literary* work it has a very elaborate structure. It is this structure that, with the numbering of the statements as a guide, we shall try to analyse in this chapter.

## I. THE FORMULATED PRINCIPLE OF THE NUMBERING

According to a note on page 30[1] the principle on which the numbering has been made is:

> Die Dezimalzahlen als Nummern der einzelnen Sätze deuten das logische Gewicht der Sätze an, den Nachdruck, der auf ihnen in meiner Darstellung liegt. Die Sätze n.1, n.2, n.3, etc. sind Bemerkungen zum Satze[2] No. n; die Sätze n.m1, n.m2, etc. Bemerkungen zum Satze No. n.m; und so weiter.

Here Wittgenstein is speaking like a mathematician. Instead of writing 'Propositions 1.1 and 1.2 are remarks on proposition 1, propositions 1.11 and 1.12 remarks on proposition 1.1 and so on' he introduces the letter '*n*' to express an arbitrary number: in other words, if *n* is the whole number of a certain proposition (the propositions 1, 2, 3, 4, 5, 6, 7), then propositions *n*.1, *n*.2, etc. comment on proposition number *n*. Again, if a proposition is numbered *n.m*, where *n* and *m* are arbitrary whole numbers, then

---

[1] The Tractatus was first published in German with the title 'Logisch-philosophische Abhandlung' in Ostwald's *Annalen der Naturphilosophie* (1921) and afterwards in the well-known German-English parallel version. All references are to the latter version.

[2] In the original *Sätze* is in place of *Satze*. This is one of the many printing errors retained in all editions of the Tractatus. Wittgenstein seems to have taken very small interest in the printed text of the Tractatus. (Cf. von Wright: 'Wittgenstein', p. 536, n. 12.)

propositions *n.m*1, *n.m*2, etc., comment on proposition number *n.m*; and so on. It is amusing to note, however, that despite their general mathematical form these directions can be said to be formally insufficient. On page 30 itself we find a proposition numbered 2.01—but what is it a comment on? According to the directions it comments on proposition 2.0, but such a proposition does not exist. Now Wittgenstein certainly means that 2.0=2 and that thus proposition 2.01 is a comment on 2—but it is not at once clear that one may apply the rules of equality between the values of decimal numerals (2.0=2) to an enumeration. This should therefore be expressly pointed out in an exact formulation of the rule.

Numbers of the 2.01 type (and even numbers like 3.001 are to be found) are problematic in another respect, too. According to Wittgenstein's instructions 'the decimal figures as numbers of the different propositions indicate the logical importance of the propositions, the emphasis laid upon them' in the exposition. And that can only be understood to mean that the numbers with *few* decimals have a greater 'logical importance' and 'emphasis' than those with more decimals. The existence of propositions numbered 2.01, 2.02, etc., beside propositions numbered 2.1, 2.2, and so on, ought, according to this general characterization, to mean that Wittgenstein divides his comments on proposition 2 into two categories: less important comments, which are given first under the numbers 2.01, 2.02, etc., and more important ones under the numbers 2.1, 2.2, etc. But if this is so one cannot but ask oneself whether Wittgenstein's principle of numbering really serves its purpose. The above-mentioned grading of the comments on a proposition by means of inserting a nought seems particularly to be putting the arrangement in a strait-jacket. Since the decimal numbers follow each other in order of size, this means that to be consistent Wittgenstein ought to mention the less important comments on a proposition first and then the more weighty ones—and this would hardly be advantageous. But in fact Wittgenstein does not follow his rule consistently—in so far as he follows any rule it is, as we shall see, partly a different rule from this one. But (thank heaven!) he does not keep consistently to any rule. It quite often happens that one has to look for explanations and remarks on a given statement in places which have no numerical relation at all to the statement itself. And as for the principle that the more important and emphatic propositions should be indicated by fewer digits than the less important—this rule, too, is not one on which one can rely too much. One could perhaps say that the propositions which have short numbers are usually more *general* than those with longer numbers. But in fact the closest one can come to what the numbering shows is a kind of rhythm of emphasis; propositions 1, 2, 3, 4, 5, 6, 7 can be regarded as 'forte' places in the rhythm, which are naturally enough followed by decrescendos—but also preceded by crescendos. If one looks at the numbering in this way as a counterpart to the arrows and other signs with which accent is marked in musical notation, one gets a certain idea of the undulating rhythm in Wittgenstein's work and of its division into main and subsidiary themes, of its melody and accompaniment.

## 2. THE MAIN LINE OF THOUGHT OF THE TRACTATUS

To elucidate these points of view we will try, with the help of Wittgenstein's numbering, to form a kind of general survey of the contents of the Tractatus. The seven main theses in the book are as follows:

1 Die Welt ist alles, was der Fall ist.

2 Was der Fall ist, die Tatsache, ist das Bestehen von Sachverhalten.

3 Das logische Bild der Tatsachen ist der Gedanke.

4 Der Gedanke ist der sinnvolle Satz.

5 Der Satz ist eine Wahrheitsfunktion der Elementarsätze.
(Der Elementarsatz ist eine Wahrheitsfunktion seiner selbst.)

6 Die allgemeine Form der Wahrheitsfunktion ist: $[\bar{p}, \bar{\xi}, N(\bar{\xi})]$.
Dies ist die allgemeine Form des Satzes.

7 Wovon man nicht sprechen kann, darüber muss man schweigen.

We have seen that Wittgenstein summarizes the contents of his book by saying 'What can be said at all can be said clearly; and whereof one cannot speak, thereon one must be silent'. One would expect the seven main theses to develop this thought. If one tries to conceive them as such and reads them one after the other one comes upon a fundamental difficulty: this is that they contain certain technical terms which need further explanation in order to be understood. The word *Wahrheitsfunktion*—truth-function—which appears in thesis 5 may be regarded as such a term, though it has nowadays been adopted into general use, partly because of the Tractatus' influence; so the modern reader who knows the basic elements of symbolic logic does not need to rack his brains over its meaning. The symbolism in thesis 6, however, is peculiar to Wittgenstein, and terms such as *Sachverhalt* —state of affairs—and *Tatsache*—fact—are given special senses by him. So one cannot understand the meaning of the theses straight away. But if one abandons the attempt to understand the statements in detail one can see none the less that theses 1-7 can possibly be read as a connected whole and that they then express a continuous line of thought. In the first thesis we learn that 'the world' is everything that 'is the case'. The second thesis says that that which is the case, i.e. a fact, is formed by the existence of something which Wittgenstein calls *Sachverhalte*, i.e. a special kind of states of affairs. In the third thesis we proceed from 'the world' to the relation between this and thought; we can read thesis 3 to mean that a 'thought' is something which may be called a 'logical picture' of a fact. The fourth thesis says further of 'a thought' that it is 'a meaningful sentence'[1], and this obviously means, roughly, that what can rightly be called thoughts can always be expressed in 'meaningful sentences'. The fifth thesis also deals with such 'meaningful sentences' and it says that they are characterized by the fact that their truth or falsehood depends on and is determined by the truth and falsehood of certain sentences called elementary sentences. In the terminology of symbolic logic this is expressed by saying that the 'truth-value' of a proposition is a function of the truth-values of atomic propositions. The sixth thesis states that the relationship between a 'sentence' and 'elementary sentences', as mentioned in thesis 5, is of a definite, generally characterizable form, and that thus every sentence which can be called meaningful is of that general form. The seventh thesis says, on the other hand, that everything which can be said at all can be said through sentences of the form characterized in 6— what cannot be said in that form cannot be said at all and about that one must be silent.

Perhaps this rough analysis—which moreover must be open to

---

[1] With a few exceptions, I have translated the German *Satz* as 'sentence' throughout this book since I think this word corresponds better to Wittgenstein's thought than the word 'proposition'.

different modifications on a closer scrutiny—is enough to indicate that the seven main theses in the Tractatus really form stages in the pursuit of a line of thought.

## 3. COMMENTS AND PREAMBLES

It would be tempting on the basis of this observation to try to continue reading the Tractatus by picking out the theses in the order given by the *emphasis* suggested through the numbering. To begin with we shall pick out some of the statements with one-decimal numbers. The main comments on thesis 1 are:

1.1 Die Welt ist die Gesamtheit der Tatsachen, nicht der Dinge.

1.2 Die Welt zerfällt in Tatsachen.

The first of these propositions forms an illuminating comment on thesis 1. When Wittgenstein says that the world *is* everything that is the case, that it is the totality of all facts, this thesis forms an antithesis to another thesis which common sense is liable to consider the right one—that the world is the totality of all things. The world is the totality of *facts* and *not*—as common sense rather would have it—of *things*.

Why Wittgenstein says so we shall analyse in later chapters. At this point we wish only to fasten our attention on Wittgenstein's style. Would he not have expressed his thought more clearly if he had started with thesis 1.1 instead of thesis 1? Why then does he prefer to start from formulation 1? One might suppose that he does so chiefly for stylistic reasons; that he prefers the less explicit formulation to the more explicit on the grounds of its greater literary force, because it has more of a ring to it. But one must at the same time remember that even if this is so Wittgenstein's mode of expression is not without importance for the content. He must have at least partly *wished* to leave room for the associations called forth by formulation 1, and which perhaps 1.1 does not call forth.

We shall not at this point discuss what proposition 1.2 could express which is not already included in 1.1.

The statements whose numbers have the form '2.*m*' are these:

2.1 Wir machen uns Bilder der Tatsachen.

2.2 Das Bild hat mit dem Abgebildeten die logische Form der Abbildung gemein.

When we read these statements we become confused. Is the statement that 'we form pictures of facts' to be a 'remark' or 'comment' on thesis 2, that a fact is formed by the existence of *Sachverhalte*? It is difficult to imagine how number 2.1 could explain, motivate or clarify number 2. And it is still more difficult to understand how number 2.2 could do so: what has the circumstance that the picture and the pictured have the logical form of representation in common to do with the circumstance that what is the case is that *Sachverhalte* exist?

But if 2.1 and 2.2 are really comments on 2, if, let us say, Wittgenstein wants to point out that to realize the correctness of 2 we must first notice what *pictures* of facts we form—then theses 3 and 4 and everything which is said in connection with them concerning the nature of a logical picture must be taken as comments on 2 and not as a development of a line of thought of which 2 is a part.[1]

It seems, therefore, as if statements 2.1 and 2.2 will be given a much more plausible place in Wittgenstein's structure of thought if we do not conceive of them as *comments* on 2 but as *preambles*, as *introductory* remarks to thesis 3—which does indeed deal with thought as a logical picture of facts.

Consider now the statements numbered 2.0*n*:

2.01    Der Sachverhalt ist eine Verbindung von Gegenständen. (Sachen, Dingen.)

2.02    Der Gegenstand ist einfach.

2.03    Im Sachverhalt hängen die Gegenstände ineinander, wie die Glieder einer Kette.

2.04    Die Gesamtheit der bestehenden Sachverhalte ist die Welt.

2.05    Die Gesamtheit der bestehenden Sachverhalte bestimmt auch, welche Sachverhalte nicht bestehen.

[1] From the point of view of 'psychology of thought' and perhaps also of 'epistemology' the starting point of the whole of Wittgenstein's system is his logical and semantical investigations. From this point of view one could, therefore, say that the 'primary' in Wittgenstein's philosophy is concentrated around the statements 4 and 5 and that what precedes or follows is motivated by this. (The thoughts in these parts seem also to be chronologically the oldest.) But from the point of view of Wittgenstein's philosophical *system* in the Tractatus this circumstance is irrelevant; here the order *is* reversed. It is especially to be noted that Wittgenstein's ontological statements are *not* 'disguised' statements about language (cf. below, Ch. X, section 3). The 'epistemological' order of knowledge is often the reverse of the 'systematical'. ('What is first to God is last to man.')

2.06 Das Bestehen und Nichtbestehen von Sachverhalten ist die Wirklichkeit.
(Das Bestehen von Sachverhalten nennen wir auch eine positive, das Nichtbestehen eine negative Tatsache.)

Of these, 2.01 says of a *Sachverhalt* as mentioned in 2 that it is a connection of objects, and 2.02 says of these objects that they are simple. 2.03 further characterizes the kind of connection mentioned in 2.01. 2.04 is a re-formulation of 1 and the first part of 1.1 having regard to what has been said in 2. Number 2.05 is a corresponding re-formulation of a remark (1.12) of 1, and 2.06 also deals with this. In other words we see that the propositions numbered 2.0*n* can very naturally be taken as *comments* on thesis 2, while in the statements 2.*n* is begun the new theme which culminates in thesis 3. The impression that this is so is strengthened if we notice that it is just in proposition 2.1 that what could be called the *main concept* in thesis 3—the concept of a 'picture'—is first introduced. All the statements between 2 and 2.1 deal with essentially the same sphere of subjects as number 2.

We will now see whether the observation made here about the statements between 2 and 3 is valid also in respect of the statements between 3 and 4. Statements 3.1–3.5 read:

3.1 Im Satz drückt sich der Gedanke sinnlich wahrnehmbar aus.

3.2 Im Satze kann der Gedanke so ausgedrückt sein, dass den Gegenständen des Gedankens Elemente des Satzzeichens[1] entsprechen.

3.3 Nur der Satz hat Sinn; nur im Zusammenhange des Satzes hat ein Name Bedeutung.

3.4 Der Satz bestimmt einen Ort im logischen Raum. Die Existenz dieses logischen Ortes ist durch die Existenz der Bestandteile allein verbürgt, durch die Existenz des sinnvollen Satzes.

3.5 Das angewandte, gedachte Satzzeichen ist der Gedanke.

Statements 3.01–3.05, on the other hand, are as follows:

3.01 Die Gesamtheit der wahren Gedanken sind ein Bild der Welt.

---

[1] Wittgenstein here lets the word *Satzzeichen* denote the sentence as written or spoken sign (for reasons that will be clear later I translate it as 'sentence-token'; cf. below, p. 129 n.). This departs strangely from the usual German dictionary meaning, according to which *Satzzeichen* means 'punctuation mark'.

3.02   Der Gedanke enthält die Möglichkeit der Sachlage die er denkt. Was denkbar ist, ist auch möglich.

3.03   Wir können nichts Unlogisches denken, weil wir sonst unlogisch denken müssten.

3.04   Ein a priori richtiger Gedanke wäre ein solcher, dessen Möglichkeit seine Wahrheit bedingte.

3.05   Nur so könnten wir a priori wissen, dass ein Gedanke wahr ist, wenn aus dem Gedanken selbst (ohne Vergleichsobjekt) seine Wahrheit zu erkennen wäre.

We can again notice the same points as held for the statements between 2 and 3. While the propositions with a nought as the first decimal are only concerned with the sphere of the *preceding* main thesis, the propositions with one-decimal numbers refer to the *following* main thesis, and what can be regarded as the *main concept* of this is introduced in the *first* of the propositions with one-decimal numbers. Proposition 3.01 concludes from 3 that, since thought is a logical picture of facts, the totality of all true thoughts is a picture of the world. The idea in 3.02 can roughly be expressed thus: the logical 'possibility' of things being thus or thus consists in nothing but our being able to imagine (picture) their being thus or thus. 3.03–05 develop this idea in respect of the concepts 'logically impossible' and '*a priori* true' (i.e. 'logically necessary'). 3.05 is immediately followed by statement 3.1 in which 'the main concept' of thesis 4—the concept of a 'sentence'—is introduced. 3.1 in fact is only a more cautious formulation of 4 and the thought expressed in it is developed in more detail in the following statements.

## 4. THE SENTENCE AS A 'PICTURE' AND AS A 'TRUTH-FUNCTION'

Does this principle of construction hold good in the rest of the book? We may say: not at least as *obviously* as in the statements between 2 and 3, or 3 and 4. Yet it would be remarkable if it should not hold good in the main. Since the expressly stated principle of numbering does not hold good, one may say that Wittgenstein rather 'felt' than 'knew' the principle on which the numbering was made. But it would be psychologically improbable that this feeling should have changed its character after proposition 4. And just because the principle of structuring stated above does *not* appear so obviously between 4 and 5, or 5 and 6, or 6 and 7 as it does between 2 and 3, and 3 and 4, it is so much the more important to be conscious of it here; otherwise we can easily misinterpret the discussion. It is important to be clear the whole time that it is not when the whole-number digit changes that a new theme in the work begins, but that the thematic change is rather to be sought where the numbers end which have o as their first decimal.

Statement 4.01 reads:

4.01   Der Satz ist ein Bild der Wirklichkeit.
        Der Satz ist ein Modell der Wirklichkeit, so wie wir sie uns
        denken.

'A sentence is a picture of reality.' This can be said to be a comment on 4, as it is nothing more than a consequence of 3 and 4. In 3 it is said that thoughts are pictures of facts (which according to 1 form the world and therefore reality) and in 4 that a thought is a meaningful sentence. It follows therefore, as is stated in 4.01, that a sentence is a picture of reality.

In 4.02, on the other hand, we read:

4.02   Dies sehen wir daraus, dass wir den Sinn des Satzzeichens
        verstehen, ohne dass er uns erklärt wurde.

'This we see from the fact that we understand the sense of the sentence-token, without having had it explained to us.' The word 'this' refers here formally to what was said in 4.016, but in fact the meaning of the statement becomes clearer if we let the word refer to what was said in 4.01. We can perceive the correctness of 4.01 in the way mentioned in 4.02 (and as 4.01 is a consequence of the earlier reasonings their validity is thus supported).

We need not dwell further on the numbers 4.0*n*, which continue to comment on the proposition as a picture. Let us instead consider proposition 4.1.

4.1    Der Satz stellt das Bestehen und Nichtbestehen der Sachverhalte
        dar.

Now this statement *seemingly* belongs to the same sphere as 4. It talks of what a sentence 'presents' (*darstellen*) and what seems to be the main concept in 5—the concept of a 'truth-function'—is not yet mentioned. But one would certainly misunderstand 4.1 if one did not take into consideration that it is precisely here that the theme is introduced whose treatment is culminated in thesis 5 and continued in the 5.0's. That this is so is obscured by two circumstances. First the word *Satz* has a vague meaning in Wittgenstein's work. In the comments on 4 a 'sentence' is treated as a *picture* and this idea applies—as we shall see later—directly only to (logically) *simple* sentences. One could therefore say that in the 4.0's Wittgenstein essentially thinks of sentences as simple, and one might therefore be tempted to suppose it is this type of sentences with which thesis 4.1 deals too. Secondly, many of the statements *between* 4.1 and 4.2 are of such a nature as to show that it is just this type of sentence which is meant here. Yet it is quite obvious that it is mainly *complex, compound* sentences that Wittgenstein is thinking of in number 4.1; for we shall only understand such sentences if we realize that they 'present' the existence *and* non-existence of *Sachverhalte*. The same is true of the concept 'sentence' as used in 5. We find on a closer analysis (cf. Chapter III) that in Wittgenstein's terminology the word *Sachverhalt* means an *atomic* state of affairs which is linguistically described by a logically simple sentence, called *Elementarsatz*—'elementary sentence'—which is *true* if the atomic state of affairs described *exists, false* if it *does not exist*. If we take the main concept of 5 as *that* concept of a sentence according to which the meaning of a sentence is determined by its being a certain *truth-function* of elementary sentences, then we can, therefore, say that this main concept is introduced in 4.1. The correctness of this interpretation is corroborated by 4.2, in which the sense of a sentence is defined by means of its agreement or disagreement with the possibilities of existence and non-existence of atomic states of affairs:

> 4.2    Der Sinn des Satzes ist seine Übereinstimmung und Nichtübereinstimmung mit den Möglichkeiten des Bestehens und Nichtbestehens der Sachverhalte.

After 4.2 the thought expressed in 5 is developed without interruption.

## 5. THE PREPARATION FOR THE NECESSITY OF SILENCE

The change over in 5.1 from the theme of 5 in that of 6 is obscured by 5.1's consisting of two paragraphs, of which only the first is

introductory to 6, while the second refers to a subsidiary subject.
5.1 reads:

> 5.1   Die Wahrheitsfunktionen lassen sich in Reihen ordnen.
> Das ist die Grundlage der Wahrscheinlichkeitslehre.

The *Wahrscheinlichkeitslehre* (theory of probability) is treated
more in detail in the statements from 5.15 to 5.156, but what
immediately follows after 5.1 refers to its first paragraph only and
is of direct importance to the propounding of thesis 6.

In 6 the general form of a meaningful sentence is set down.
A closer analysis shows that this is the general form of a sentence
which is a truth-function of elementary sentences. Every meaningful
sentence can be brought into this form. That 'boundary' of thinking
is thus indicated, of which it is said in the preface: 'The book
will, therefore, draw a limit to thinking, or rather—not to thinking,
but to the expression of thoughts; for, in order to draw a limit to
thinking we should have to be able to think both sides of this
limit (we should therefore have to be able to think what cannot
be thought). The limit can, therefore, only be drawn in language
and what lies on the other side of the limit will be simply nonsense.'
According to 7 one must be silent outside this boundary. If we
regard 6.1–6.5 as a preparation for this final chord we must consider
Wittgenstein's coda[1] magnificent. Because every one of these
propositions bars a way on which one might feel tempted to try
and overstep this boundary:

> 6.1   The propositions of logic are tautologies.
>
> 6.2   Mathematics is a logical method.
> The propositions of mathematics are equations, and therefore
> pseudo-propositions.
>
> 6.3   The investigation of logic means the investigation of *all*
> conformity to *laws*. And outside logic all is accident.
>
> 6.4   All propositions are of equal value.

---

[1] One is constantly tempted to use musical terms to describe the construction of the
Tractatus. Wittgenstein himself, in fact, was according to von Wright ('Wittgenstein',
p. 531) 'exceptionally musical, even if one judges by the highest standards'. I believe
one can say with more reason than of most works so characterized that the construction
of the Tractatus is 'musical'.

6.5   For an answer which cannot be expressed the question too
cannot be expressed.
*The riddle* does not exist.
If a question can be put at all, then it *can* also be answered.

These propositions will be treated in Chapter XI.

## 6. THE COMMENTS ON THE COMMENTS

We have thus analysed the structure of the Tractatus first by
trying to read the seven main theses—i.e. the theses with the
strongest emphasis—as an expression of the thought which was
said in the preface to be a summary of the whole work; secondly
we have tried to look at the statements with the next strongest
emphasis—i.e. the statements numbered *n.m* and *n.om*—as a more
detailed expression of the line of thought indicated in the main
theses. One might feel tempted to continue in the same way and
try to pick out the statements with a 'third degree' emphasis and
look at them as a further expression of the line of thought expressed
in the statements of a second degree emphasis. For many reasons
this is not worth while. First, the statements with a third degree
emphasis form too great a part of the book; it would be to no
purpose to study them omitting all that is left. Secondly, we must
realize that the division of the 'comments' on a thesis into 'real'
comments and 'preambles' as was made above with regard to the
comments on the main theses is not possible with statements whose
numbers contain many decimals. Thirdly, Wittgenstein's directions
on emphasis show what he *himself* stresses. But an outsider who
perhaps may have thoughts similar to Wittgenstein's though not
exactly the same, may often feel a need to lay the emphasis in another
place in order to make clear which points in Wittgenstein's way of
thinking differentiates it from his own. But more important than
all these points of view is that to continue the analysis on the lines
of the above principles would give a *wrong* picture of the structure
of the Tractatus.

To explain why I think so I shall start from an example. Thesis
number 1.13 reads:

1.13   Die Tatsachen im logischen Raum sind die Welt.

What does this mean? In what way are we to understand that 'the
facts in logical space' form the world? Is it an explanation of thesis

1.1 that the world is the totality of facts and not of things? For clarity's sake we must try to discover what idea Wittgenstein connects with 'logical space'. The term 'logical space' (or the term 'space' used in roughly this sense) recurs in rather few statements: in 2.013 and 2.0131, which can be said to comment on the concept 'thing'; in 2.11, which comments on the concept 'picture'; in 3.4 and 3.42, which comment on the concept 'sentence'; and in 4.463, which comments on the concepts 'tautology' and 'contradiction'. These statements can be said to form a totality of their own, since they explain each other. The statement 1.13 quoted is not a basis on which one might build up an understanding of other statements in this group—the contrary is equally true. We could therefore best characterize the function of 1.13 by saying that it is a first hint of a motif which weaves together different parts of the work into a fabric where everything is connected with everything else. To understand this fabric one must notice that some of the comments on a thesis can be regarded as thematic cross-references indicating how a subject treated in one place is connected with a subject treated in another. And these references from an earlier point in the exposition to a later one and *vice versa* come about through the use of the same *terminology* in different connections. A really thorough study of the Tractatus demands a comprehensive index— much more comprehensive than is to be found in the latest edition.

To sum up we can say that to understand the exposition in the Tractatus one must notice that on the one hand it *is* a continuous presentation whose structure we can study on the basis of the numbering; on the other hand, however, this continuous thread of thought is crossed by other threads in different directions which can be discerned on the basis of the recurrence of the motifs. Whether one is only intent on a vague 'aesthetic' experience of the Tractatus as a whole or on a thorough analysis of its contents, one must constantly have both these points of view before one's eyes. And if it is the analysis one is interested in one must subject the text to extremely penetrating 'exegetic' enquiry.

Is such an arduous analysis of a work like the Tractatus worth while? Well, what is really 'worth while' as a subject of philosophical analysis? It is true that the author of the Tractatus has disclaimed much that is written in it. Its preface ends as follows:

'If this work has a value it consists in two things. First that in it thoughts are expressed, and this value will be the greater the better the thoughts are expressed. The more the nail has been hit on the head.—Here I am conscious that I have fallen far short of the possible. Simply because my powers are insufficient to cope with the task.— May others come and do it better.

'On the other hand the *truth* of the thoughts communicated here seems to me unassailable and definitive. I am, therefore, of the opinion that the problems have in essentials been finally solved. And if I am not mistaken in this, then the value of this work secondly consists in the fact that it shows how little has been done when these problems have been solved.'

Thus in 1918 Wittgenstein was of the opinion that the truth of the thoughts he expressed was unchallengeable. Twenty-seven years later he writes in the preface to *Philosophical Investigations* (p. x):

'Four years ago I had occasion to re-read my first book (the *Tractatus Logico-Philosophicus*) and to explain its ideas to someone. It suddenly seemed to me that I should publish those old thoughts and the new ones together: that the latter could be seen in the right light only by contrast with and against the background of my old way of thinking.

'For since beginning to occupy myself with philosophy again, sixteen years ago, I have been forced to recognize grave mistakes in what I wrote in that first book. . . .'

And since Wittgenstein himself disclaims his Tractatus it might be regarded as a superseded work. But this would of course be a wrong conclusion. In fact we see that Wittgenstein himself thinks that his new thoughts can only be understood against the background of his earlier ones. Further the Tractatus is one of the starting-points of an important current in modern intellectual life, and for this reason it is of great historical interest. But the Tractatus is also interesting in itself—I share the often-expressed feeling that Wittgenstein overshoots the mark when in his later work he criticizes his earlier thought.

I think the best way of characterizing the position of the Tractatus is by pointing out that those trends in modern philosophy which are based on, or otherwise connected with, the thoughts expressed in it stand in the same position to it as Wittgenstein himself. Admitted that Wittgenstein is right in saying that it contains 'grave' mistakes, the book can still not be dismissed, because the statements in it are 'profound' enough to provide a tempting path for thought to wander along. By travestying Wittgenstein's own saying (6.54) one might say that even if he who understands the statements in the Tractatus finally realizes that they are incorrect or misleading they are still illuminating because in order to see clearly one must understand in what way they are incorrect or misleading. The statements in the Tractatus must be surmounted; only then one can see the world, or to put it in less solemn terms, the philosophical problems aright. And this characteristic the Tractatus has in common with all other 'good' philosophy.

# II

# THE WORLD AS A FACT

After our survey of the general structure of the Tractatus we will now turn to a first analysis of main thesis number 1. I say a 'first' analysis, because we cannot regard the more important statements as having received final treatment until we have gone through a great part of the work. As the starting-point of the analysis we will take, in addition to thesis 1, statements 1.1 and 1.2:

1    Die Welt ist alles, was der Fall ist.

1.1   Die Welt ist die Gesamtheit der Tatsachen, nicht der Dinge.

1.2   Die Welt zerfällt in Tatsachen.

The statements between 1 and 2 form an exception to the general principles for the construction of the Tractatus which we laid down in the previous section. 1.1, as has already been pointed out, can really be regarded as a comment on 1 and as an illuminating one: 'The world is everything that is the case; it is the totality of *facts* and not'—as common sense is inclined to think—'of things.'

## 1. CAN THE WORLD MEANINGFULLY BE SAID TO BE THE TOTALITY OF FACTS?

There seems therefore to be a difference in view between Wittgenstein and common sense concerning the structure of the world. This difference is certainly of a special kind. I shall illustrate the kind by a rather similar difference between the view held by Anaxagoras concerning the structure of matter and the one implicit in Aristotle's objections to it

When Anaxagoras built up his philosophical system to explain what remains constant and what changes in the universe, the starting-point for his speculations was the rhetorical question: 'How can hair come from what is not hair, or flesh from what is not flesh?' He arrived at this question by pondering how it could be possible that the same nourishment, such as bread and water, could give rise to many different things such as hair, flesh, bone, nails and sinews. He answered it by saying that flesh, hair, bone, nails and sinews must be *included* in the food, since all change is really only a mingling or separation of things. With a rapid generalization he concluded that 'in everything there is a portion of everything else'; what each thing 'seems to be' is merely its predominant constituent.

Aristotle's objections to this were roughly as follows: If everything contains everything else, he argued, then every drop of water must contain a little piece of meat and every piece of meat a little drop of water. Consequently a drop of water would contain a little piece of meat, and this little piece of meat an even smaller drop of water, and this tiny drop of water a still smaller piece of meat, and so on *ad infinitum*. This Aristotle found absurd.

Surely Anaxagoras must have also found such a Chinese Box of a structure absurd. If we are to follow what I believe to be the correct interpretation of Anaxagoras, then in saying that bread and water contained such things as hair, flesh and bone he meant that bread and water contained the *qualities* of hair, flesh and bone. Matter was simply a *mixture of qualities* and all change was merely a re-mingling of qualities in a new way.[1]

It is, of course, a matter of dispute whether this interpretation of Anaxagoras' doctrine is really correct. What interests us here, however, is not that, but whether the theory we have ascribed to Anaxagoras presents a structure of matter which is *logically possible*. Can one *think* of matter as a 'mixture' of qualities and of the conversion of matter as a new mingling of qualities?

One can answer both 'yes' and 'no' to this question. 'Yes' means that it is not hard to formulate in modern mathematical terminology a theory which in its content agrees with this version of Anaxagoras' theory. But one has to answer 'no' on the other hand, because the assertion that a (material) 'thing' is a 'mixture' of qualities is logically incorrect *in its formulation* and so represents something which cannot be 'thought' in the proper sense of the word. It would, for instance, be logically incorrect to say that a piece of gold is a 'mixture' of the qualities 'yellow', 'shining', 'heavy', 'metallic', etc. If one is to explain how it happens that gold is yellow, proceeding from a theory of the 'constituents' of gold, one must

[1] See my book *Tankens Gryning*, pp. 127 ff.

assume that gold contains a constituent which *is* yellow, not that the quality 'yellow' *itself* is a constituent of gold. For, on the one hand, that which can be said to form a 'constituent' of a 'thing' must itself have the logical nature of a 'thing': it must, to use Aristotle's terminology, belong to the 'category' of things. On the other hand it belongs to the logical nature of a 'quality' that any mention of a quality presupposes 'things' which either 'have' or 'do not have' this quality—it is incorrect to call something a 'quality' if one does not think of something or other as possible bearer of the quality. If 'yellow' is a part of gold, then—granting that we use the word 'part' in the usual way—yellow is not a quality. Therefore its existence as a 'part' of gold does not explain why gold is yellow.

In his interpretation of Anaxagoras' doctrine Aristotle speaks for 'common sense'. Common sense rightly says that if one takes Anaxagoras at his own words and thinks that 'everything is part of everything', one must think of every drop of water as containing a piece of meat and every piece of meat a drop of water, and so on.

Common sense, however, might similarly object to Wittgenstein's thesis that the world is the totality of *facts* and not of *things*. 'Facts', too, do not belong to the category of 'things'; facts also have a different logical nature from things. *If*—as might seem most natural —we conceive of the *world* as a *thing*, even though a very complex thing, and *if* we interpret 'to be the totality of' in the usual way, then the world cannot be conceived of as the totality of facts. What the world can be thought to be a totality of is precisely—things. And thus far, I think, common sense is right. I believe, moreover, that Wittgenstein thought so too.

## 2. CATEGORIES

The distinction we have touched upon between different 'categories' of concepts is of fundamental importance in a clarification of what Wittgenstein might or might not mean in the Tractatus. We must therefore deal with it a little more fully even at this stage.

To define such a concept as 'man' means, according to Aristotle and scholastic logic, firstly to state a general concept, a *genus*, of which the concept to be defined forms a part, a *species*; secondly to state the quality, the *differentia*, which distinguishes an object of the *species* in question from another object within the same *genus*. The concept 'man' is thus defined as a *species* of the concept 'animal', which in this case is the *genus*. The distinguishing *differentia* is 'rational'[1]. So the definition is: *homo =animal rationale*. The concept 'animal' (i.e. the concept which in this definition forms the *genus*) can in turn be defined by the same method as a *species* within a more general *genus* and one can proceed in this way until one comes to the concept 'thing', or 'substance' as it is called in scholastic terminology —i.e. that which exists 'independently'—which is the highest *genus, summum genus*. Scholastic logic thus clearly emphasizes[2] that the concept 'substance' cannot in its turn be conceived as a *species* of a more general *genus*; the concept of a 'substance' is already *genus generalissimum*, the most general of all concepts, than which nothing more general can be found.

When the concept 'substance' is nevertheless made into a special 'category' (*praedicamentum*) along with nine others, amongst which 'quality', 'relation' and 'quantity' may be mentioned, it must be understood that the division of concepts into 'categories' is a *completely different kind of division* from that which occurs within a particular category. The difference could be characterized thus: the division of concepts into 'categories' is not based on the *contents* of the concepts but on their 'logical nature'. And although the Aristotelian division into categories is unsatisfactory in its details, yet the idea which lies at its root is of great importance: it is necessary to make a division of concepts on the basis of their 'logical nature' and a division on this basis is different in kind from a division of entities of the same logical nature. A similar principle underlies Russell's 'theory of types', even if its details are unsatisfactory too.

What categories would be reached by a correct division of concepts according to their 'logical nature'? This is a difficult question —the difficulty lies partly in the fact that the meaning of the term 'logical nature' is not clear. The categories we need to deal with in the following discussion are (a) the category of (*individual*) *things* (substance)[3], (b) the category of the *predicates*[4] of individual things,

---

[1] I disregard the additional *differentia* of 'mortal' according to the Arbor Porphyrii.

[2] See, for instance, Petrus Hispanus, 2.06 (p. 16.)

[3] *Only* individual things (i.e. what in Aristotelian scholastic terminology is called *substantia prima*) are here counted as belonging to the category 'substance'. *Substantia secunda*, the general concept answering to a *genus* of individual things—the concept 'man', for instance—I count as belonging to the category of qualities.

[4] What I call 'predicates', i.e., qualities and relations, are often called 'universals'. I think this terminology is very misleading and the source of many philosophical errors. The same is true of calling individual things 'particulars'. If it is possible to make any 'logical' distinction between 'universals' and 'particulars', it must not, in any case, be identified with the difference in logical nature between 'individual things' and 'predicates'.

which is subdivided into *monadic* predicates (i.e. qualities), *binary* predicates, *ternary* predicates, etc. (i.e. relations with different numbers of places), (c) the category of *facts*. How these categories can be said to have different 'logical natures', and why the distinction between them is so important, we shall see later. It must only be added here that the above list of categories is by no means complete; we must allow for there being an infinite number of categories, infinite in different dimensions. Russell's 'predicates of higher types' can be mentioned as examples of other categories.

We have seen here that if we use the words 'world' and 'totality of' in the way that seems most natural, then thesis 1.1 implies a confusion between the categories 'things' and 'facts' which Wittgenstein himself puts in opposition to each other. The formulation of it might therefore be regarded as a *paradox*, and in addition a complicated paradox. One could say, that is, that on this assumption the formulation of 1.1 is a striking example of the fact that the theses in the Tractatus are what Wittgenstein calls *unsinnig*, i.e. 'nonsensical'—or perhaps one ought rather to say 'anti-sensical'. One could add—with a certain concession to German romanticism— that this 'anti-sensicalness' allows a sentence to be 'profound' at the same time as it is nonsensical.

Less romantically, one could characterize the sentence as an 'elliptical' expression. This holds good on the assumption that Wittgenstein accepts the opinion that the word 'world' denotes something which belongs to the category of things. But even if he does not, even if by 'world' he *means* something which belongs not to the category of things but of *facts*—and such a change in the meaning of the word is not inconsistent with at least the majority of its uses in the Tractatus—even so, the formulation of the statements must be regarded as 'elliptical'. For then propositions 1 and 1.1 ought rather to be regarded as a kind of 'persuasive definition'. According to this interpretation Wittgenstein means firstly something which could be formulated thus: 'By the "world" I *understand* everything which is the case. By the "world" I *understand* the totality of all facts, not of all things.' He also means secondly that this is a 'philosophically' *important* meaning of the word 'world'. If we call the world 'the world as a fact' (*die Welt als Tatsache*) we could set it up as a polar opposite to the ordinary 'universe', which we would call 'the world as a thing' (*die Welt als Ding*). We could also assert that 'the world as a fact' is the philosophically important world; it is *this* which is fundamentally involved when we speak of a 'theory of the world' or a 'conception of the world'. Our task is then to understand *why* the world as a fact is regarded as the philosophically interesting world.

## 3. ENIGMATIC 'THINGS'

Once, many years ago, I sat with my mother on a veranda. On the table was a vase of roses. 'Look at that rose,' I said. 'Look at its red colour, how the petals enfold each other and how the thorny stem sticks out over the side of the vase. We can say all these things *about* a rose. And the philosophers have racked their brains as to why we can always say things *about* a rose, but never what the rose really is in itself.'

'What an uninteresting question,' said my mother.

'Yes, isn't it,' I said. 'But one need only give the question another turn to arrive at an absorbing problem. Since what we experience is always only *about* a thing and never the thing in itself, why do we always give our experiences such a structure that we presuppose things—like the rose in this instance—which these experiences deal with? Now that I think an interesting question.'

My mother agreed with me, for we often have the same feelings about what is interesting.

Later, as a professional philosopher, I have pondered on the psychological reason why philosophers have posed the former question rather than the latter. I have come to the conclusion that the reason is that the former question is thought of as having a connection with feelings of the 'mystical'. I have further concluded that the latter question contains an answer to the former—or rather that if the latter question cannot be answered, if we simply have to realize that we do presuppose things with which our experience deals, then it shows that the former question is put in the wrong way. I suppose that it is along these lines one should look for the 'profundity' in regarding the 'world' as a world of facts.

## 4. THE STRUCTURE OF THE FIELD OF PERCEPTION

To illustrate this association with Wittgenstein's theses further I shall take as a starting-point an example from the psychology of perception. How does our visual impression of an object such as a flag arise? Older 'atomistic' psychology answers that it is through an integration of perceptions of different parts of the flag. 'Gestalt Psychology' contests this. Our perception of the entire flag is not preceded by a perception of different parts of the flag. The process is the reverse: we first perceive the whole, and if we perceive the details at all it is the result of a later analysis of the whole. The problems of the psychology of perception do not consist of an inquiry into how a total perception is built up of partial perceptions but of how an initially undifferentiated whole—the so-called 'field of perception'—is differentiated and how this leads to the whole being 'structured', analysed into its elements.

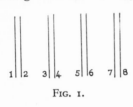

FIG. 1.

Gestalt Psychology has drawn up well-known rules for this structuring. One of them is the so-called 'law of proximity' which is illustrated by an example of the following kind: On perceiving Figure 1, a pattern of lines arises which is so organized that adjacent elements are combined into units; we see the figure, that is, as a composition of four narrow bands separated by wider spaces.

If we look at this example from what one might call in a wide sense a 'logical' point of view there are two things we should particularly observe. The first concerns the 'elements' which appear in the organized field. The four objects of which the figure consists are not four 'things' in general, they are four things of a certain kind—something which can be called 'bands'. This means that the four things have a common *quality*: the quality of being a 'band'. In this instance the bands have also the common quality of being equally broad. Furthermore, the four objects are not just 'four bands' in general but four bands which stand in a certain definite spatial relation to each other. In our particular case the bands are in pairs at the *same distance* from each other. Because the four objects have certain definite qualities and stand in a certain definite relation to each other we can say that the picture apprehended has a *structure*. This 'structure' of the apprehended 'field' is determined not by the things, nor by the qualities and relations as such, but by certain definite *facts*. These facts are *that* the figure consists of four separate objects, *that* these objects are bands of the same width, and *that* the bands are the same distance from each other. Without noticing these facts, in which things and their predicates are contained as elements, we cannot perceive the things themselves. The organization of the 'field' is thus an analysis of it in terms of more or less simple and easily recognizable *facts*.

The second thing to consider concerns the *whole* that is analysed. What is the 'field'?—The figure as a whole? To say so would be incorrect. We cannot be said to perceive a 'figure' at all until we have organized the 'field' and perceived the elements and the facts in which they occur.[1] If there should be any purpose in introducing the concept of a 'field of perception' to be organized, this 'field' therefore must be distinguished from the 'figure' perceived. It seems to me that the simplest way of showing the difference is to say that the 'field' *does not belong to the category of things* but to that of 'facts'. If we make this logical distinction we can characterize the analysis of the field in this way: the 'unanalysed' field 'breaks up' (*zerfällt*) into simpler facts and thus becomes *structured* into things and their predicates. This holds good not only in this instance of perception: we can also express ourselves in the same way in more general cases.

To sum up: The concept of *a field of perception* can be regarded as a concept within the category of *facts*. To organize it means that the field of perception *breaks up* into *simpler* facts. The particular objects are perceived because this breaking-up is combined with a *structuring* of the simpler facts into *things* and *predicates* of things (i.e. into objects and qualities of objects and/or relations between objects). *The things and predicates* enter into the field of perception only as *elements* of facts, and this is their function.

Now it is a well-known fact that the field of perception resulting from an observation of a figure like Figure 1 can be organized otherwise than in the manner above. The validity of the law of proximity is conditional and can in special circumstances be set aside. If, for instance, we omit lines 1 and 8 on the outside of Figure 1 we tend to combine 2 and 3, 4 and 5, 6 and 7 into units. Yet even as the figure now appears we can with a certain effort apprehend it in this way: we see it as made up of *five* objects (instead of four) formed by the lines 1, (2, 3), (4, 5), (6, 7) and 8. Three of these objects are then regarded as 'gates' of equal width, close to and at the same distance from each other, while the two remaining ones are 'posts' at each side of the three gates and at the same distance from the outermost gates as the gates are from each other. The two apprehensions are *different* breakings-up of the field into simpler facts, and just as the facts they break into are different so too are the things which arise

---

[1] The example of the flag is misleading in this respect.

as elements of these facts. The 'complex' wholes we see can also be said to be *different* (psychologically speaking), although for different reasons we are naturally convinced that, objectively speaking, it is the same figure.

Thus the same field of perception can be analysed into simpler facts in different ways; the way in which it is analysed is determined by 'psychological' factors. The first division is dominant in Figure 1 because it means the simplest way of surveying the total fact—we could say that it is an interest of a 'theoretical' kind which here determines what partial facts the field is analysed into. In other situations the structure of the field of perception is known to depend on what one might call more 'practical' interests. The field of perception is thus organized so that those facts emerge which are of theoretical or practical 'interest' to the person perceiving—it is analysed so that what could be called *relevant facts* emerge. And what *things* and *predicates* are perceived depends on what facts are relevant.

## 5. THE ORGANIZATION OF THE 'WORLD FIELD'

At one point in the Tractatus Wittgenstein touches upon the observations of the psychology of perception. This is in sentence 5.5423 where we read: 'To perceive a complex means to perceive that its constituents are combined in such and such a way.' He illustrates this remark by an example of the 'double meaning' of figures of perception and the comment that we perceive *different* facts when we interpret the figure in different ways. We may infer from this that Wittgenstein conceives of the field of perception as belonging to the category of facts. However, our analysis of the phenomenon of perception has not been an attempt to reconstruct one of Wittgenstein's lines of thought but a heuristic method from which to arrive at a possible interpretation of theses 1, 1.1 and 1.2.

Firstly we can state that if the 'field of perception' is substituted for the word 'world' in these theses we get formulations which approximately express what has previously been said. Thus transformed, Thesis 1 can be taken as expressing that the field of perception is a 'whole' belonging to the category of facts; 1.1 expresses that the field of perception, seen in this way, is a totality of facts and not of things;[1] and 1.2 expresses something we have

---

[1] I here disregard the fact that by *Dinge* Wittgenstein does not mean 'individual things', 'things belonging to the category of things', but something more general. On this, see further below, Ch. V.

already formulated; that the *field of perception breaks up into facts*.

Secondly we can state that what we have said of the field of perception must also apply to the whole of our *world picture*. Even our knowledge of the world as a whole is primarily a knowledge of facts; even here the role of things and predicates is to appear as elements in a structure which is the product of an analysis of these facts. It holds good even of our knowledge of the world that 'the facts as a whole' can be analysed in different ways. Revolutionary advances in science have, in effect, been connected with a 're-structuring' of facts applying to the world. The most often quoted example is that of Newton and the apple.[1] When Newton saw the fall of the apple not only as a movement peculiar to the apple but as a relation between two bodies, 'the apple' and 'the earth', the way lay open to the general law of gravity. Another example is the new way in which Faraday looked at the facts of electricity. Faraday, so to speak, regarded the 'things' of this theory not as 'particles of electricity', as was the classical conception, but as the electrical field lying between the charged objects; and instead of the mutual attraction and repulsion of the particles he introduced the tension of the field. What Faraday made was only a *re-arrangement* of facts already known; he described them in a new way. Only with Maxwell's electromagnetic waves do we come across phenomena which can be described only from Faraday's point of view and not from the classical one.

In short, it is natural to introduce 'the world' as a fact as a *primary* conception in relation to 'the world' as a thing. And in many respects we can make the same observations of this 'world as a fact' as we did of 'the field of perception'. 'The world as a fact' is also a whole which can be analysed in different ways into 'relevant facts'. The simple 'things' and 'predicates' which enter into 'the world' do so as 'elements' of facts, and this determines their function in the world picture. Things and predicates are what one might call *complementary*: they presuppose each other. The role of things in the world picture is to act as 'bearers' of predicates and that is their *raison d'être*. If a 'thing in itself' means a 'thing' without predicates then the assumption of a thing in itself has no purpose; indeed such a thing cannot be thought of as a thing: it is inconceivable. That is why we can never really say what a thing is in itself. The same is true of a 'predicate in itself'.

The *structure* of the world is determined by the way the world as a

---

[1] Cf. Langer: *Feeling and Form*, pp. 8-9.

fact is analysed into more simple 'facts' and by how these are apprehended as 'things' and 'predicates'. The world as a *thing* is a complex
thing within this structure.

I shall summarize the above views in a number of statements
which may be regarded as an attempt to characterize approximately
the meaning of Wittgenstein's sentences 1, 1.1 and 1.2. It should be
understood, however, that they do not claim to do this exhaustively.

(II.1)   *Our knowledge of the world is primarily a knowledge of facts, not
         of things.*

(II.2)   *The concept of 'the world as a fact' is prior to 'the world as a
         thing'. Our world picture results from an analysis of the world
         as a fact into simpler facts. How this analysis is carried out
         determines the structure of the world.*

(II.3)   *Things and predicates are complementary. Things enter into the
         world (whether this is understood as a 'thing' or as a 'fact') as
         elements of facts.*

(II.4)   *'The world as a thing' is a complex thing within the structure of
         the world.*

I have pointed out that these statements do not claim to exhaust
the meaning of the theses under consideration. There is one point
I particularly want to make in this connection. Wittgenstein's first
main thesis strikes a special note because it is in the form of an answer
to the question as to *what* the world *is*. Is this note significative, and
in that case what does it mean? We will return to this question in
the last chapter.

# III

# THE CONCEPT OF A *SACHVERHALT*

Before we go on to discuss the statements 1.11–1.13 and 1.21 we must consider some terminological questions which mainly concern the word *Sachverhalt* and other related expressions. The term *Sachverhalt* appears for the first time in statement 2:

2 Was der Fall ist, die Tatsache, ist das Bestehen von Sachverhalten.

In the English version of the Tractatus this is rendered as follows: 'What is the case, the fact, is the existence of atomic facts.' This translation seems confusing, and the confusion is increased by the interpretation of Wittgenstein's terminology given by Russell in his introduction to the Tractatus. Russell says (p. 9): 'Facts which are not compounded of other facts are what Mr Wittgenstein calls *Sachverhalte*, whereas a fact which may consist of two or more facts is called *Tatsache*: thus, for example, "Socrates is wise" is a *Sachverhalt*, as well as a *Tatsache*, whereas "Socrates is wise and Plato his pupil" is a *Tatsache* but not a *Sachverhalt*.' Though Russell's formulation is founded on an explanation given in a letter[1] by Wittgenstein himself, this is *not* the way in which the two concepts are in reality related to one another in the Tractatus.

## I. ALL *SACHVERHALTE* ARE NOT *TATSACHEN*

The relation between the concepts *Sachverhalt* and *Tatsache* can be examined from two points of view which must be treated separately. Etymologically the German word *Sachverhalt* is a *Sich-Verhalten* of *Sachen* or *wie sich die Sachen verhalten*, i.e. something which could be rendered as a 'relatedness of things' or 'of matters' or as a 'how matters stand'. There is no counterpart in English of the word *Sachverhalt*; among others the following translations have been

[1] Of August 19th, 1919, from a prison camp in Italy.

suggested: 'situation', 'circumstance', 'state of affairs'; but the use of each of these expressions differs from the German use of the word *Sachverhalt*. The third of them is employed in the English version of the Tractatus as a rendering of the German word *Sachlage*, which refers to a concept of the same category as the concepts *Sachverhalt* and *Tatsache*, and differs from both of them. We must therefore on the one hand examine which is the difference, according to Wittgenstein's terminology, between the concepts *Sachverhalt* and *Sachlage*, on the other hand how these concepts differ from the concept *Tatsache*. I shall begin with the latter distinction.

We have stated that a *Sachverhalt* according to German usage is a 'how matters stand'. Also a *Tatsache*—i.e. a 'fact'—is a 'how matters stand'. Is there any difference between the two concepts? I think it is in accordance with at least one way of using the words in question if we make a distinction of the following kind: The sentence

(1)                    The moon is smaller than the earth

expresses that something is the case. What the sentence asserts as being the case, i.e. that the moon is smaller than the earth, I shall call the *descriptive content*[1] of the sentence. The sentence

(2)                    The earth is smaller than the moon

also expresses that something is the case. Its descriptive content is that the earth is smaller than the moon. Now the first sentence is true, the latter false. This difference we can state thus: The descriptive content of sentence (1) is not only *asserted* to be the case, it is really the case; hence this descriptive content is a *fact*, a *Tatsache*. The descriptive content of sentence (2) is *only* asserted to be the case, but is not really the case—hence it is *not* a *fact*, *not* a *Tatsache*. Now I think it is in accordance with German usage if we call the descriptive content of a sentence of this kind a *Sachverhalt independently* of its being a fact or not. According to this terminology both (1) and (2) can be regarded as describing *Sachverhalte*. The difference between them is that the *Sachverhalt* described by (1) is a *bestehender Sachverhalt* —an 'existing' *Sachverhalt*—i.e. a *Tatsache*, whereas (2) describes a *nicht bestehender Sachverhalt*—a 'non-existing' *Sachverhalt*—which is not a *Tatsache*.

---

[1] I prefer the expression 'descriptive content' to the expression 'cognitive content', which has sometimes been used in approximately the same sense. The expression 'descriptive content' is, however, also misleading in a way. Cf. below, p. 109.

Thus a *Sachverhalt* is something that could *possibly* be the case, a *Tatsache* something that is *really* the case. What a sentence like (1) or (2) describes and asserts to be the case is a *Sachverhalt*; it is a *Tatsache* as well, if the sentence is true, but not a *Tatsache* if the sentence is false.

So far we have only emphasized what from the point of view of German usage could be thought as a natural distinction between a *Sachverhalt* and a *Tatsache*.[1] That Wittgenstein in fact makes this distinction seems clear from statement 2 alone. Here we are told that what is the case, *die Tatsache*, is *das Bestehen von Sachverhalten*, i.e. that *Sachverhalte* 'exist'. This must imply that *Sachverhalte* as such are thought of as either 'existing' or 'non-existing', and that, in the first case only, they belong to what is the case and form *die Tatsache*. In fact Wittgenstein's use of the words *Sachverhalt* and *Tatsache* is throughout in accordance with this distinction being made between their meanings[2]—perhaps with the exception of 2.034 and 4.2211. In particular I want to point to statement 2.04, in which the world is characterized as the totality of *die bestehenden Sachverhalte*, which can be compared to the characterization of the world as the totality of *Tatsachen* in 1.1; and to 2.05, in which the totality of *die bestehenden Sachverhalte* is said to determine also which *Sachverhalte* do not *bestehen*, while in 1.12 the totality of *Tatsachen* is said to determine all that is the case and also all that is not the case. Note also 4.25: *Ist der Elementarsatz wahr, so besteht der Sachverhalt; ist der Elementarsatz falsch, so besteht der Sachverhalt nicht.*

The English version of the Tractatus translates *Sachverhalt* as 'atomic fact', *bestehen* as 'exist', and *Tatsache* as 'fact'. The reason for giving the *Sachverhalte* the characteristic 'atomic' I shall consider in a moment. In this connection I only want to call attention to the circumstance that this terminology leads to the absurdity in the formulation of 2 that 'the fact' is said to be 'the existence of . . . facts'. A corresponding absurdity is not, of course, found in the original, in which the one 'fact' corresponds to *Tatsache* and the other to *Sachverhalt*. If the word 'fact' is to be used in English in such a way that *Sachverhalte* can be considered a kind of 'facts', which accord-

---

[1] Grimm's *Deutsches Wörterbuch* defines *Sachverhalt* as *statum rerum*, *Tatsache* as *factum*, i.e. something that 'really has happened', etc.

[2] Mr. D. S. Shwayder has earlier (in an unpublished thesis, deposited in the Bodleian Library, Oxford) made a similar observation concerning Wittgenstein's use of the words *Sachverhalt* and *Tatsache*, and compared it with Husserl's usage. Since I have not had the opportunity of a detailed study of Mr. Shwayder's dissertation, this is the only reference to it.

ingly can be thought of both as 'existing' and as 'non-existing', then
the word *Tatsache* cannot be translated as 'fact' but must be rendered
as 'existing fact'. If, on the other hand—which seems more natural—
the word 'fact' is taken as corresponding to *Tatsache*, then it is
nonsense if one—as for instance in 2.06—speaks of 'the non-existence
of facts', whether these 'facts' are atomic or not. For then 'non-
existent' facts are *no* facts at all.

The above distinction between *Tatsache* and *Sachverhalt* could be
transferred into English in, for instance, this way: We translate the
word *Tatsache* as 'fact', *bestehend* as 'existing' or 'real', *Sachverhalt* as,
say, 'circumstance', and adopt the following rule: 'A circumstance is
something that may exist (be real) or not exist (not be real). An
existing (real) circumstance is a fact.' Statement 2 could then be
rendered as follows: 'What is the case, the fact, is that circumstances
exist.'[1]

However here are some additional difficulties to be taken into
consideration.


## 2. *SACHVERHALTE* ARE 'ATOMIC'

What has been stated above of the term *Sachverhalt* holds true of
the term *Sachlage* as well. Like a *Sachverhalt* a *Sachlage* is something
*possible* in contradistinction to a *Tatsache*, that is something existing,
real. (Cf. 2.203, 3.11, etc.) In some statements the words *Sachverhalt*
and *Sachlage* may seem to be used synonymously, but in fact they are
not. The difference between the concepts signified by them appears
from an examination of two related characteristics of the concept
denoted by *Sachverhalt* in Wittgenstein's technical use of that word.

We have stated that a *Sachverhalt* is the descriptive content of a
factual statement. From this, however, does not follow that the
descriptive content of every factual statement is a *Sachverhalt*. I
think there may be a tendency to take the word *Sachverhalt* as
applicable to the descriptive contents of a special kind of factual
statements only. Assume for the moment that 'The earth is round'
and 'The earth is bigger than the moon' describe *Sachverhalte*. How
are we then to consider the sentence 'The earth is round and bigger
than the moon'? I think there is a tendency in German usage to

---

[1] The translation 'that circumstances exist' for *das Bestehen von Sachverhalten* is to be
preferred to the translation 'the existence of circumstances', because the latter expression
could also be taken as meaning 'that there exist circumstances'—which is not a possible
interpretation of the German text.

consider this as not describing a *Sachverhalt* but a conjunction of *Sachverhalte*. Such a tendency seems still more manifest for the sentence 'The earth is round *or* bigger than the moon', which may be said to describe not one *Sachverhalt* but a disjunction of two *Sachverhalte*. If this analysis is correct there is a tendency in German usage to take *Sachverhalte* as in some sense 'simple'. That this is implied in Wittgenstein's use of the word is obvious from 4.21:

> 4.21 Der einfachste Satz, der Elementarsatz, behauptet das Bestehen eines Sachverhaltes.

For this means that the descriptive contents of 'elementary sentences' only, i.e. of statements which according to Wittgenstein's terminology are 'logically simple', are to be considered as being *Sachverhalte*.

This is taken into account in the English version of the Tractatus, in which *Sachverhalte* are called 'atomic'. The rendering is to a certain degree disputable because it is not obvious that a *Sachverhalt* is always to be taken as 'atomic' in an absolute sense; as we shall see later it will in some contexts be more convenient to take the 'atomicity' in only a *relative* sense, relative, that is, to some fixed context. Nevertheless I think it inevitable that the word 'atomic' or some equivalent of it should be used in English to qualify the concept which is introduced as a translation of the German concept *Sachverhalt*. If we, for instance, translate *Sachverhalt* as 'circumstance', we must put the word 'atomic' in front of it, for there is no connotation of simplicity in the concept of a 'circumstance' as such. But then it seems more natural to use the expression 'state of affairs' instead of the word 'circumstance'. As will be shown later every *Sachverhalt* is also a *Sachlage*, though the converse need not to be true: a *Sachlage* need not be atomic, but if it is so, it is a *Sachverhalt*. It will not, therefore, lead to misunderstandings if we preserve the translation 'state of affairs' for *Sachlage* and at the same time translate *Sachverhalt* as 'atomic state of affairs'. *These translations will be used in the following discussion.*

## 3. *SACHVERHALTE* ARE INDEPENDENT OF ONE ANOTHER

There is another characteristic of the concept of a *Sachverhalt* which is logically connected with its atomicity. The *Sachverhalte*

D

are said to be independent of one another. The statements most relevant to this idea are the following:

1.21    Eines kann der Fall sein oder nicht der Fall sein und alles übrige gleich bleiben.

2.061   Die Sachverhalte sind von einander unabhängig.

2.062   Aus dem Bestehen oder Nichtbestehen eines Sachverhaltes kann nicht auf das Bestehen oder Nichtbestehen eines anderen geschlossen werden.

4.211   Ein Zeichen des Elementarsatzes ist es, dass kein Elementarsatz mit ihm in Widerspruch stehen kann.

Taking into consideration that an atomic state of affairs is the descriptive content of an elementary sentence these statements can be regarded as four different formulations of the same thought. From the existence or non-existence of one atomic state of affairs we cannot infer the existence or non-existence of any other atomic state of affairs (2.062), for the atomic states of affairs are *independent* of one another (2.061); an atomic state of affairs can, that is, 'be the case' or 'not be the case' independently of what holds true in respect of other atomic states of affairs (1.21): therefore two elementary sentences cannot contradict each other (4.211).

This general mutual independence of the atomic states of affairs presupposes their logical 'simplicity'. Whether or not the descriptive content of what is usually called a (logically) compound sentence is the case, is, of course, not independent of the truth or falsehood of, for instance, its components—that is, of whether the descriptive contents of the components are or are not the case.

## 4. *SACHLAGE* AND *TATSACHE*

As stated above a *Sachlage* seems to differ from a *Tatsache* in that it is something possible that need not be 'existent', and from a *Sachverhalt* in that it need not be atomic. Wittgenstein seems to use this concept mainly in the same sense as for instance Carnap. It seems to signify a 'possible' state of a larger or smaller portion of the world. It follows that not all factual sentences describe 'states of affairs'. If the sentences '$p$' and '$q$' describe atomic states of affairs, the sentences '$p \ \& \ q$', '$\sim p \ \& \ q$', '$p \ \& \sim q$', and '$\sim p \ \& \sim q$' describe 'states of affairs'. But a disjunction of sentences which describe states of affairs—as for instance '$p$ v $\sim p$' or '$(p$ & $q)$ v $(p$ & $\sim q)$' does not describe a state of affairs—we could say that its descriptive content is an alternative of states of affairs—for it does not describe one possible state but gives an alternative between different possible states. A closer analysis of this usage of the term *Sachlage* will be given in next chapter.

As for the term *Tatsache* we have stated that it should be rendered as 'fact'. But it is uncertain whether Wittgenstein means everything that might naturally be considered a 'fact' to fall under the concept of a *Tatsache*. In 2.06 'the existence of atomic states of affairs' is called a 'positive fact', 'the non-existence of atomic states of affairs' a 'negative fact'. Assuming that

(1)    The moon is smaller than the earth

and

(3)    The sun is smaller than the earth

describe atomic states of affairs, this means that the descriptive content of (1) is a *positive* fact, whereas the descriptive content of

(3')    The sun is *not* smaller than the earth

is a *negative* fact. However, Wittgenstein, as will be shown more in detail later, in 1.11 seems to take 'facts' only in the sense of 'positive facts', and the same is probably true of 2. In 2 'the fact' (*die Tatsache*) seems to be considered as compounded, whereas the 'facts' which the world is the totality of according to 1.1 or in which it is 'divided' according to 1.2 certainly must be regarded as 'atomic'. We may infer that Wittgenstein's terminology varies with regard to what facts are to be considered 'facts' in the technical sense of the word. To this may be added that an *existing* state of affairs is also called 'reality' (*Wirklichkeit*) in 2.06 (cf. 2.063).

To create a more uniform terminology I shall in the following discussion call an 'existent *atomic* state of affairs' an 'atomic fact'. It should be noted that according to this convention my use of the expression 'atomic fact' is *different* from that of the English version of the Tractatus. In concordance with 2.06 I shall make the further convention that a 'positive fact' is to mean the same as an 'atomic fact'.[1] A 'positive fact' accordingly means 'that an atomic state of affairs exists' or 'an existent atomic state of affairs'.[2] By a 'negative fact' I mean 'that an atomic state of affairs does not exist'. The word 'fact' we shall use to denote the descriptive content of any true sentence whatsoever, whether it is a state of affairs or not.

Finally an important point should be emphasized. In our division of concepts into categories in Chapter II we introduced a category named the 'category of facts'. It is, however, obvious, that states of affairs belong to the same category *independently* of their being facts or not. When using the expression 'category of facts' we therefore must be clear that this category comprises not only 'facts' in our sense of the word, but also all that could *possibly* be a fact. Facts alone cannot form a category because whether a state of affairs is a fact or not does not affect its *logical nature* but is a question of the 'material' properties of reality (cf. 2.0231).

## 5. SUMMARY

By use of the terminology adopted above statement 2 may be formulated as follows:

2′   What is the case, the fact, is that atomic states of affairs exist.[3]

The concept of an (atomic) state of affairs fulfils the following conditions:

(III.1)   *An (atomic) state of affairs can be existent (real) or non-existent. An existent atomic state of affairs is called an atomic fact.*

---

[1] The formulation of 2.06 seems to indicate that Wittgenstein regards every conjunction of atomic facts as a 'positive fact'. However, we need that term only to signify single atomic facts. A similar remark is to be made on 'negative facts'.

[2] I use the word 'exist' in connection with the expression '(atomic) state of affairs' according to the following rules of logical grammar:

'The state of affairs that the moon is smaller than the earth exists' = 'the moon's being smaller than the earth is an existent state of affairs' = 'the moon is smaller than the earth'.

'The state of affairs that the sun is smaller than the earth does not exist' = 'the sun's being smaller than the earth is a non-existent state of affairs' = 'the sun is not smaller than the earth'.

What here appears on the left side of the equals sign is to be regarded only as a complicated way of saying the same thing as what is said by the sentence on the right side. Cf. below, p. 145.

[3] Cf. above, p. 32 n.

(III.2) *Atomic states of affairs are independent of one another. The existence or non-existence of one atomic state of affairs is independent of the existence or non-existence of any other atomic state of affairs.*

(III.3) *As a general rule this independence holds only for atomic states of affairs. States of affairs are not in general independent of one another.*

(III.4) *An atomic state of affairs is described in language by an elementary sentence.*

# IV

# LOGICAL SPACE

In our second chapter we stated that objects and predicates enter into the world only as constituents of facts. This could be called a feature of the 'logical structure' of the world—the word 'logical' being taken here in the wide and somewhat vague sense in which it is used by Wittgenstein. In Chapter III we pointed out a circumstance which, according to the Tractatus, forms another such feature: the world as a fact breaks up into existent 'atomic states of affairs' which are thought of as being 'independent' of one another.

The present chapter is mainly devoted to the analysis of the concept of 'independence' as it is to be understood in this context.

The 'independence' of 'the atomic states of affairs' belongs, we said, to the *logical* structure of the world. If $p$ and $q$ are two states of affairs which exist in our world, then it is the case that $p$ and $q$ exist, it is a *fact* the statement of which belongs to a description of our world as it is. If, however, we are to say that $p$ and $q$ are 'independent' of each other, then we no longer simply state a fact about the world as it is, but rather something about the world as it *might* possibly be: though $p$ and $q$ *are* both existent, each of them *might be* existent *or* non-existent independently of what is true of the other. The 'independence' does not refer in particular to the real world; it refers likewise to all possible worlds. And therefore the question whether a state of affairs is *independent* of another state of affairs involves the question of *what kind of worlds are to be considered 'possible worlds'*.

## I. A MODEL OF A 'LOGICAL STRUCTURE' OF THE WORLD

This question will, I think, be illuminated by considering a model of the following kind. Assume that what is called the 'world' (as a thing) consists of a number—say five—rectangular parallelepipeds (see Fig. 2), and that the only facts considered relevant in this 'world'—it may be called P—are the size and shape of those parallelepipeds. A description of the world would then take the following form:

$$
\begin{array}{llll}
& \text{1. } P_1 \text{ is 2.3 yds long.} & P_1 \text{ is 1.5 yds wide.} & P_1 \text{ is 0.8 yds high.} \\
& \text{2. } P_2 \text{ ,, 4.0 ,, ,,} & P_2 \text{ ,, 3.2 ,, ,,} & P_2 \text{ ,, 2.5 ,, ,,} \\
(P) & \text{3. } P_3 \text{ ,, 5.9 ,, ,,} & P_3 \text{ ,, 5.1 ,, ,,} & P_3 \text{ ,, 4.4 ,, ,,} \\
& \text{4. } P_4 \text{ ,, 2.0 ,, ,,} & P_4 \text{ ,, 2.1 ,, ,,} & P_4 \text{ ,, 0.5 ,, ,,} \\
& \text{5. } P_5 \text{ ,, 3.1 ,, ,,} & P_5 \text{ ,, 4.3 ,, ,,} & P_5 \text{ ,, 3.8 ,, ,,}
\end{array}
$$

(P) is thought of as giving a complete description of the world as it *is*. Now it seems natural to consider the fifteen facts described by sentences (P) as mutually *independent* states of affairs. For we may plausibly think that each of these states of affairs could possibly be

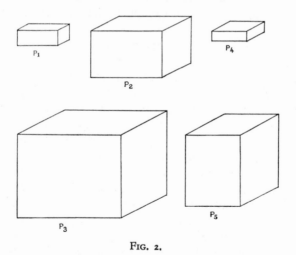

P₁
P₄
P₂
P₃
P₅

FIG. 2.

changed while all the others remained the same. So, for instance, the length of $P_1$ could be changed from 2.3 yds to, say, 3.5 yds without any change of its width or height, because 'length', 'width' and 'height' belong to different 'dimensions'. Of course we could also imagine the length of $P_1$ changed without any changes in the measurements of the other parallelepipeds—because there is no logical connexion between the dimensions of different parallelepipeds.

Now I think the fact that the length of a parallelepiped is naturally considered as being logically independent of its width or height throws light on the concept of 'independence' as it is used in this context. For it seems plausible to say that what is essential to the notion of different 'dimensions' is the idea that states of affairs which refer to different dimensions are *independent* of one another while states of affairs not belonging to different dimensions are logically connected. When a parallelepiped is said to have three dimensions, this means that its length, width and height can be fixed independently of one another, whereas any *other* measurement of it is logically dependent on these three measurements and can be calculated from them. With the aid of Pythagoras' Theorem the diagonal of $P_1$ can be calculated to be 2.9 yds, and therefore this measurement cannot be changed without a change of at least one of the dimensions of $P_1$. In the same way, for instance, the volume of $P_2$ can be calculated from its dimensions—it is found to be 32.0 cub. yds—and, again, this measurement cannot be changed without a change of at least one of the dimensions.

We could therefore generalize the concept of 'dimensions' by stating that a world has as many dimensions as it has mutually independent components of description. According to this terminology our model world $P$ has 15 dimensions.

Now the fact that there are 15 dimensions in the world $P$ in the sense of 15 mutually independent components of description implies an assumption concerning what variations of measurements are considered possible, and hence an assumption concerning what *worlds* are considered possible. That no necessary connections are assumed between the different dimensions of each parallelepiped or the dimensions of different parallelepipeds implies, on the one hand, that *all* worlds consisting of five parallelepipeds are considered *possible* worlds, independently of the measurements of each parallelepiped. That the measurements of the diagonal of a parallelepiped is regarded as 'logically dependent' on its three dimensions presupposes, on the other hand, that *only* such worlds are considered possible as consist of *rectangular* parallelepipeds with Euclidean geometrical properties. The fixation of the dimensions limits the range of 'all' possible worlds, and conversely, the number of dimensions will—at least under some additional conditions—be determined by the system of all possible worlds.

Perhaps the model $P$ and the terminology attached to it may seem a very artificial experiment of thought, and certainly it is so in many respects. But in some important regards it is not. The notion of mutually independent components of description as 'dimensions' is not an uncommon metaphor in ordinary language. A generalized concept of 'dimensions' with an import of this kind is also found in physics. But above all the number of mutually independent components of description has been an important factor in physical world description. Our world is considered by the physicists as a world with an immense number of 'dimensions' in this sense, and therefore our model can in this respect serve as a model of descriptions in physics.[1] Also a more 'phenomenal' description of the world must—it seems to me—employ a system of dimensions of an essentially similar kind.

We will now go on to a more detailed discussion of our model world. We have considered the sentences ($P$) as a complete description of this world. Further we have regarded the state of affairs described by any of these sentences as being *independent* of any other such state of affairs. And we have assumed that this implies that every 'possible' world consists of five parallelepipeds with three dimensions each. We shall now consider the states of affairs described by ($P$) as 'atomic states of affairs' and raise the question whether the atomic states of affairs, thus defined, fulfil the conditions (III.1)–(III.4) of the preceding chapter. Then an important point can immediately be noticed: condition (III.2) is *not* satisfied as formulated there. Atomic states of affairs of *different* dimensions are, to be sure, independent of one another. But in every dimension there is an infinite number of atomic states of affairs which belong to the *same* dimension and hence are not independent of one another but on the contrary mutually *inconsistent*. So, for instance, $P_1$ must have *some* length in every possible world, and this might differ from that indicated by ($P$), but $P_1$ cannot have more than one length in any possible world. The two states of affairs '$P_1$ is 2.3 yds long' and '$P_1$ is 3.5 yds long' are both possible in themselves, but they exclude one another. The same holds true of all other dimensions of the system.

This means that condition (III.2) in our model world must be replaced by the following weaker condition:

[1] A view of this kind is developed, for instance, in Hertz's *Mechanics*. Cf. below p. 83, n. 1.

(III.2') *Atomic states of affairs of different dimensions are independent of one another. The existence or non-existence of the atomic states of affairs of one dimension is independent of the existence or non-existence of the atomic states of affairs of any other dimension.*

The conditions (III.3) and (III.4) should be modified in a corresponding way.

In fact Wittgenstein in his paper 'Some Remarks on Logical Form' (1929) modified his conception of the logical structure of the world in the direction indicated by (III.2'). In this paper he is chiefly concerned with properties which admit of gradation and in particular the colour concepts. For the last mentioned there is an old problem whether it is to be considered an empirical or logical truth that the same patch of the visual field cannot be, for instance, both red and blue. On this subject Wittgenstein makes the following observation in the Tractatus, 6.3751: 'For two colours to be at the same place in the visual field is impossible, and it is *logically* impossible, for it is excluded by the logical structure of colour.' A similar statement is repeated in the 1929 paper, with the additional remark that it is therefore incorrect to believe that atomic propositions cannot exclude one another.[1] So here Wittgenstein can be said to admit the possibility of different atomic states of affairs of the same dimension which are not logically independent.

## 2. 'LOGICAL SPACE'

We therefore could find support in Wittgenstein of 1929 for objecting against the Tractatus that it seems to accord better with the actual descriptions of physics, if we think of the logical structure of the world on the analogy of our model world rather than in the way assumed by the author of the Tractatus. In order to see the import of this objection we must try to form a more precise idea of the differences between the two views. To this end an examination of the concept of 'logical space' introduced in 1.13 is useful:

1.13    Die Tatsachen im logischen Raum sind die Welt.

'The facts in logical space are the world.' If applied to our model world this statement could be given the following interpretation: We have stated that P has 15 'dimensions' in the sense of 15 mutually

[1] 'Logical Form', p. 168. Cf. also Waismann: 'Was ist logische Analyse?', pp. 280 ff.

independent components of description. Now this system of 'dimensions' must be clearly distinguished from the system of three dimensions belonging to our ordinary geometrical space. The three-dimensionality of the geometrical space is a characteristic of the 'world as a thing' whereas the fifteen dimensions of our model world refer to this world as a *fact*. That *P* has 15 dimensions means that the description (*P*) is complete, not only positively in the sense of indicating what is the case, but also negatively in that it *excludes* all other possibilities. Our description comprises 'the totality of facts' and 'the totality of facts determines what is the case and in addition all that is not the case' (1.12).[1] This is important, because a proposition cannot have a factual content unless, in stating something as being the case, it *excludes* something else from being the case. It is essential to the 'logical structure' of our model world that it be fitted into a *logical space* of *possible* states of affairs. Of those states of affairs a complete description singles out one as existent, as real, excluding all others. This 'logical space' is a fifteen-dimensional 'space' of possible places of *states of affairs*, whereas the ordinary geometrical space is a space of possible places of *things*. What the places in logical space are places of belongs to the category of *facts* whereas what the places in ordinary geometrical space are places of belongs to the category of *things*. And the real world occupies only one 'point' in the logical space of possible worlds.

The general conception of a logical structure of the world, of which our model world is an instance, might be summed up in the following theses:

(IV.1) *The world as a fact is fitted into a 'logical space' of possible worlds. The dimensions of this logical space are determined by the mutually independent components of a world description.*

(IV.2) *Every dimension comprises a system of atomic states of affairs which mutually exclude one another.*

(IV.3) *A combination of atomic states of affairs which consists of one atomic state of affairs of each dimension determines a 'possible world', i.e. a possible state of affairs of the world as a whole.*

(IV.4) *In order to give a complete description of the real world we have to indicate, for each dimension, which atomic state of affairs of this dimension is a fact.*

---

[1] On this interpretation of 1.12, cf., however, below, pp. 48 ff.

## 3. YES-AND-NO DIMENSIONS

The logical space characterized by the theses (IV.1–4) corresponds to a system of atomic states of affairs which fulfils the condition (III.2′). According to the Tractatus, however, the 'logical space' is related to atomic states of affairs which fulfil the condition (III.2) instead of (III.2′). But how are we to imagine a 'logical space' in which *all* atomic states of affairs are independent of one another?

The transition from (III.2′) to (III.2) could be carried out by using an argument of the following kind. We have regarded the world P as fitted into a logical space which, on the one hand, does not allow for any other 'possible worlds' than such as consist of five rectangular Euclidean parallelepipeds, but which, on the other hand, does not impose any further restriction as to what is considered 'possible'. This means, for instance, that the dimensions of the different parallelepipeds may take any positive values whatsoever independently of one another. But why should the logical space around P have exactly this structure? Even if we take it as granted that all possible worlds are composed of five rectangular parallelepipeds we might ask ourselves whether *all* worlds composed of five rectangular parallelepipeds are really possible. Is there anything to prevent us from regarding as 'possible' worlds only such systems of five parallelepipeds as are submitted to certain additional conditions? So long as there are no criteria for what is possible it is difficult to see how such a view could be refuted. We might, for instance, regard as possible only such worlds as have the ratio between length, width and height in common with the real world. This means that we regard the *size* of each individual parallelepiped as variable, whereas its geometrical shape is regarded as belonging to its 'essence' and therefore unchangeable. Then the length, width and height of each rectangular parallelepiped are not considered independent of one another. In order to state what is the case in the actual world, we need only indicate, e.g., the *length* of each parallelepiped, the width and height being calculable from the length by means of the ratios given *a priori*. Thus our world would not possess fifteen but only five dimensions.

It is also possible to decrease the number of the 'possible' worlds without changing the number of the dimensions. We might simply restrict the number of *values* that are regarded as possible in each dimension. We could for instance for some reason admit as 'possible' only those worlds in which the length of $P_1$ is, say, either 2.3 yds, 4.6 yds, 6.9 yds or 9.2 yds, while the length of $P_2$ takes, for instance, one of the values 2.0 yds, 4.0 yds, 6.0 yds and 8.0 yds, and so on, assuming for each dimension only four different possible values. We could call this a world with fifteen four-valued dimensions. Incidentally the assumption of such 'discrete' dimensions cannot be regarded as too artificial in the age of quantum theory[1].

Here the possibility of each dimension allowing for only *two* different values is of special interest.

Assume that the possible values of the length, width and height of $P_1$ are, say, 4.6 yds and 2.3 yds, 3.0 yds and 1.5 yds, and 0.8 yds and 0.4 yds, only two values (the one of which is double the other) being considered logically possible in each dimension, and that a corresponding restriction holds true for the remaining parallelepipeds. We have then a fifteen-dimensional two-valued logical space. Now the circumstance that every dimension allows for only two possible values means not only that the *assertion* of one of the values logically implies the *negation* of the other, but also that the converse is true. The assertion of one of the values of a dimension is in that case logically *equivalent* to the negation of the other. The only possible values of the length of $P_1$ being 2.3 yds and 4.6 yds, '$P_1$ is 2.3 yds long' means the same as '$P_1$ is not 4.6 yds long' and conversely. But if this is so, then we could agree upon regarding the assertion of *one* of these values only—say the greater one—as a *positive* statement, whereas the assertion of the other value is regarded as a mere *negation* of this. If now the positive statement is considered to describe an *atomic* state of affairs, then according to this interpretation the *negative* statement does not describe an atomic state of affairs—because the negation of an atomic state of affairs is not atomic but logically compounded. So according to this interpretation every dimension contains only *one* atomic state of affairs properly so called, and therefore *all atomic states of affairs* properly so called are *independent of one another*. And so a logical space the dimensions of which are all two-valued is transformed by means of this interpretation into a logical space in which (III.2) is valid instead of (III.2').

The assumption that only 4.6 yds and 2.3 yds are logically possible

[1] From a physiologist's point of view a 'phenomenal' description of the world too can be assumed to be founded on discrete dimensions. Cf. Reenpää: 'Wahrnehmnen', pp. 104 ff.

values of the length of $P_1$ makes, of course, the mention of exactly *these* values irrelevant for the description of the world; what is relevant is only that there are two and only two different values. And then the mention of any special values at all is superfluous and may be omitted—indeed *should* be omitted, if we are to apply Occam's razor (cf. 3.328 and 5.47321)—so we might say instead that there is a yes-value and a no-value. Instead of writing '$P_1$ is 4.6 yds long', we might write only '$P_1$ is long' and accordingly instead of '$P_1$ is 2.3 yds long' simply '$P_1$ is not long' and similarly for all other dimensions. The description ($P$) then takes the form

$P_1$ is not long.     $P_1$ is not wide.     $P_1$ is high.
($P'$)  $P_2$ is...................................................
.....................................................

Written in this form some of the sentences of our description indicate 'positive' facts while the rest of them indicate 'negative' facts. Of the facts belonging to $P_1$ only one is positive and atomic; the other two are negative and logically compounded.

We arrive at the following result:

(IV.5)   *If the dimensions of the logical space allow for only two values each, these values may be considered as a yes-value and a no-value, which means that only one of the states of affairs in each dimension is considered atomic. A logical space of this kind can therefore be described as one in which all atomic states of affairs are independent of one another.*

If a two-valued logical space is interpreted in this way I shall call it a *yes-and-no* space. By use of this term (IV.4) can be formulated as follows:

(IV.5')   *A two-valued logical space can be considered as a yes-and-no space. In a yes-and-no space every atomic state of affairs has a dimension of its own.*

4. IS EVERY LOGICAL SPACE REDUCIBLE TO A
   YES-AND-NO SPACE?

A logical structure of the world fulfilling the condition (III.2) might thus be considered a *special instance* of a logical structure fulfilling the condition (III.2'). We can therefore state that Wittgenstein at the beginning of the Tractatus regards this special instance as the 'general' form of a logical structure of the world as a fact. Now one might be tempted to infer from the statement 6.3751 quoted above (p. 42) that Wittgenstein at the end of the Tractatus abandons this view and thinks instead of a logical space with continuously gradeable dimensions. But this is not so. That a patch in the visual field is red excludes indeed logically, according to the Tractatus, its being blue, yellow or green, but obviously Wittgenstein did not regard states of affairs of the type 'this patch is red' as atomic, but on the contrary held them to be compounded in a complicated way. He apparently was of the opinion that all states of affairs of this kind could be *reduced* by a more thorough analysis to a system of atomic states of affairs which are all independent of one another, a view which in 1929 he explicitly states he had held earlier,[1] but had now abandoned. I shall not discuss here the question, which of Wittgenstein's two standpoints is to be considered more true. I only want to state that *if* the author of the Tractatus was in some sense right contra Wittgenstein of 1929, then one has to infer that the possibility of regarding a logical space as a yes-and-no space exists not only for a space with two-valued dimensions, but also, in some sense, for spaces with many-valued dimensions. If this were so, the condition (III.2') could be regarded as only seemingly more general than (III.2).

## 5. THE LOGICAL STRUCTURE OF THE WORLD IN A YES-AND-NO SPACE

We have noticed that the transition from a logical space with two-valued dimensions to a yes-and-no space can be effected simply by regarding half of those states of affairs which, according to the two-value view, are considered 'atomic' as logically compounded 'negative' states of affairs. It follows that the world as a fact, if analysed in terms of a yes-and-no space, does not break up into *atomic* facts alone, as it does if analysed in terms of many-valued dimensions: the description (P') does not, like (P), comprise only 'positive' facts, which are atomic, but 'negative' facts as well. If 'positive' facts together with 'negative' facts are called 'simple', the difference might be summarized as follows:

[1] 'Logical Form', p. 167.

(IV.6)   *In a yes-and-no space the world as an analysed fact does not break up into atomic facts only, but is built up of 'simple' facts that are either 'positive' atomic facts or 'negative' compounded facts, the latter consisting in the non-existence of an atomic state of affairs.*

But how is this result to be reconciled with statement 2? According to this statement, 'what is the case' i.e. the world as a fact, is that atomic states of affairs *exist*—there is no room left for negative facts.

Now statement 2 and also statements 1.11–1.13 in fact get a simpler interpretation if we assume a logical space with many-valued dimensions than if we assume a yes-and-no space. But there is a reasonable interpretation at least of the last mentioned statements on the latter assumption too. They run as follows:

1.11   Die Welt ist durch die Tatsachen bestimmt und dadurch, dass es a l l e Tatsachen sind.

1.12   Denn, die Gesamtheit der Tatsachen bestimmt, was der Fall ist und auch, was alles nicht der Fall ist.

1.13   Die Tatsachen im logischen Raum sind die Welt.

As we have stated before, the word *Tatsache* has a vague use in the Tractatus. In these statements, however, it seems obvious that *Tatsachen* is taken in the sense of positive facts only. The world is determined by (an indication of) all positive facts and by (the indication of) these being *all* the positive facts (1.11). For the totality of positive facts determines also all negative facts (1.12). Hence the world is the totality of all positive facts in relation to logical space (1.13).

If we assume a logical space with many-valued dimensions these statements can be naturally interpreted thus: the world as an analysed fact breaks up into positive facts alone—one for each dimension. These positive facts, however, being fitted into a logical space, determine not only positively all that is the case, but also negatively all that is *not* the case because every positive fact excludes all other atomic states of affairs of the same dimension. 1.11 then means that the world is determined by an indication of one fact for each dimension and the additional statement that these are *all* the dimensions, 1.12 that the totality of these positive facts excludes all other atomic states of affairs, 1.13 that this is so because the positive facts are surrounded by a logical space.

Assuming a yes-and-no space the interpretation becomes more complicated. Let us think of all atomic states of affairs as ordered into a series:[1]

$$(p) \qquad\qquad p_1, p_2, \ldots .$$

According to what is the case this series can be divided into two sub-series: the series of all *existent* atomic states of affairs, which may be denoted

$$(p+) \qquad\qquad p_{+1}, p_{+2}, p_{+3}, \ldots ,$$

and the series of all non-existent atomic states of affairs, which may be denoted

$$(p-) \qquad\qquad p_{-1}, p_{-2}, p_{-3}, \ldots .$$

('$p_{+1}$' indicates the first of the atomic states of affairs in $(p)$ that exists, '$p_{-1}$' the first of them that does not exist, etc.).

The expressions '$p_1$', etc., we may consider as abbreviations of the elementary sentences describing the corresponding atomic states of affairs. We then obtain a complete description of the world by asserting all the statements of $(p_+)$ and negating all the statements of $(p_-)$. A description of this kind is given above in (P'), (p. 46). I shall call it a description of the *first* kind.

We could, however, give a complete description of the world in a different way, too. Granted that the atomic states of affairs in $(p)$ are given in advance and also the elementary sentences describing them—which means that the series of *all* elementary sentences is given in advance—we could give a complete description of the world by asserting the sentences of $(p_+)$ and adding that what then has been asserted is *all* true elementary sentences. The series $(p)$, namely, being given in advance, the series $(p_-)$ can be obtained by a subtraction of the series $(p_+)$ from the series $(p)$, and it follows that all sentences of $(p_-)$ are false. Leaving out the reference to language this could be expressed thus: *If the series of all atomic states*

[1] I assume, for the sake of simplicity, that the set of dimensions is either finite or, if infinite, denumerable. It will not, however, make any essential difference if the set of dimensions is assumed to be non-denumerable.

E

*of affairs is given in advance, then we can indicate all simple facts of the world by indicating* (a) *all positive facts and* (b) *that what then has been indicated is* ALL *positive facts.* This method I shall call a description of the *second* kind.

Here an important point should be noticed. A description of the second kind could be said to contain two steps: (a) the indication of the series $(p)$ of *all* atomic states of affairs, (b) the selection of the positive facts from these series. Of these steps, however, only the second constitutes what can properly be said to belong to the *description* of our world, whereas the first is only a preparatory step for this description. For the series (a) is not peculiar to the real world—it determines only the 'logical space' to which this world belongs. But the logical space is common to *all* 'possible' worlds, and this means that an indication of the structure of the logical space does not form a proper part of the description of the world but only determines a *framework* for such a description and thus is *prior* to all actual description. An actual description of the world consists in the division of all atomic states of affairs into existent and non-existent states of affairs.

Our interpretation of 1.11–13 in respect of a yes-and-no space is accordingly the following. In 1.13 the world is characterized as the positive facts *in* logical space—that is as the system $(p_+)$ as a part of the system $(p)$. 1.11 and 1.12 state of this system that it—being the system of *all* positive facts—also determines the system $(p_-)$.

## 6. WELT AND *WIRKLICHKEIT*

We might therefore from the point of view of a yes-and-no space suppose that the main purpose of statements 1.11–1.13 is to emphasize the *priority* of the system of atomic states of affairs to a description of the world. As we shall see from the following discussion this is a very important idea in the Tractatus. Thus, I think, we have arrived at an interpretation of these statements on the assumption of a yes-and-no space which, though it is more complicated, is nevertheless as natural as the interpretation assuming a space with many-valued dimensions. But in one respect it remains unsatisfactory: why is the world in 1.13 *identified* with the system of the *positive* facts only? The dissatisfaction is increased by the fact that this identification is made still more explicit in 2.

One thing must be emphasized here. In 2 Wittgenstein mentions only the *existent* atomic states of affairs: this cannot be due to a pure lapse. The same formulation is repeated in 2.04, where the world is characterized as the 'totality of the existent atomic states of affairs' with the additional remark made in 2.05, that the 'totality of the existent atomic states of affairs also determines which atomic states of affairs do not exist', which may be regarded as a more exact formulation of 1.12. Moreover 2.04 may be contrasted to 2.06, where reality (*Wirklichkeit*) is stated to be the existence *and* non-existence of atomic states of affairs. But why is reality said to be composed of both positive and negative facts, if the world (*Welt*) consists of positive facts only?

There is a possible explanation of this difference between *Wirklichkeit* and *Welt*. According to our earlier analysis *Wirklichkeit* means a larger or smaller part of the world as a fact—we might call it 'a piece of reality' rather than 'reality'. A description of *Wirklichkeit* therefore consists of the affirmation of a smaller or larger part of $(p_+)$ and the negation of a smaller or larger part of $(p_-)$. This is the way, that is, in which a piece of reality is described according to our *first* method of description. And it corresponds to the concept of *Wirklichkeit* as the existence *and* non-existence of atomic states of affairs. Now it should be noticed that our *second* method of description is not applicable to a piece of reality. Consider a piece of reality R. The corresponding subseries of $(p_+)$ and $(p_-)$ may be called $(p_{+R})$ and $(p_{-R})$. Together they form a subseries of $(p)$ which may be called $(p_R)$. Assume that we have indicated only the positive facts in R together with the statement that these are all positive facts in R. Then we have indicated which are the atomic states of affairs belonging to $(p_{+R})$—but we cannot infer from this which are the atomic states of affairs belonging to $(p_{-R})$, because we have left open the question whether an atomic state of affairs not belonging to $(p_{+R})$ belongs to $(p_{-R})$ or falls outside $(p_R)$ altogether.

We may conclude, then, that Wittgenstein thinks of a description of the first kind when speaking of 'reality' and a description of the second kind when speaking of the 'world'. The fact that the world can *also* be described by a description of the first kind accounts for the formulation of 2.063—inconsistent as such with the differentiation made in 2.04 and 2.06—according to which the world is 'the whole of reality'. But this circumstance still does not explain why the world should anywhere be identified with the system of the positive facts alone. As a matter of fact I think this identification can be given a natural interpretation *only* in relation to a logical space with many-valued dimensions. And there are other points, too, in the Tractatus where Wittgenstein's thought seems to oscillate between the explicitly stated principle of a logical space in which all atomic states of affairs are mutually independent and the idea of a logical space with many-valued dimensions. And whether or no this is so it is of interest that many of Wittgenstein's views in the Tractatus can be maintained even if the latter conception is accepted. On the other hand it should be noticed, that, though the idea of the *priority* of the system ($p$) to any description of the world is fundamental to the philosophy of the Tractatus, the 'second method' of dividing this system into existent and non-existent states of affairs is not of any importance in the rest of the book. In the following discussion we shall therefore—with the support of 2.063— regard the world as the totality of both the positive and the negative facts in accordance with (IV.6).

## 7. THE LOGICAL SPACE AS A SPACE OF 'POSSIBLE WORLDS'

The priority of the system ($p$) to a description of the world is due—we have said—to the fact that ($p$) determines the 'logical space' and thus the common framework of all 'possible' worlds. We shall here—assuming the logical space to be a yes-and-no space—try to give a more precise account of this idea.

We have earlier characterized the logical space as a space of 'possible states of affairs' (*Sachlagen*), or, since these states of affairs refer to the world as a whole, as a space of 'possible worlds' ('worlds', that is, of the category of facts).

This should be understood in the following way. The world is determined by a division of the system ($p$) into the sub-systems ($p_+$) and ($p_-$) of the existent and non-existent atomic states of affairs. Thus there is one, and only one, division which holds for the *real* world. Now the different atomic states of affairs in ($p$) determine the dimensions of the logical space, and this means that, though only one division holds for the real world, there are nevertheless other divisions which are *logically* possible. And each logically possible division defines a *possible world* in the logical space of ($p$).

Every world which is 'possible' in this sense has therefore the system ($p$) in common with the real world and differs from it only by corresponding to a different division of $(p)$ into 'existent' and 'non-existent' atomic states of affairs.

When in the last sentence we used the words 'existent' and 'non-existent' we meant 'existent' and 'non-existent' in a certain *possible* world. This *relative* use of the words 'existent' and 'non-existent'—with reference to a *possible* world—must not be confused with their *absolute* use in the sense of 'existent' and 'non-existent' in the *real* world. An atomic state of affairs which is 'existent' in the *absolute* sense is a *fact*, whereas an atomic state of affairs which is 'existent' in a possible world $W$ need certainly not be a fact—it must be so only if $W$ is the real world.

In the same way the words 'existent' and 'non-existent' (and their derivatives) can be taken relatively to a state of affairs which does not comprise the whole world. A state of affairs $S$ is determined by a division of a sub-system $(p_S)$ of $(p)$ into two classes, the class $(p_{+S})$ of atomic states of affairs which are 'existent' in $S$ and the class $(p_{-S})$ of atomic states of affairs which are 'non-existent' in $S$. But this does not mean that the members of the first class *exist*, nor that the members of the second class *do not exist* in the absolute sense—it is so only if $S$ is a *real* state of affairs, i.e. a piece of *reality*.[1]

This point should be taken into account in the interpretation of 2.11. Here 'existence' and 'non-existence' of atomic states of affairs are referred to a *Sachlage* and must be understood in a relative sense.

It will be convenient to call an atomic state of affairs 'positive in a state of affairs $S$' if it belongs to $(S_+)$ and 'negative in $S$' if it belongs to $(S_-)$, and correspondingly in respect of a possible world $W$. (If $S$ is a *real* (existing) state of affairs, then the positive atomic states of affairs in $S$ are *positive facts*, whereas the *negation* of the negative states of affairs in $S$ are *negative facts*.)

We could then simply *define* a possible state of affairs $S$ as a division of a certain sub-system $(p_S)$ of $(p)$ into two classes the members of which are called the positive and negative atomic states of affairs in $S$. Similarly we define a 'possible world' $W$ as a division of the whole system $(p)$ into positive and negative atomic states of affairs in $W$. In this way the system $(p)$ as a whole determines a 'logical space' of possible worlds and every sub-system of $(p)$ a logical space of possible states of affairs.

---

[1] The 'relative' use of the terms 'existent' and 'non-existent' corresponds to an analogous use of the terms 'true' and 'false' in truth-tables. Cf. below, p. 150.

If the logical space possesses only a finite number of dimensions, say $n$, so that $(p)$ has $n$ members, then it can be divided into positive and negative atomic states of affairs in $2^n$ different ways, and therefore contains $2^n$ possible worlds.

## 8. LOGICAL POSITION

We have said that the individual 'places' of the logical space are places of possible worlds (as facts). These places correspond to the 'points' of the ordinary geometrical space. If the logical space contains only three atomic states of affairs, say, $p_1$, $p_2$, and $p_3$, this correspondence enables us to visualize the idea of 'logical space'. The atomic states of affairs $p_1$, $p_2$ and $p_3$ may correspond to the three axes of an orthogonal coordinate system within the three-dimensional geometrical space (Fig. 3).

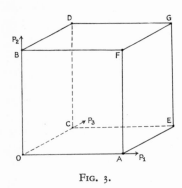

FIG. 3.

On each of the axes we take two values, say o and I, to correspond to the no-value and the yes-value in this dimension. The determination of a possible world by a division of the atomic states of affairs into positive and negative states of affairs in $W$ corresponds to the determination of a point in geometrical space by its three coordinates. That $p_1$ is positive in $W$ means geometrically that the $p_1$-coordinate of $W$ is I; that $p_1$ is negative in $W$ means that the $p_1$-coordinate of $W$ is o, and so on. Our logical space consists in this instance of $2^3 = 8$ possible worlds, which correspond to the 8 corners of a cube (the points $O$–$G$ in Fig. 3). If we denote the non-existence of $p_i$ by $\bar{p}_i$ the possible worlds corresponding to the points $O - G$ may be indicated as follows:

$O:$ $(\bar{p}_1, \bar{p}_2, \bar{p}_3)$    $A:$ $(p_1, \bar{p}_2, \bar{p}_3)$    $B:$ $(\bar{p}_1, p_2, \bar{p}_3)$    $C:$ $(\bar{p}_1, \bar{p}_2, p_3)$

$D:$ $(\bar{p}_1, p_2, p_3)$    $E:$ $(p_1, \bar{p}_2, p_3)$    $F:$ $(p_1, p_2, \bar{p}_3)$    $G:$ $(p_1, p_2, p_3)$

The expressions occurring inside the parentheses we could call the 'logical coordinates' of a possible world as a state of affairs. A state of affairs the atomic states of affairs of which are only two—e.g. $p_1$ and $p_2$—corresponds to a point in a two-dimensional space; the position in the third dimension is left undetermined.

It may be useful to examine some of the statements of the Tractatus containing the expression 'logical space' with reference to Fig. 3. One of these statements is the following:

3.4 Der Satz bestimmt einen Ort im logischen Raum . . .

The word *Satz* we translate as 'sentence'. The word *Ort* should, I think, be rendered as 'position' rather than 'place' (*Stelle*). According to thesis 5 every sentence is a truth-function of elementary sentences. In this context we may regard the signs '$p_1$', '$p_2$', '$p_3$' as elementary sentences (cf. 4.24.) If a sentence $q$ is a truth-function of '$p_1$', '$p_2$' and '$p_3$' every combination of truth-values of these elementary sentences determines a truth-value for $q$. Now a 'combination of truth-values' for '$p_1$', '$p_2$' and '$p_3$' indicates a division of the atomic states of affairs of our logical space into positive and negative atomic states of affairs and hence determines a possible world, and conversely. It follows that every possible world determines a truth-value for sentence $q$, and that $q$ determines a division of all possible worlds into two classes, those which correspond to the truth-value true and those which correspond to the truth-value false for $q$, i.e. in 'positive' and 'negative' instances for $q$. Now the assertion of $q$ states that the real world is one of the positive instances for $q$. The totality of these positive instances is what is called the logical 'position' of $q$.

According to this principle the 'logical position' of $p_1$ & $p_2$ & $p_3$ is $G$, whereas the logical position of $p_1 \vee p_2 \vee p_3$ is the whole logical space except $O$, etc.

In 3.41 Wittgenstein states of the 'sentence-token' (*Satzzeichen*) and the 'logical coordinates' that they are the 'logical position'. Wittgenstein seems here to use the notion of 'logical coordinates' in a sense which is related to, though not identical with, the notion of 'logical coordinates' as used above. In 3.411 the geometrical and logical positions are said to agree in that each determines a 'possibility of existence'. This could be interpreted thus: just as the 'geometrical position' is a position that a body might occupy and in this sense means a possibility for the existence of a body, the logical position means a 'possibility for the existence of worlds'. 3.42 runs:

3.42 Obwohl der Satz nur einen Ort des logischen Raumes bestimmen darf, so muss doch durch ihn schon der ganze logische Raum gegeben sein.

(Sonst würden durch die Verneinung, die logische Summe, das logische Produkt, etc. immer neue Elemente — in Koordination — eingeführt.)

(Das logische Gerüst um das Bild herum bestimmt den logischen Raum. Der Satz durchgreift den ganzen logischen Raum.)

This statement could be interpreted as follows.[1] Consider an elementary sentence, e.g. '$p_1$'. This sentence determines a logical position. *Prima facie* we could think of this position only as a 'point' without taking into consideration what there is outside this point. But now we form the negation of '$p_1$'. This must determine a logical position *other* than does '$p_1$' (cf. 4.0641). If we start with thinking that '$p_1$' determines an isolated point the negation of '$p_1$' introduces a 'new element' into the logical space. If '$p_1$' is given there is therefore given a logical position not only for '$p_1$', but also for the negation of '$p_1$'. Thus we obtain a two-valued one-dimensional logical space. But again we can think that the logical space has this structure only if we take '$p_1$' in isolation without paying regard to the possibility of its entering into logical combinations with other elementary sentences. If we have two elementary sentences '$p_1$' and '$p_2$' there must be positions not only for these sentences and their negations, but also for their 'logical sum, logical product, etc.' As a 'dimension' in a two-dimensional logical space $p_1$ has therefore a function different from its function in an isolated one-dimensional space. And as a dimension in a three-dimensional space it has again a function different from its function in a two-dimensional space, and so on. 'Although a sentence may determine only a position in logical space, the whole logical space must be given by it.'

What is of essential interest in this argument is only the fact that the logical position of '$p_1$', for instance, in a space of many dimensions is *not* a point. Considered as a 'truth-function of elementary sentences' sentence '$p_1$' is, to be sure, in the first place a truth-function only of *itself*.[2] But taken as a truth-function of itself '$p_1$' determines a logical position only in the one-dimensional logical space, the dimension of which is the $p_1$-dimension. If it is to deter-

---

[1] I leave the reference to a picture in the first sentence of the last paragraph out of consideration in the present context.

[2] Cf. the second paragraph in 5.

mine a position in the three-dimensional logical space of Fig. 3 it must be regarded as a truth-function of the arguments '$p_2$' and '$p_3$' as well. In fact this is possible: '$p_1$' is a truth-function of the arguments '$p_1$', '$p_2$' and '$p_3$' taking the value 'true' for those four combinations of truth-values of the arguments in which the truth-value of the first argument is 'true' and taking the value 'false' for the remaining combinations.[1] The logical position of '$p_1$' in the space of Fig. 3 consists therefore of all points the $p_1$-coordinate of which is 1, i.e. points $A$, $E$, $F$ and $G$. In the same way every sentence can be regarded as a truth-function not only of those elementary sentences which it contains, but also of all other elementary sentences. Thus every sentence 'reaches through (*durchgreift*) the whole logical space'.

In 4.463 the first paragraph runs: 'The truth-conditions determine the range which is left to the facts by the sentence.' This range (*Spielraum*) can be identified with the logical position, because the logical position is the range of those alternative worlds whose existence is compatible with the sentence. The range is limited by the range of all those possible worlds the existence of which is incompatible with the sentence, and thus the sentence is 'in the negative sense like a solid body, which restricts the free movement of another'—as we read in the continuation of 4.463—whereas the sentence is 'in the positive sense, like the space limited by solid substance, in which a body may be placed'. The logical position is the 'space' inside which a world compatible with the sentence must be situated. This means—again according to 4.463—that 'tautology' 'leaves to reality the whole infinite logical space'; i.e. the logical position of a logical truth is the whole logical space, whereas the logical position of a contradiction is empty, i.e. in the 'negative' sense it 'fills the whole logical space and leaves no point to reality'.[2]

To sum up: every sentence which is a truth-function of elementary sentences can be considered a truth-function of *all* elementary sentences and determines thus a 'logical position', i.e. the range of those alternative possible worlds the existence of which is compatible with and verifies the sentence. This view can be said to form an important feature of Carnap's treatment of logic in *Meaning and*

---

[1] Cf. 5.101, where, for instance, '$p$' is analysed as a truth-function of '$p$' and '$q$' in this way.

[2] On the concept *Spielraum*, cf. also Waismann: 'Wahrscheinlichkeit', p. 268.

*Necessity.* We shall use it in our discussion of the descriptive content of logical compounds in Chapter VIII.

If we are dealing with many-valued dimensions a three-dimensional logical space can be visualized in the same way as a yes-and-no space has been visualized in Fig. 3. The only difference is that we then may have more than two possible values on each coordinate axis and that there are therefore possible worlds corresponding not only to the corners of the cube but also to other points in the space. If in particular every dimension is continuous, and if certain additional conditions are fulfilled *every* point of the three-dimensional geometrical space may correspond to a possible world and conversely.

## 9. HUME'S THESIS

The instances of a logical space given by the space around $P$ or the three-dimensional space considered in the preceding section differ from Wittgenstein's idea of a logical space in that the number of their dimensions is *finite*. In one of the passages from 4.463 quoted above Wittgenstein says that the logical space is *infinite*. But a yes-and-no space can be infinite only if the number of its dimensions is infinite.

That the number of dimensions is to be regarded as infinite we can see also from the treatment of Hume's thesis in the Tractatus. By 'Hume's thesis' I understand the assertion often so called, that there cannot be any *necessary* connection between what is the case at one point of time and what is the case at another point of time, and that therefore all inductive inferences are hypothetical. Wittgenstein approves of this view in the Tractatus, and his treatment of the subject is closely connected with his conception of the world as constructed of mutually independent atomic states of affairs. That the atomic states of affairs are to be considered mutually independent we have inferred in particular from 2.061, 2.062 and 4.211. Similar formulations are, however, repeated later in the book in connection with the treatment of Hume's thesis. The statements most relevant to this theme are the following:

5.134    Aus einem Elementarsatz lässt sich kein anderer folgern.

5.135    Auf keine Weise kann aus dem Bestehen irgend einer Sachlage auf das Bestehen einer, von ihr gänzlich verschiedenen Sachlage geschlossen werden.

5.136    Einen Kausalnexus, der einen solchen Schluss rechtfertigte, gibt es nicht.

5.1361   Die Ereignisse der Zukunft k ö n n e n wir nicht aus den gegenwärtigen erschliessen.
         Der Glaube an den Kausalnexus ist der A b e r g l a u b e .

6.36311  Dass die Sonne morgen aufgehen wird, ist eine Hypothese; und das heisst: wir  w i s s e n  nicht, ob sie aufgehen wird.

6.37     Einen Zwang, nach dem Eines geschehen müsste, weil etwas anderes geschehen ist, gibt es nicht. Es gibt nur eine l o g i s c h e Notwendigkeit.


A comparison of 5.135 with 5.136 shows what kind of inference Wittgenstein is thinking of, when in 5.135 he says that an inference cannot be made 'from the existence of one state of affairs to the existence of another entirely different from it'. Since in 5.136 he says that 'there is no causal nexus which justifies such an inference', the 'entirely different states of affairs' referred to in 5.135 must be different in such a way as would permit us to infer from the one to the other *if* there were a causal nexus. This argument leads us to the following interpretation of Wittgenstein's thought. Assume a system $Q$ which is in a state $S$ at a point of time $t$. If there were a 'causal nexus' one could from this fact infer to what state $S'$ system $Q$ is in at point of time $t'$. Now there is no causal nexus, and this means that the two states of affairs described as '$Q$ is in state $S$ at time $t$' and '$Q$ is in state $S'$ at time $t'$' are 'entirely different'—which in view of 5.134 is to mean that these two states of affairs do not have any *common* atomic states of affairs among their constituents. Thus every atomic state of affairs which belongs to one point of time $t$ is *different* from and, therefore, logically independent of any atomic state of affairs belonging to another point of time $t'$, even if those atomic states of affairs are in all other respects similar. We may say, then, that every point of time is surrounded by a *separate* system of dimensions in the logical space. And since we have to regard the number of time-points as infinite it follows that the total number of dimensions is infinite.

Since atomic states of affairs, and as a consequence also states of affairs in general, which belong to different points of time are mutually independent, 'the events of future *cannot* be inferred from those of the present' (5.1361). 'That the sun will rise to-morrow is', therefore, 'an hypothesis; and that means that we do not *know* whether it will rise' (6.36311).

A world which is similar to our world in respect of all that has happened hitherto, but in which the sun will not rise to-morrow is logically possible.

There is no other kind of necessity than *logical* necessity (6.37). Therefore the belief in the causal nexus is a form of *superstition*, if we are to believe Wittgenstein (5.1361). What Wittgenstein means here is not that the belief in causal connections is as such a superstition. By 'causal nexus' he obviously means the aprioristic *certainty* of causal connections. And it is the belief in this he regards as superstitious.

But what interests us here is only the fact that Wittgenstein connects Hume's thesis with the idea that the world is analysable into the existence and non-existence of mutually independent atomic states of affairs.

So far we have treated Wittgenstein's conception of the world's logical structure without taking into consideration the inner structure of the separate atomic states of affairs. Our next task is an examination of Wittgenstein's view on this subject.

V

# THE CONCEPT OF SUBSTANCE

Wittgenstein introduces the discussion of the inner structure of an atomic state of affairs in 2.01:

> 2.01 Der Sachverhalt ist eine Verbindung von Gegenständen.
> (Sachen, Dingen.)

This statement indicates that the words *Ding, Sache, Gegenstand* should be regarded as synonyms. There is nothing in the Tractatus to show that this practice is not followed. We shall therefore translate these three words by the same word 'thing'.

## 1. 'THINGS': INDIVIDUAL OBJECTS AND PREDICATES

What does Wittgenstein mean by a 'thing'? There are two aspects of this question. The first concerns the category to which a 'thing' belongs. In Chapter II we have stressed the importance of distinguishing between the categories of (individual) 'things', 'predicates' with different numbers of places, and 'facts'. Does Wittgenstein maintain this distinction when he talks of 'things'? In other words, do what Wittgenstein calls 'things' always belong to the category of things?

Let us first examine the terms 'thing', 'fact', *Sachverhalt*. When Wittgenstein says in 1.1 that the world is the totality of facts and not of things his formulation implies that he makes a definite distinction between what are called 'things' and what are called 'facts'. When stating in 2.01 that a *Sachverhalt* is a 'connection of things'[1] he likewise seems to presuppose that a *Sachverhalt* is not itself a 'thing'. Even though Wittgenstein sometimes expresses himself somewhat vaguely in this respect, we can assert that not

---

[1] I think the word 'connection' is to be preferred here as a translation of the German word *Verbindung* to the word 'combination' used in the English version of the Tractatus.

only does he constantly maintain the terminological distinction between what can be characterized as 'things' and what belongs to the category of facts (facts, states of affairs, etc.), but that he also lays great stress upon it. We can therefore sum up as follows:

(V.1) *What Wittgenstein characterizes as 'things' cannot belong to the category of facts.*

The formulation of 2.01, however, seems to indicate that Wittgenstein does not terminologically make the distinction between the categories of 'things' and 'predicates'. As is pointed out in Chapter II (individual) things and predicates are 'complementary' in that things can only enter into facts or states of affairs as bearers of predicates. A 'connection' between individual things only, therefore, cannot form an atomic state of affairs. And so, it seems, a predicate must be included amongst the 'things' of which an atomic state of affairs forms a connection.

However, the truth of this conclusion can be questioned on the grounds that we do not *a priori* know what Wittgenstein means by a 'connection'. Perhaps 2.01 is to be understood in such a way that the 'connection' is the predicate—i.e. the 'things' spoken of in 2.01 are individual objects which are 'connected' by a predicate into an atomic state of affairs?

Yet such an interpretation is certainly incorrect as is clear on an analysis of the statements in the Tractatus. I will content myself with the following observations:

(1) It could be plausible to say of a many-place predicate that it 'connects' individual objects into an atomic state of affairs, as for instance, if we say that in '$A$ is greater than $B$' the greater-than relation 'connects' the objects $A$ and $B$ into a state of affairs, or that in '$A$ lies between $B$ and $C$' the between relation 'connects' the objects $A$, $B$ and $C$ into a state of affairs. But to say such a thing would be extremely misleading if we are dealing with an atomic state of affairs with a one-place predicate, since one cannot possibly say that in '$A$ is red' the predicate 'red' connects the object $A$ into a state of affairs —if such a state of affairs is to be regarded as a 'connection' between things one must surely mean that redness is also to be regarded as a 'thing'.[1]

---

[1] Wittgenstein seems to express himself in this way in the *Philosophical Investigations*, too; see in particular §§ 46 and 48.

(2) While an atomic state of affairs is said in 2.01 to be a 'connection' of things, 2.0272 says that it is formed by the 'configuration' of things, and 2.03 that things 'hang one in another' in it, 'like the links of a chain' (*Kette*). The impression that not only the individual objects but also the predicate is meant here by 'things' is strengthened by comparing 2.03 with the statement that an elementary sentence 'consists' of names since it forms a 'concatenation' (*Verkettung*) of names (4.22); and that the 'names' deputize, in the sentence, for the 'things' (3.22). And as an elementary sentence is said to consist of names in 4.22, so in 4.2211 an atomic state of affairs is said to consist of 'things'. The idea of an atomic state of affairs as a connection of things is thus closely tied up with the idea that an elementary sentence 'consists of names in immediate connection' (4.221)—and here not only names of individual objects must be meant but also 'names' of predicates.

We can sum up thus:

(V.2)   *Wittgenstein counts as 'things' not only individual objects but also predicates with different numbers of places.*

Though Wittgenstein does not distinguish terminologically between 'things' and 'predicates' it does not follow that he makes no distinction between the contents of these categories. To this we shall return later. But one cannot reason away the fact that the characterization of predicates as 'things' tends to make one think that the construction of an atomic state of affairs from individual objects and predicates is more similar to the construction of a sentence from words than it really is. It leads among other things to an obscuring of the *difference* between the ways in which things and predicates enter into an atomic state of affairs. Thus the statements in the Tractatus which deal with 'things' acquire a somewhat different meaning if we mean by 'things' individual objects than if we mean predicates. We must bear this in mind when we interpret them.

## 2. THE SIMPLENESS OF 'THINGS'

What we have said above is one aspect of what is meant by 'things' in the Tractatus. The second is the question of *what* kind of individual things and predicates are characterized as 'things'. 2.011 reads

2.011  Es ist dem Ding wesentlich, der Bestandteil eines Sachverhaltes sein zu können.

At first sight this statement might seem to be only an expression
of what we have already stated—that 'things' enter into the world
only as components of facts. But actually it is something more
specific, since here instead of 'facts' we find 'atomic states of affairs':
'It is essential to a thing that it can be a component of an atomic
state of affairs.' This implies among other things that not everything we characterize in daily speech as individual objects or
predicates is a 'thing' in Wittgenstein's sense. Only those individual
objects and predicates which as components fit into *atomic* states
of affairs are regarded as 'things':
We read further:

2.02  Der Gegenstand ist einfach.

According to Wittgenstein, it is true of 'things' that besides
being components in atomic states of affairs they are also 'simple'.
When a thing is characterized as 'simple' it is contrasted with something that is called a 'complex' and which is mentioned for the first
time in 2.0201. This terminology refers to a view of the kind which
Russell characterizes as 'logical atomism' and which I shall here
briefly touch upon.
When Russell put forward his much admired theory of 'descriptions' in the article 'On Denoting' in 1905, this theory was fitted
into a more general theory of the interpretation of what he called
'denoting phrases'—amongst which are counted not only such expressions as 'the present King of England', 'the present King of
France', or 'a man' (which are later characterized as 'descriptions')
but also expressions such as 'some man', 'all men', etc. The main
principle of the theory is stated as 'that denoting phrases never have
any meaning in themselves, but that every proposition in whose
verbal expression they occur has a meaning' (p. 43). This means that
the expression 'all men' in the proposition 'all men are mortal' is not
used to 'denote' anything—the proposition acquires its meaning in
another way. Similarly, in the statements (written in 1905) 'the
present King of France is bald', 'the present King of England is
bald' *neither* the expression 'the present King of France' *nor* the
expression 'the present King of England' are used to denote any-

thing. These statements also acquire their meaning in a different way—in that they can be analysed into propositions which do *not* contain the expressions in question. An essential characteristic of this analysis is that the statement 'the present King of France is bald' is neither understood, nor on analysis appears, as meaningless —'it is plainly false'.—Russell has later added that a similar analysis holds good of certain proper names—of the name 'Apollo',[1] for example.

If we place this theory by the side of Tractatus 2.0201, 3.24, 3.25, 3.26 and 3.261 we arrive at the following characterization of what we might call Wittgenstein's logical atomism. Every (meaningful) sentence can be 'completely analysed' in only one way. On this analysis the sentence proves to be either an elementary sentence or a truth-function of elementary sentences. Among the latter belong certain sentences which perhaps 'to the eye' have the form of elementary sentences but which are distinguished from them on the grounds that they deal with 'complexes'. And it appears that a sentence contains a symbol which characterizes a complex when on a logical analysis it proves 'definable' as a truth-function of other sentences which do not contain this symbol (cf. 3.24). If one supposes that in the sentence 'Socrates is a man' both the subject 'Socrates' and the predicate 'man' are understood as 'complexes', then this sentence is thought to be analysable into a statement about the 'constituents' of the concept 'Socrates' and the concept 'man' together with a description of these complexes (2.0201). The sentence of which 'Socrates is a man' appears on analysis to be the equivalent is not 'nonsensical', if Socrates does not exist, but simply false (3.24)—which shows that the word 'Socrates' is not in the proper sense a 'name'—the word 'Socrates' has a meaning only *via* the signs which appear in the analysed statement (3.261). On this analysis we come in the end to elementary sentences which consist of 'names' in immediate connection with each other (cf. 4.221 and 4.2211). These 'names' cannot be further analysed by definition— they are 'primitive signs' (3.26)—which means that an elementary sentence is understood through our knowing what 'things' the names are names of. These things are 'simple' in the *logical* sense— they are not complexes. We might say that the 'things'—i.e. the individual objects and predicates—which appear as components in atomic states of affairs are 'logically *atomic* things'.

[1] *Principia Mathematica*, p. 31.

F

3. THE 'THINGS' AS THE SUBSTANCE OF THE WORLD

2.0201 (cf. 2.0211 and 2.0231) gives a hint that 'logical atomism' should be considered the basis for regarding 'things' as 'simple'. Formally a more explicit reason for the simpleness of things is, however, given in the statement which immediately follows:

> 2.021 Die Gegenstände bilden die Substanz der Welt. Darum können sie nicht zusammengesetzt sein.

The reason why things must be simple is according to this that they form the 'substance' of the world. But what meaning, then, did Wittgenstein attach to the word 'substance'?

The following is a possible interpretation. We have seen that only those objects and predicates included as components in atomic states of affairs are regarded as 'things'. Thus all 'things' enter as components into the system of all atomic states of affairs—i.e. into the system ($p$) (see p. 49). But the series ($p$) is *prior* to the description of the world and thus in that sense *common* to all 'possible' worlds. Now it seems that an essential characteristic of that which Wittgenstein calls the 'substance' of the world is that it forms what all possible worlds have in common: 'that which exists independently of what is the case', as 2.024 says. But the 'things' common to all possible worlds—Wittgenstein possibly reasoned—cannot be compounded, since if they were then the 'parts' could be thought to be configured in different ways in different worlds (cf. 2.0231).[1]

This thought is not very clear. However, it is important that the conception of simpleness of 'things' is linked with the idea that they form something *common* to all 'possible' worlds and that in this sense they form the 'substance'[2] of the world. This idea is developed in different ways in statements 2.011–2.0271. We shall now attempt to trace the main line of thought in these statements.

4. THE INDEPENDENCE AND NON-INDEPENDENCE OF 'THINGS'

As a starting-point we take statement 2.0124:

> 2.0124 Sind alle Gegenstände gegeben, so sind damit auch alle m ö g l i c h e n Sachverhalte gegeben.

[1] Cf. *Phil. Inv.*, §§ 55 ff.

[2] In the following discussion I accept Wittgenstein's use of the word 'substance' though Wittgensteinian 'substance' comprises entities which do not belong to the Aristotelian *category* of substance. Cf. above, p. 21.

Since all possible atomic states of affairs are given by the system $(p)$, and since 'things' are atomic objects and predicates, we may paraphrase 2.0124 thus:

(V.3)   *If the system of all atomic objects and predicates is given, then the system $(p)$ of all atomic states of affairs is given too.*

Consider a 'thing' $a$—which may be either an object or predicate. If we pick out from $(p)$ all those atomic states of affairs which contain $a$ we obtain a subsystem of $(p)$ which may be denoted:

$(p_a)$                    $p_{a1}, p_{a2}, \ldots$

The system $(p_a)$ determines a *subspace* in the logical space. It consists of all the states of affairs obtained if $(p_a)$ is divided in different ways into positive and negative atomic states of affairs (2.013).[1] What (V.3) says of a particular thing could then be expressed as follows: As soon as a thing $a$ is given (as an element in substance), then the system $(p_a)$ is given too—'if things can occur in atomic states of affairs, this (possibility) must already lie in them' (2.0121), because 'in logic nothing is accidental: if a thing *can* occur in an atomic state of affairs the possibility of that atomic state of affairs must already be prejudged in the thing' (2.012). As soon as a thing is 'known' the series $(p_a)$ is known too—this belongs to the 'nature' of the thing.

What has been explained here as included in the nature of a 'thing' is connected with something called 'the *form* of a thing'; thinking of the statement 2.012 just quoted I shall for clarity's sake say 'the *logical form* of a thing'.[2] This concept is introduced in 2.0141, where we are given the 'definition':

2.0141   Die Möglichkeit seines Vorkommens in Sachverhalten ist die Form des Gegenstandes.

This means: (a) that what decides which atomic states of affairs a 'thing' *can* enter into is something called its '(logical) form' and conversely that (b) a thing's 'logical form' is determined by the

---

[1] Wittgenstein speaks in 2.013 of logical space as being formed of *atomic* states of affairs, not of states of affairs in general. He is obviously thinking of the atomic states of affairs which occur as the dimensions of the space. Cf. below, p. 73n.

[2] Wittgenstein uses the term 'logical form' of 'things' in 2.0233.

atomic states of affairs into which it *can* enter. Thus it is true that not only is the way in which the system $(p_a)$ is formed from *a* determined by the logical form of *a* but also that conversely the logical form of *a* is clear from $(p_a)$. This leads one to the thought that (V.3) could also be converted so as to get:

(V.4)   *As soon as the system $(p)$ of all atomic states of affairs is given, the substance—i.e. the system of all atomic objects and predicates of the world—is given too.*

Knowledge of a thing *a* implies knowledge of how $(p_a)$ is formed but it does not imply knowledge of how this system is divided up into 'existing' and 'non-existing' atomic states of affairs. That Wittgenstein meant this is corroborated by 2.0231 where he points out that the substance can only determine a 'form' and not 'material properties', 'for these are not presented but by the sentences—they are formed only by the configuration of the objects.'[1] The things do not determine their actual configurations.

2.01231 says much the same when it points out that to know a thing one does not need to know its '*external* qualities' but to know all its '*internal* qualities'. We have established earlier (Ch. II §§ 4 and 5) that objects and predicates enter into the world only as elements of facts, and that objects and predicates in isolation are unthinkable. The conception proposed here by Wittgenstein might be said to be a modification of this thesis. 'Things' are in a *certain* sense 'independent' (2.0122), since one can always imagine that an object has *other* predicates than it *really* has or that a predicate belongs to other objects than it *really* does. 'This form of independence is a form of . . . dependence', however, since one cannot think of a thing or predicate except in connection with *some* atomic state of affairs.

In the statement 2.0122 just quoted a remark is included which refers to language and which suggests that there is a theory of 'names' and 'elementary sentences' analogous to the one of 'atomic states of affairs' developed here. Such a theory—which, however, deals not only with names and elementary sentences but also with 'expressions' and 'sentences' in general—is developed in statements 3.31 onwards and suggests associations between Wittgenstein's theory of the logical form of 'things' and Russell's theory of types (cf. below, p. 133 n. and Ch. X, §§ 4 and 7). At this point, however,

---

[1] The translation in the English version of the Tractatus is very confused here.

we shall deal with the theory of the world without more than sporadic references to the corresponding theory of language.

The concepts '(logical) form' and 'internal qualities' (or 'internal relations') appear in many places in the Tractatus, and in different contexts they are used in ways which differ from each other to a greater or lesser extent. It is not easy to be clear on how these usages are related to each other.[1] We shall content ourselves for the moment with stating that the 'logical form' of a 'thing' is obviously to be regarded as an 'internal quality' of that 'thing' leaving open the question whether there are also 'internal predicates' in 'things' which do not belong to their 'logical form'. One should notice that 'internal qualities' and 'internal relations' are not 'qualities' or 'relations' properly so called. 'Internal predicates' are not genuine predicates belonging to the category of predicates— they can be characterized as 'qualities' or 'relations' only in a metaphorical way. The fact than an atomic quality, for instance, belongs to a thing is seen from the *existence* of an atomic state of affairs, not from its mere possibility; thus it forms an 'external' and not an 'internal' predicate. It follows from this that the logical form of a 'thing' is not a genuine quality of that 'thing' either.

We shall sum up what we have established about the logical form of a 'thing' in the following theses:

(V.5) *The way in which the system* $(p_a)$ *is formed from a 'thing' a is determined by the logical form of the 'thing' and conversely the logical form of a 'thing' a is determined by* $(p_a)$.

(V.6) *That a 'thing' is 'given' ('known') implies that its logical form is given (known), but it does not mean that any of its 'material predicates' is given (known).*

## 5. THE LOGICAL FORM AND THE CATEGORIES

I shall now try to illustrate the import of the concept 'logical form' in a yes-and-no space in connection with a model. Consider a 'world' $M$ consisting of five atomic objects denoted by '$a$', '$b$', '$c$',

---

[1] In 4.122 Wittgenstein gives an explanation of his use of the terms 'internal' and 'external', which, however, does not give us much information. And the information given seems not to be in accordance with his actual use of those terms, at least not with their use in the beginning of the book. In the following discussion we shall attribute 'internal qualities' and 'internal relations' only to 'things', not to 'facts' or 'states of affairs' as in 4.122. Cf., however, below, pp. 182 ff.

'*d*', '*e*' which are in an atomic dyadic relation R to one another as the arrows in Fig. 4 show. To the elements of our world belongs further an atomic quality $Q$: objects possessing this quality have the letters which stand for them circled in the diagram. Thus the 'substance' of our world consists of the five atomic objects, the relation R and the quality $Q$. The set ($p$) corresponding to M comprises the following 30 atomic states of affairs:

$(p_M)$

$$R(a,a), \quad R(a,b), \quad R(a,c), \quad R(a,d), \quad R(a,e),$$
$$R(b,a), \quad R(b,b), \quad R(b,c), \quad R(b,d), \quad R(b,e),$$
$$R(c,a), \quad R(c,b), \quad R(c,c), \quad R(c,d), \quad R(c,e),$$
$$R(d,a), \quad R(d,b), \quad R(d,c), \quad R(d,d), \quad R(d,e),$$
$$R(e,a), \quad R(e,b), \quad R(e,c), \quad R(e,d), \quad R(e,e),$$
$$Q(a), \quad Q(b), \quad Q(c), \quad Q(d), \quad Q(e).$$

M is described through the division of $(p_M)$ into existent and non-existent atomic states of affairs. The diagram shows that $R(a,b)$, $R(a,c)$, $R(c,d)$, $R(c,e)$, $Q(b)$, and $Q(e)$ are existent; the rest are non-existent.

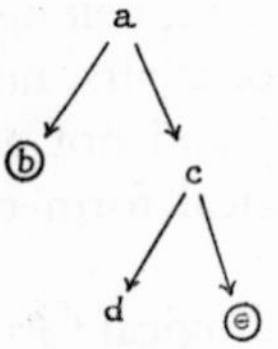

The *logical space* round M comprises $2^{30}$ (i.e. over a milliard) different possible worlds, corresponding to the various possible ways of connecting some of the letters '*a*', '*b*', '*c*', '*d*', and '*e*' with arrows in combination with circling some of them.

FIG. 4.

Let us now consider the 'thing' $Q$. The subsystem of $(p_M)$ that corresponds to the logical form of this 'thing' reads:

$(p_Q)$ $\qquad\qquad Q(a), Q(b), Q(c), Q(d), Q(e).$

$Q$ can thus be 'connected' with the 'things' $a$, $b$, $c$, $d$, or $e$ into an atomic state of affairs. From this we infer its 'logical form'. The 'things' $a$, $b$, $c$, $d$, and $e$ are those elements in M which belong to the category of *objects*. We can thus characterize the logical form of $Q$ by saying that it can be connected with a *single* atomic *object* into an atomic state of affairs. This can be formulated more shortly by saying that $Q$ is a *one-place predicate*, i.e. a quality. If we make a corresponding analysis of the 'thing' R we find that its logical form is to be a *two-place* predicate, i.e. a dyadic relation. Finally, for an atomic object—*a* for example—the corresponding subsystem takes the form

$(p_a)$ $\qquad\qquad R(a,a), R(a,b), R(a,c), R(a,d), R(a,e), Q(a).$

It is, however, characteristic of a 'thing' $a$ as an individual *object* that it fits into exactly *those* atomic states of affairs. As a general rule, we can state that the following is true, if we assume a logical space of the type represented by the logical space round model $M$—I shall call it a *logically homogeneous* yes-and-no space for reasons which I will give later:

(V.7) *The logical form of a 'thing' is its category—i.e. its logical nature of being an individual object or a predicate with a definite number of places.*

Thus Wittgenstein here makes the division into categories as a division of 'things' on the basis of their 'logical form'.

When Wittgenstein speaks of the form of 'substance' he sometimes seems to mean not the logical form of the individual elements but a 'form' of the substance as a *system* of elements, which can be defined as the *totality of the logical forms of the different elements*. The 'form' of the substance of world $M$ can in this sense be said to be that the substance consists of seven elements, five of which are individual objects, one of which is a two-place and one a one-place predicate. I call this 'form' the *internal structure* of the substance. The *internal structure* of the substance, which is a logical characteristic of it, must be carefully distinguished from the *external structure* of the world, which is shown for $M$ by Fig. 4.

If the number of elements is finite the internal structure of the substance can be described as follows:

The elements of the world consist of

$(S_1)$

$n$ individual objects,
$m_1$ one-place predicates,
$m_2$ two-place predicates,
........................................
$m_r$ $r$-place predicates.

This description can be said to be exhaustive with regard to a world of the type represented by $M$. As soon as $(S_1)$ is given, the system of all atomic states of affairs is given, too, and thus also the logical space. If we take for granted that the logical space is a homogeneous yes-and-no space the internal structure of the substance can be said to coincide with its division into categories, and then the logical form of a 'thing' is given as soon as we know to which category it belongs. In other cases the situation is more complicated, as we shall see.

## 6. LOGICALLY HOMOGENEOUS SPACES WITH MANY-VALUED DIMENSIONS

Let us now inquire how the concept 'logical form' could be applied in a logical space with many-valued dimensions. As a starting-point we will take this statement:

> 4.123　Eine Eigenschaft ist intern, wenn es undenkbar ist, dass ihr Gegenstand sie nicht besitzt.
> (Diese blaue Farbe und jene stehen in der internen Relation von heller und dunkler eo ipso. Es ist undenkbar, dass d i e s e beiden Gegenstände nicht in dieser Relation stün- den.)
> . . . . . . .

We will first take Wittgenstein's words in the parenthesis literally so far as concerns the use of the word *Gegenstand*. Since in Wittgen- stein's terminology a *Gegenstand* is an atomic 'thing' we must regard the two blue colours as atomic 'things'—i.e. as constituents of atomic states of affairs. Since colours are 'gradeable' the paren- thesis thus comes to refer to a world with many-valued dimensions. As a difference in brightness between two colours is considered an 'internal' relation, the same must be true of a difference in hue. Since 'internal relations' of this kind are closely connected with the division of predicates into 'dimensions' we may assume that the fact that two predicates belong to the *same* dimension or to *different* dimensions (see above, pp. 39 ff.) is also due to their 'internal relations'. We might express this by saying that to be of a certain dimension is an *internal* quality of a predicate.

If we are dealing with an atomic predicate we are faced by the question whether such an 'internal' quality of a 'thing' shall be said to belong to its 'logical form' or not. Naturally enough Wittgen- stein does not explicity mention this in the Tractatus, since he pre- supposes that the logical space is a yes-and-no space. It is, however, important also to give a precise account of the concept of logical form if this assumption is dropped.

According to 2.0141 the 'form' of a 'thing' is the possibility of its occurrence in *atomic* states of affairs. This we have interpreted in (V.5) as meaning that the way in which the system $(p_a)$ of all atomic states of affairs containing $a$ is formed is determined by the logical form of $a$, and conversely. We could express this by saying that the logical form of $a$ manifests itself in $(p_a)$. However, Wittgenstein in the statement 2.014 immediately preceding 2.0141 refers to states of affairs in general (*Sachlagen*) instead of atomic states of affairs (*Sachverhalte*). Now all possible states of affairs which can be obtained by a division of $(p_a)$ into positive and negative states of affairs form a subspace of the logical space (cf. above, p. 67). This subspace belonging to an object $a$ I shall call $T_a$.[1] In a yes-and-no space *every* division of $(p_a)$ into positive and negative states of affairs determines a state of affairs in $T_a$. Therefore, if we *presuppose* that the logical space is a yes-and-no space the space $T_a$ is uniquely determined by $(p_a)$ (and conversely), and if the logical form of $a$ is said to manifest itself in $(p_a)$ it can also be said to manifest itself in $T_a$.

In a space with many-valued dimensions, however, some divisions of $(p_a)$ into positive and negative states of affairs do not correspond to any states of affairs in $T_a$, since two atomic states of affairs of the same dimension exclude one another and cannot both occur positively in the same state of affairs. Therefore, if we allow for spaces with many-valued dimensions we do not know $T_a$ as soon as we know $(p_a)$. But then we have to decide whether we want to let the 'logical form' of $a$ manifest itself in the system $(p_a)$ or the logical space $T_a$. The latter alternative seems to lead to greater clarity. If we choose it, however, we must put the following formulation instead of (V.5) so as to include the possibility of many-valued dimensions:

(V.5′)    *The logical form of a 'thing' a determines how the logical space $T_a$ is formed from a, and conversely the logical form of a is determined by the logical space $T_a$.*

If we give this meaning to the concept 'logical form', $(S_1)$ does not give an exhaustive description of the internal structure of substance. A classification of substance into elements of different logical forms then demands that, in addition, the predicative elements

---

[1] It is to be noted that $T_a$ does not contain *all* the states of affairs into which $a$ enters, but only such states of affairs as are formed of atomic states of affairs *all* of which contain $a$.

of every category should be classified according to the different dimensions. If the number of elements is finite the description can be given the following form:

The elements of the world consist of

$(S_2)$ 
    $n$   individual objects,
    $m_1$  one-place predicates, of which $m_{11}$ belong to one dimension, $m_{12}$ to another, etc.
    $m_2$  two-place predicates, of which $m_{21}$ belong to one demension, $m_{22}$ to another, etc.

If in description $(S_2)$ every dimension comprises only one predicate $(m_{11}=m_{12}= \,.. \,=m_{21}= \ldots =1)$ the logical space is a yes-and-no space.

Description $(S_2)$ could of course be replaced by a description of the type $(S_1)$, supplemented by information as to which predicates exclude each other. The fact that the one-place predicates $Q_1$ and $Q_2$ belong to the same dimension means that every proposition of the form '$Q_1(x)$ & $Q_2(x)$' is a contradiction. If '$x$' is taken as a free individual variable and '$L$' as a sign for 'logical necessity', this can be written:

(1) $$L(\sim(Q_1(x) \,\&\, Q_2(x))).$$

Thus we can replace $(S_2)$ by a description of the type $(S_1)$, supplemented by an indication of a system of 'logically necessary' connections between the atomic predicates.

This method of description can in fact be used under more general conditions than those presupposed in $(S_2)$. Hitherto we have assumed that the atomic states of affairs are at least sufficiently independent to be classified according to 'dimensions'. But suppose that the relation $R$ in Fig. 4 is intransitive and asymmetrical in the same way as, for instance, the father-son relation and that this is so not as a 'synthetic' fact but as a consequence of the existence of an 'internal quality' of the relation $R$. Then the existence of this 'internal quality' can be expressed by the propositions:

(2) $$L(R(x,y) \,\&\, R(y,z) \supset \sim R(x,z))$$
$$L(R(x,y) \supset \sim R(y,x)),$$

which in this instance belong to the description of the logical form

of 'things'. And these propositions cannot be replaced by any classification according to dimensions. We thus obtain the following
result for spaces of the type dealt with here:

(V.8)    *In the logical form of 'things' is included not only their categories
         but also their classification according to dimensions and other
         logically necessary connections between the atomic states of
         affairs in which they occur.*

It should be noted that an indication of *what* logical connections
hold between the elements belongs to a description of the internal structure of substance as soon as we take into consideration
the *possibility* of logically necessary connections between the atomic
states of affairs. If this possibility is taken into consideration $(S_1)$
is not an exhaustive description of the internal structure *even* if the
logical space 'happens' to be a yes-and-no space, because to characterize the internal structure in such a space we have then to add
to $(S_1)$ that the logical space *is* a yes-and-no space, i.e. that there
are *no* logical connections between the atomic states of affairs.

This point might be expressed thus: Not only the *existence* but
also the *non-existence* of logical connections forms a kind of *logical
interrelation* between the elements. If the logical interrelations between
the elements are counted as belonging to their 'logical form', then a
description of the internal structure of substance must comprise an
indication of those logical interrelations. The logical space is a
yes-and-no space if *every* logical interrelation between the elements is
'negative', i.e. consists in the non-existence of logical connections.
And to say that this is so belongs to the description of the internal
structure of a substance of this kind.

However, a description of the internal structure of substance
of the form $(S_2)$, or of the form $(S_1)$ supplemented by an indication
of all logical connections between the atomic states of affairs,
can in its turn be said to be *exhaustive* only if we presuppose that
the logical space fulfils certain conditions to be discussed in the
next section. A logical space fulfilling these conditions I call *logically
homogeneous*.

When the possibility of logically necessary connections between
the atomic states of affairs is taken into consideration it would be
most natural to say that (V.4) (p. 68) is *not* valid. For a 'thing' to
be 'given', its logical form must be given. The 'logical interrelations'

belong to this form, and thus for 'things' to be given, not only must the system of atomic states of affairs be given but also the system of all logically necessary connections between those atomic states of affairs.

According to 6.1 the sentences of logic are tautologies. It is obviously meant by this that 'logical truths' are tautologies. And that they are tautologies means two things: (a) that they are 'sense-less' (*sinnlos*) in that they say nothing about reality and (b) that they have 'tautological truth-conditions'—i.e. are true for all the 'truth-possibilities' of the elementary sentences (4.46, cf. 4.3).

If one regards—as Wittgenstein, thinking of logical space as a yes-and-no space, does in the Tractatus—*every* combination of truth values for the elementary sentences as a 'truth-possibility', then (b) is not of course valid for all logical truths in respect of a logical space with many-valued dimensions or in which we have other logical connections between the atomic states of affairs. Sentences the logical truth of which is stated in (1) or (2) have not tautological truth-conditions in this sense.

But this does not prevent the validity of (a). It follows from (1) that the sentence $\sim(Q_1(a) \& Q_2(a))$, for instance, says nothing about $a$ and consequently nothing about the external structure of the world.[1]

There can be no 'internal relations' of the types expressed by (1) or (2) between atomic 'things' in a yes-and-no space, because in it all atomic states of affairs are independent of each other. If we wish to apply 4.123 to a yes-and-no space we cannot conceive of two 'things' between which an internal relation of this kind exists as *genuine*, i.e. *atomic*, 'things'—the existence of such an internal relation shows that the things are *not* simple. We must therefore take for granted that colours and other qualities which 'logically exclude' each other are 'complex'. We could say that (1) then expresses an internal relation between complexes. The sentence $\sim(Q_1(a) \& Q_2(a))$ must therefore be analysable as a truth-function of elementary sentences and, of course, a 'tautological' truth-function. If analysed in this way the sentence will be transformed into a logical truth in the propositional or predicate calculus.

---

[1] Wittgenstein emphasizes that statements of this kind are to be considered tauto-logical in 'Logical Form', p. 167. The analysis of the situation given there amounts to the view that such truth-values of the elementary sentences as exclude each other logically cannot be combined since they do not represent 'existing' truth-possibilities (cf. *l.c.*, p. 169).

## 7. LOGICALLY UNHOMOGENEOUS SPACES

Besides the types of internal structure discussed in the preceding section there is another complication of which we also find hints in the Tractatus. This complication may occur in a yes-and-no space as well as in a space with many-valued dimensions. We will first look at the statement:

2.0251 Raum, Zeit und Farbe (Färbigkeit) sind Formen der Gegenstände.

This statement is not so closely connected with statement 4.123 as one might think at first sight. While 4.123 speaks of an 'internal' relation between the colour qualities themselves, 2.0251 deals with the question of the 'form' of an object that *has* (or can have) these qualities. 2.0251 obviously means that to the 'form' of a 'thing' belongs its being a spatial or a temporal object or having (or being capable of having) a colour. While being of a certain dimension belongs to the logical form of a *predicate*, the 'form' we now come into contact with is a form of individual *objects*.

This interpretation is supported, as far as space and time are concerned, by the fourth paragraph in 2.0121 and for colouredness by 2.0131, where we read:

2.0131  ............
Der Fleck im Gesichtsfeld muss zwar nicht rot sein, aber eine Farbe muss er haben: er hat sozusagen den Farbenraum um sich. Der Ton muss e i n e Höhe haben, der Gegenstand des Tastsinnes e i n e Härte usw.

One might add to this statement: but the spot in a visual field can have no pitch or hardness, the note no colour or hardness, the object of feeling no colour or pitch. The *note* has no 'colour space' around it.

This means a deviation from the internal structure of substance treated in the preceding section. We have described the logical space around our model world $M$ as 'logically homogeneous'. This means that, when constructing this logical space, we have presupposed that we get an atomic state of affairs whatever object the quality $Q$ or whatever pair of objects the relation $R$ is combined with. We call the *logical space* (or substance) *logically homogeneous* if *every t-place predicate* appearing as an element of the substance *can be combined in an atomic state of affairs with every t-tuple of individual objects* in the substance. If the logical space (or substance) does not fulfil this condition we will call it *logically unhomogeneous.*

In order to describe the internal structure of a logically un-homogeneous substance we must indicate for each predicate what objects it can be combined with in an atomic state of affairs. We might say of a one-place predicate that these objects form the *subject field* of the predicate. When dealing with many-place predicates we must reckon with the possibility that the subject fields are different for the different places of the predicate.

A logically unhomogeneous substance differs from a logically homogeneous one in that if the substance is logically unhomo-geneous the set $(p)$ *does not comprise all the atomic states that one might possibly form on the mere basis of the category to which the elements belong.* If the substance is unhomogeneous certain combinations correctly formed according to a $(S_1)$ (or $(S_2)$) type description must be excluded, because in fact they do not form atomic states of affairs.

The unhomogeneity means linguistically that certain sentences must be struck off as 'nonsensical' from the set of 'syntactically' correct elementary sentences. If colour and pitch were atomic predicates one might quote the following as examples of this kind of nonsensical sentences:

'This spot in the visual field has the pitch of middle C.'

'This note is red.'

In a logical space with many-valued dimensions two predicates belonging to the same dimension must necessarily, I think, have the *same* subject fields. On the whole it is natural to think that the individual objects in the substance can be divided into *groups* which form *common* subject fields for different predicates (or places of predicates). If this is so, the logical unhomogeneity means a fine-structuring of the logical form of individual objects. The category of individual objects must be divided into 'subject fields' of different predicates.

The distinction between 'logically homogeneous' and various kinds of 'logically unhomogeneous' substance could serve as a model for various metaphysical views. That the substance of the world is supposed to be logically homogeneous could be called a form of metaphysical 'monism'. The view that the category of objects can be divided into two subject fields, each with its own separate set of predicates, could be called a form of metaphysical 'dualism', etc.

## 8. LOGICAL FORM AND INTERNAL QUALITIES

With the aid of our analysis of the concept of an 'internal structure' of substance we can give a more precise account of the relation between the 'logical form' of a 'thing' and its 'internal qualities'. Whereas the *external* structure of the world as a fact (or some other possible world) refers to what is *actually* the case in a given world, the *internal* structure of substance pertains only to what could *possibly* be the case in any world. Now the 'logical form' of a 'thing' must obviously be taken as the totality of the 'qualities' it has as an element in a substance with a given *internal* structure, and which it consequently possesses independently of what is actually the case. The 'logical form' of a 'thing' therefore comprises its category together with its logical relations to other things and so on.

We have earlier (p. 69) pointed out that the 'logical form' of a 'thing' is to be regarded as an 'internal' quality of it. But we have left open the question whether the 'things' perhaps have internal qualities not contained in their logical form. Although certain passages in the Tractatus rather suggest that the concepts 'internal quality' and 'logical form' are synonyms, I find it clearer to use the concepts in a way that makes possible the existence of internal qualities other than those contained in the logical form.

The reason for such a terminology is this: In statement 2.025 Wittgenstein makes a distinction which is not developed further in the Tractatus but which is nevertheless important. We read:

2.025   Sie (i.e. die Substanz) ist Form und Inhalt.

Substance is form and content. A corresponding formulation is given in 3.31 of an 'expression', but apart from this the word *Inhalt* occurs only once more (3.13) in the Tractatus and then it relates not to substance but to sentences. There is moreover a contrast between 2.025 and 2.0231, where we read that the substance can *only* characterize a 'form'—and not 'material qualities'. (Logical) 'form', on the one hand, seems to be the contradictory opposite of the 'material qualities', i.e. those qualities that correspond to the 'configuration of things', and thus to comprise *everything* that 'exists independently of what is the case'. But on the other hand, *substance* is also precisely that which 'exists independently of what is the case' (2.024) and has nevertheless not only 'form' but 'content' as well.

What could such a 'content' be? Let us bear in mind that a description of the 'internal structure' of substance—which includes a description of the logical form of the elements—leaves open the question of what are the elements of the world. Or to be more explicit: the fact that the internal structure of substance is such and such can, to be sure, exclude a certain set of given predicates from belonging to the elements of the world. If the internal structure of substance corresponds to a yes-and-no space then, for instance, all hues cannot occur as elements, since they form a many-valued dimension. But even if the structure of the substance is such that all hues *can* occur among its elements it does not follow that they really do so. There are other sets of qualities which have the same internal structure as the system of hues. If the logical form of substance determines only its internal *structure* (cf. above, pp. 71 f.), then substance—even if it is regarded as what is common to all possible worlds—possesses 'content' as well as 'form', the 'content' being determined only by an indication of *what* are the elements of the substance.

Consider now the 'quality' of being a colour, which is a quality of a quality. This second-order quality cannot be *external* (cf. above, p. 69), because the fact that a first-order quality is a colour has nothing to do with how atomic states of affairs are divided into existing and non-existing atomic states of affairs. To be a colour must therefore be described as an *internal* quality, and of course this internal quality of a predicate characterizes not only its logical form but also its content. Thus we are to reckon with 'internal qualities' which do not belong to logical form.

To this argument one might object that the question what are the elements of the world according to some epistemologists lies outside our faculty of knowledge and therefore is nonsensical—we can never describe anything but the structure of the world. The attitude one adopts towards this idea depends, I think, on one's starting-point in describing the world. But even if a closer logical analysis would lead one to hold that the content of the elements of the world is unknowable, it is important to distinguish between 'form' and 'content' of substance.

However, we have based our argument leading to this distinction on the examination of a predicative element. A corresponding distinction in respect of elements belonging to the category of objects leads to difficulties: it is not quite easy to make clear what is to be meant by the 'internal' content of an *object*.[1] Nevertheless it is important to distinguish between structure and content also with regard to objects, though the important opposition seems here to concern not internal but *external* structure as opposed to content.

And this brings into the foreground the fact that the distinction between the concepts 'structure' and 'content' is different in kind from the distinction between the concepts 'external' and 'internal'. Wittgenstein seems to tend to an identification of those distinctions, but this leads to much confusion (cf. below, Ch. VI, § 10). We must therefore take into account four possible concepts of this kind: 'external structure', 'external content', 'internal structure' and 'internal content'. If we differentiate between 'logical form' and 'content' for the quality 'red', the former belonging to the internal structure of predicates, the latter to their internal content, we must make a corresponding distinction for *red objects*, though the distinction here is a matter of *external* structure as opposed to *external* content. The sentence '*a* is red' states something external of *a*: this is partly a matter of *structure*—in so far as we take the logical form of the predicate into consideration—partly a matter of *content*—in so far as we pay attention to the content of the predicate.

These distinctions will become clearer in the next chapter. Here I only wish to add, that, though the distinction between what is 'external' and what is 'internal' seems to be of great importance, when we are dealing with *structure*, the corresponding differentiation with regard to *content* seems to be of small interest in the present investigation. When speaking of content it is often best to refrain from adopting an attitude to the question whether the content spoken of is to be regarded as 'external' or 'internal'.

## 9. THE SUBSTANCE AS WHAT IS PERSISTENT IN TIME

We have interpreted 2.024 as saying that the substance is the same in all possible worls. But 2.024 could be rendered in English

---

[1] This is possibly what Wittgenstein is thinking of in 2.0233.

not only as 'substance is what exists independently of what is the case' but also as 'substance is what remains unchanged independently of what is the case', i.e. as stating that substance is what remains unchanged in the course of time. That the latter interpretation conforms with a Wittgensteinian view is confirmed by 2.0271, where we read:

> 2.0271   Der Gegenstand ist das Feste, Bestehende; die Konfiguration ist das Wechselnde, Unbeständige.

This cannot be translated as in the English version of the Tractatus but must rather be rendered: 'The thing is the fixed, the persistent, the configuration is the changing, the mutable.'

We see from this passage that Wittgenstein vindicates not only the view that 'things' *are* persistent, but also that they are *all* that is persistent in a changing world. We shall not discuss the latter thought here. The former, however, is of fundamental interest.

In connection with our comments on Wittgenstein's treatment of Hume's thesis (Ch. IV, § 9) we pointed out that Wittgenstein provides every point of time with a separate system of dimensions in the logical space; i.e. an atomic state of affairs belonging to one point of time $t$ belongs *only* to that point of time and is therefore independent of any atomic state of affairs belonging to a different point of time $t'$. In our present context we seem to arrive at a different view. We have stated earlier that the 'things' in the world *uniquely* determine the atomic states of affairs which can be formed out of them. It follows that if the 'things' are persistent then the atomic states of affairs must be persistent too. There is no possibility of different atomic states of affairs for different points of time. But in fact we can infer from 2.0271 that *changes* are never internal but always external: the 'things' do not change, only their configurations are variable.

There is something attractive to intuition in the idea that all that is changing is 'external' whereas the 'logical space' remains the same in the course of time. In fact one could argue that the concept of logical space loses a good deal of its significance unless this is assumed. Why is there any interest in the question what worlds are possible besides the real one? Assume that we could give a complete description of the real world as a fact, i.e. a description that includes all that is, has been or will be the case—what additional interest could there be in knowing what might be, have been, or come to be, as a logical possibility? But really we cannot give such a description, and in so far we can do so, our description is always a product of *induction*, founded on what is believed to be the case in a *limited* part of the world (i.e. limited in space and time). Induction, however, occurs within a presupposed framework. Thus the 'logical space' is a framework within which we describe such facts as we believe we know and within which we also make predictions as to facts not yet known. What makes 'logical space' important is essentially that it determines a persisting framework for what *can* be the case in the future.

However, the idea of persisting elements can in one way be combined with the idea of different atomic states of affairs for different points of time, if certain conditions are fulfilled. Let us start from the latter view, but add to it two presuppositions: (a) the *internal structure* of the systems of elements belonging to two different points of time $t_1$ and $t_2$ is always the same, and (b) the *predicative* elements are always identical in both systems. Thus we assume that the predicative 'things' are persistent, whereas the 'things' belonging to the category of individual objects exist only instantaneously. But since the systems of elements belonging to time points $t_1$ and $t_2$ have the same internal structure there is a *one-one* correspondence between the individual objects existing at the time point $t_1$ and the individual objects existing at time point $t_2$. Moreover, the corresponding elements in this correspondence always have the same logical form. It is therefore possible to consider the corresponding elements *as* being identical.[1] This 'identification' of corresponding elements means that two atomic states of affairs, instead of being regarded as belonging to two different objects, are taken as referring to different *states* of the same object, which are independent of one another. It should be noticed that such an 'identification' of different instantaneous objects, giving rise to a persistent object, is necessary for it to be possible to say that anything 'changes' or remains 'unchanged'. The use of these expressions presupposes that there is an object which can be *thought* of as having different predicates at different times.[2]

---

[1] Cf. Hertz: '*Definition* 1: A material particle is a characteristic by which we associate without ambiguity a given point in space at a given time with a given point in space at any other time.—Every material particle is invariable and indestructible.' (*Principles of Mechanics*, p. 45 f.—Wittgenstein refers to this work in several places in the Tractatus.)

[2] It is often asserted that Einstein's theory of relativity does not reckon with any

## 10. FRAMEWORK QUESTIONS AND QUESTIONS ABOUT WHAT IS THE CASE

The idea of substance as what is persistent in the course of time brings out a fundamental obscurity in the Tractatus: in what sense are the 'things' common to all 'possible worlds'? We will examine two possible answers to this question.

(a) That all 'possible' worlds have their substance in common is to be understood in an *absolute* sense. There is a definite system of atomic 'things' forming the substance; and a world the substance of which is not this is unthinkable.

(b) That all 'possible' worlds have their substance in common is to be understood only in a *relative* sense. The formation of the system of atomic states of affairs is, to be sure, *prior* to a description of the world, and forms a framework for it, but this framework can be chosen in different ways, and every choice determines a separate system of possible worlds.

Many of Wittgenstein's formulations seem to confirm that he assumes alternative (a). 'It is clear that however different from the real world an imagined world may be, it must have something—a form—in common with the real world. This fixed form consists of the things', says Wittgenstein in 2.022 and 2.023. And when he says in 2.0124 that 'if all *things* are given, then thereby are all *possible* atomic states of affairs also given', he does not make any reservations indicating that he is speaking only of *those* atomic states of affairs which can be formed with *these* things. Neither here, nor in any other place in this context does he suggest that a different system of atomic states of affairs could possibly be formed from a different system of 'things'. The statements on which we have founded our exposition of Wittgenstein's 'logical atomism' point in the same direction. There is only one correct analysis of a sentence, which leads to a uniquely determined set of atomic things, named by names which occur in elementary sentences. It is also to be observed that he seems to attack a view of this kind in the *Philosophical Investigations* —see especially the arguments in §§ 46 ff.

However, what is noteworthy in the thesis that the world

---

persistent objects but only with 'world points', i.e. places in space-time. For my part I believe this view is due to a logical illusion. There is an obvious mistake in the belief that this theory totally dispenses with individual things. The mistake is due to an unfortunate terminology, according to which the 'points' of space-time are called 'events'. The points of space-time are instantaneous objects and not events, if by 'events' we understand something belonging to the category of facts.

consists of facts rather than of things seems to get lost, at least according to the view we have taken as our starting-point for the interpretation of the Tractatus, if we accept an idea of this kind. What is noteworthy in this thesis is that the 'world as a fact'—like the field of perception—can be analyséd into simple facts in *different* ways, and that the elements of the world are *different* according to how this analysis is effected. We have stated in Chapter IV that the world as a fact is a place in the logical space—but we should notice that the world is surrounded by a logical space only as an *analysed* fact, and that the structure of the logical space is dependent on *how* the world as a fact is analysed. That this is so is of particular significance in view of the following point: the construction of the logical space into which the world as a whole is fitted is based on an analysis only of a greater or smaller *part* of the world as a fact.

With regard to this argument it is important to state that Wittgenstein in other contexts in the Tractatus expresses himself in a way which seems to contradict the idea of a uniquely determined substance. Let us assume that the substance is uniquely determined, and ask ourselves by what *method* we are to decide what things the substance consists of. How are we to decide what atomic states of affairs there are in the logical space? Or if we are not interested in the content of substance but only in its internal structure, how are we to decide what *forms* of atomic states of affairs there are? This question corresponds on the linguistic plane to the question: *By what method are we to decide what forms of elementary sentences a description of the world is to contain?* The last mentioned question is dealt with in statements 5.55–5.5571. I shall give an account of their content such as I understand it.

In 5.55 we read: 'We must now answer *a priori* the question as to all possible forms of elementary sentences.' Wittgenstein here gives himself the task of indicating *a priori* all possible forms of elementary sentences. But he adds at once a remark to the import that the problem of indicating all possible forms of elementary sentences cannot be solved *a priori*: an elementary sentence consists of names, and we cannot give the number of names with different meanings *a priori*. Thus we seem to have to infer that this problem cannot be solved by logical analysis (as logical atomism presupposes), because 'our fundamental principle is that every question which can be decided at all by logic can be decided off-hand' (5.551, cf. also 5.5562 and 5.5563). Is our problem then to be solved by experience?

No, that is impossible too, because here we have to do not with a question about what is the case but about the nature of substance (a question about 'What', not about 'How'), and this means that our question is one the answer to which *precedes* any formulation of questions about experience (5.552). Then has such a question any sense at all (5.5542)? Can one ask whether the substance contains a relation with 27 places (5.5541)?

Wittgenstein's answer runs: 'The *application* of logic decides what elementary sentences there are. What lies in its application logic cannot anticipate' (5.557). Substance, which forms the framework of the description of the world, is in so far *prior* to experience, as a question about experience can be *stated* only within a certain framework. Nevertheless the choice of a framework is not independent of experience. How the framework is to be chosen is a question about the application of logic.—Even if this answer is not very informative, it obviously takes into consideration the possibility of *different* choices.

The problem what the relation is between the framework of a world description and experience is of course very important even if we admit that the framework can be chosen in different ways. Since the framework of a world description determines the form empirical questions will take, and therefore is in one way *a priori*, the fact that the framework *can* conflict with experience is of overwhelming significance. An example of a revolutionary scientific theory which essentially consists in a change of the framework of description is given by Einstein's theory of relativity. The law of additivity of velocities was probably regarded by all physicists before Einstein as an *analytical* statement. Within the framework determined by this axiom one had to adopt very complicated hypotheses in order to explain the 'apparent' constancy of light velocity in respect of systems of reference with different velocities. Einstein proved the possibility of employing a concept of velocity for which the law of additivity was *not* analytic. After this had been made clear it was easy to formulate a new law for the composition of velocities which corresponded to experience. In our time many physicists have a feeling that there is something wrong with the framework of quantum theory and atomic physics. That nevertheless no satisfactory framework has been found is a sign of the methodological difficulties involved in the treatment of framework questions.

As a final remark on Wittgenstein's conception of substance we may add that his use of the concept of 'form' reminds us of Kantian terminology.   Wittgenstein had been brought into contact with this through his acquaintance with Schopenhauer's writings and Hertz's *Principles of Mechanics*.[1]   We shall return to Wittgenstein's relation to Kant in the last chapter of the book.

[1] Wittgenstein was in his youth much influenced by Schopenhauer.   As to Hertz. note the reference to Kant in his 'Prefatory Note', (op. cit. p. 45).

# VI

# THE CONCEPT OF A PICTURE

## 1. REPRESENTATIONS OF FACTS

2.1  Wir machen uns Bilder der Tatsachen.

'We form pictures of facts.' The emphasis laid on this statement implies that it is of fundamental philosophical importance. In the present chapter, however, our main task is not to analyse the part it plays in Wittgenstein's system but to give an idea of what Wittgenstein means by a picture.

2.11  Das Bild stellt die Sachlage im logischen Raume, das Bestehen und Nichtbestehen von Sachverhalten vor.

2.12  Das Bild ist ein Modell der Wirklichkeit.

When we call something a 'picture' we do not always imply that it 'represents' or 'depicts' something—there are also 'nonrepresentational' pictures. From the formulations of 2.1, 2.11, and 2.12, however, we see that Wittgenstein, when speaking of a picture, always thinks of it as a picture *of* something. 'The picture *depicts* a state of affairs in logical space, the existence and non-existence of atomic states of affairs'; 'the picture is a *model* of reality'.

Consider the following examples of pictures *of* something:

(a) a sculpture of Venus,
(b) a bust of Shelley,
(c) a picture of a dog in a text-book of zoology,
(d) a portrait of the pet dog Fido,
(e) an illustration of a fairy tale,
(f) a photograph or a painting of a historical event,
(g) a map of Lilliput,
(h) a map of England.

(a) represents a fictitious god, (b) a real person, (c) represents an object of a certain type, (d) a real object of this type, (e) and (g) represent fictitious states of affairs, (f) and (h) real states of affairs. In (b), (d), (f) and (h) the picture has a real prototype, whereas in (a), (c), (e) and (g) there is no real prototype. From 2.12 it seems to follow that Wittgenstein always thinks of a picture as having a *real* prototype, which it represents. I shall therefore call a picture a genuine *representation* (*Abbildung*) only if it represents a real proto-type; otherwise I shall call it 'fictitious'.

What we form pictures of is *facts*, according to 2.1. Since by 'reality' Wittgenstein means a 'real state of affairs', what a picture is a model of according to 2.12 is also a fact. I think Wittgenstein must be understood literally here: that a picture has a real prototype means in his terminology that it is either a 'true' or a 'false' repre-sentation of a fact. (Cf. 2.0212, 2.17, 2.21 ff.) But what are we then to mean by a representation of a fact?

## 2. THE CONCEPT OF AN ARTICULATE FIELD

According to 2.11 a picture depicts the existence and non-existence of *Sachverhalte*. This seems to imply that a fact of which we form a picture is always thought of as analysed in terms of 'atomic states of affairs' in the sense developed in the preceding chapters. It is, however, important to notice that Wittgenstein's statements concerning the concept of a 'picture' express an idea which is as such *independent* of the idea of *Sachverhalte* as 'atomic' in any absolute sense of the word, and likewise independent of the idea of a sub-stance consisting of *atomic* elements. The only thing we need to presuppose for a development of this idea is that the fact depicted is an *analysed* fact, i.e. 'analysed' in the same way as the 'field of perception' of Fig. 1 was analysed in Chapter II.

Consider once again Fig. 4 of the preceding chapter (p. 70). We thought of it there as an illustration of a 'world', the elements of which are some unspecified atomic objects and predicates. We shall now give it a more specified interpretation, but at the same time drop the assumption that the elements of the depicted facts are atomic. The five letters *a–e* we shall take as standing for five persons of a family, say, Alan, Brian, Christopher, David, and Eric. The arrow may indicate the 'father-son relation' and the circle 'intelligence'. From our diagram, then, we can read that Alan is the father of

Brian, that Christopher is the father of David, that Brian is not the father of Eric, that Eric is intelligent, that Alan is not intelligent, and so on. Our diagram illustrates a certain *complex fact* concerning our family, which is analysed into the existence and non-existence of some—so far as the analysis goes—unanalysed states of affairs, which are built up of—again so far as the analysis goes—simple objects and predicates, namely: the five persons, the quality of intelligence and the father-son relation. So far as the analysis goes we may consider these objects and predicates the *elements* in terms of which our fact is analysed, and the states of affairs which are combinations of these elements the '*elementary states of affairs*' of the analysed fact.

In order to have a convenient terminology I shall call a fact capable of being analysed in different ways a 'field'. A field so analysed that certain objects and predicates—which need not be atomic—appear as its elements I shall call an *articulate field*.[1] To an articulate field, then, belongs (a) the fact analysed, (b) the system of elements in terms of which it is analysed. An 'articulate field' differs from an analysed 'world as a fact' only in (1) that it need not comprise more than a certain portion of the world as a fact and (2) that the elements need not be 'atomic'. With this change all that was said in the preceding chapter about the world holds true of an 'articulate field'. In respect of its elements an articulate field has a fixed 'external structure'. The 'system of elements' (which corresponds to the 'substance' of the world) has a certain 'internal structure' that determines the structure of a 'logical space' of 'possible states of affairs', in which the articulate field is a 'place'. This 'logical space' may be homogeneous or unhomogeneous, it may be a yes-and-no space or a space with many-valued dimensions, etc. The system of elements determines a system of 'elementary states of affairs', every elementary state of affairs being a possible combination of the elements. One possible state of affairs differs from another as regards its external structure, and this is determined by the way in which elementary states of affairs are divided into 'positive' and 'negative' states of affairs.

When I go on to interpret Wittgenstein's statements about a picture, I shall take the concepts *Sachverhalt, Sachlage, logischer Raum* as 'elementary state of affairs', 'possible state of affairs' and 'logical space' in *relation* to such an articulate field.

---

[1] On this terminology cf. 3.141 and Langer: *Philosophy in a New Key*, p. 75.

## 3. THE CONCEPT OF 'ISOMORPHISM'

Wittgenstein's use of the notion of 'representation' (*Abbildung*) and related concepts is not free from a certain amount of ambiguity, and I do not think it possible to grasp exactly what idea he connects with them. I shall therefore adopt the following method of analysis. First I shall define an exact concept of 'representation' called 'isomorphic representation'. Then I shall interpret Wittgenstein's statements about pictures with reference to this sort of depicting. In this way we obtain a model that satisfies many of Wittgenstein's statements on the subject. This model can be used as a system of reference for the analysis of Wittgenstein's application of the concept of a picture in his theory of language.

Before defining the concept of an 'isomorphic representation' it is convenient to introduce the more general concept of an 'isomorphism'.

We have interpreted the diagram of Fig. 4 (reproduced as diagram (i) in Fig. 5) as illustrating a fact concerning the members of a family. This fact can be considered an *articulate field*. I shall call it $F\,1$. The system of elements in $F\,1$ consists of the five persons, the father-son relation and intelligence; I shall call this system $S\,1$. Now we will compare $F\,1$ with another field, illustrated in diagram (ii) of Fig. 5. This diagram we interpret as illustrating a group of five army officers: Adams, Barratt, Colman, Denison, and Ellis. The double arrow indicates 'giving direct orders to'. We read from our diagram that Barratt and Colman take direct orders from Adams, that Denison and Ellis take direct orders from

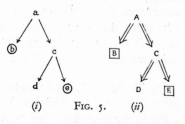

(i)  FIG. 5.  (ii)

Colman, that Colman does not take direct orders from Barratt, and so on. Those marked with squares are brave, the others not. Thus diagram (ii) illustrates an articulate field the elements of which are the five officers, the order-giving relation and braveness. I shall call this field $F\,2$ and the system of its elements $S\,2$.

A comparison of the two diagrams shows that there is some 'similarity in structure' between the articulate fields $F\,1$ and $F\,2$. This similarity can be characterized in the following way:

(1) The *internal* structures of the systems of elements in $F\,1$ and

$F$ 2 are similar, at least in that both $S$ 1 and $S$ 2 consist of *five* objects, *one* quality and *one* binary relation.[1] That is, $S$ 1 and $S$ 2 could be said to have the same *categorial structure*. Whether or no there is also a stronger similarity in internal structure between the two systems—consisting of similar logical interrelations between the elements—is unimportant in this connection.

That $S$ 1 and $S$ 2 have the same categorial structure means that it is possible to establish a one-one correspondence between the elements of each category in the two systems, for instance as follows:

|  |  |  |  |
|---|---|---|---|
| | *Objects:* | Alan | — Adams |
| | | Brian | — Barratt |
| | | Christopher | — Colman |
| $(C_0)$ | | David | — Denison |
| | | Eric | — Ellis |
| | *Qualities:* | intelligence | — braveness |
| | *Binary relations:* | Father-son relation | — order-giving relation. |

It should be noticed that the identity in categorial structure between systems $S$ 1 and $S$ 2 guarantees the *possibility* of a one-one correspondence between the elements of each category but does not uniquely determine which this correspondence is; i.e. it can be established in different ways. In our example the correspondence between the objects can be established in 120 ways. If there were more than one quality in each system the correspondence between the qualities could also be established in different ways, and so on.

(2) There is further an identity in *external structure* of the *articulate fields* $F$ 1 and $F$ 2. This holds or does not hold good in respect of a *fixed* correspondence between the elements and may be stated as follows

In respect of correspondence $(C_0)$

(a) any object of $S$ 1 has the quality of intelligence in $F$ 1 if, and only if, the *corresponding* object of $S$ 2 has the *corresponding* quality of braveness in $F$ 2;

(b) of two objects in $S$ 1 one is in the relation of 'being father of' to the other in $F$ 1 if, and only if, the *corresponding* re-

---

[1] Cf. 4.04–0412, 5.475.

lation of 'giving direct orders' holds good in $F$ 2 between the *corresponding* objects of $S$ 2.

This identity in external structure we call an *isomorphism*. The articulate fields $F$ 1 and $F$ 2 are said to be *isomorphic* in respect of the correspondence $(C_0)$.

In general the concept of 'isomorphism' can be defined as follows:

Given two articulate fields $F$ and $G$, the categorial structure of which is the same, and given a one-one correspondence $(C)$ between the elements of each category in $F$ and $G$, then $F$ and $G$ are said to be *isomorphic* in respect of $(C)$ if, and only if, the following condition is fulfilled:

*An elementary state of affairs does or does not exist in F according as the corresponding elementary state of affairs does or does not exist in G.*

Here elementary states of affairs in $F$ and $G$ are said to correspond to one another if their analogous elements correspond to one another.

Concerning the concept of isomorphism as defined here, the following features should be noticed:

(a) Isomorphism is a relation between *facts*, not between *things*.

(b) Only facts that are *analysed* in terms of fixed systems of elements can be said to be isomorphic or not.

(c) Isomorphism is a relation between two articulate fields the elements of which have the *same* categorial structure, and holds or does not hold good in respect of a fixed correspondence between the elements of each field. This correspondence we call the *key of isomorphism*.

The question whether or not two fields are isomorphic can be raised only if the categorial structure of their elements is the same, and only in reference to a fixed key of correspondence. In the last respect our terminology deviates noticeably from the usual terminology of mathematics: there we often say that two systems are isomorphic if there is only *some* key in respect of which they are isomorphic in the above sense. For our purpose, however, this more restricted use of the term 'isomorphic' is more convenient.

(d) Isomorphism is a *symmetrical* relation. It is also *transitive* in the following sense. If $F$ and $G$ are isomorphic in respect of key $(C)$ and if $G$ and $H$ are isomorphic in respect of key $(C')$, then $(C)$ and $(C')$ in combination define a correspondence between the elements of $F$ and $H$, in respect of which $F$ and $H$ are isomorphic.

With the aid of the concept of 'isomorphism' we can give a clearer account of the distinction between 'structure' and 'content' introduced in the preceding chapter. Two isomorphic fields (as for instance $F$ 1 and $F$ 2) have the *same* external structure but *different* contents. A similar account could be given of the distinction between internal structure and content.[1]

### 4. ISOMORPHIC REPRESENTATIONS

It is a remarkable fact that we are able to state the isomorphism of fields $F$ 1 and $F$ 2 simply by examining the diagrams illustrating them, without any further knowledge of these fields. We infer the isomorphism between fields $F$ 1 and $F$ 2 from an observed isomorphism between the diagrams. The conclusion is possible because of the transitivity of isomorphism and the tacit additional assumption that *a diagram and the field illustrated by it are isomorphic*. This assumption can be formulated thus: to understand a diagram as a diagrammatic *picture* implies the understanding that there is an isomorphism between the diagram and the field depicted. Understanding Diagram (i), for instance, as it is intended to be understood comprises the following steps:

(a) We see the diagram not as a 'thing' but as a complex fact, a *field*.
(b) We apprehend this field—I shall call it $D$ 1—as an *articulate field* analysed in terms of a fixed system of elements:

Objects:         the five letters '*a*', '*b*', '*c*', '*d*', and '*e*'.
Qualities:       the quality of being surrounded by a circle—
                 I shall call it the 'circle-quality'.
Binary relations: the relation of being connected by an arrow—
                 I shall call it the 'arrow-relation'.

This step is by no means trivial. For we could certainly apprehend our diagram as an articulate field in many other ways too. And the only reason why the field should be analysed in exactly this way is that this is the analysis *relevant* for the interpretation of

[1] Cf. below, p. 103 n.

$D$ 1 as a picture.[1]—It should be noticed that it is the *quality* of being surrounded by a circle, not the circle itself, and likewise the arrow-*relation* only, not the arrow itself, that appears as an element in this field.

(c) We establish the correspondence between the elements of $D$ 1 and $F$ 1, i.e. we 'interpret' the elements of $D$ 1 as 'standing for' the elements of $F$ 1 according to the following key:[2]

(C₁)

| Objects: | Letter '$a$' | — Alan |
| | „ '$b$' | — Brian |
| | „ '$c$' | — Christopher |
| | „ '$d$' | — David |
| | „ '$e$' | — Eric |
| Qualities: | The circle-quality | — intelligence |
| Binary relations: | The arrow-relation | — the father-son relation. |

(d) We *read* from $D$ 1 what is the case in $F$ 1 on the assumption that $F$ 1 is isomorphic with $D$ 1 in respect of key (C₁). $D$ 1 *shows* what is the case in $F$ 1, because $F$ 1 is understood to have the same external structure in respect of *its* elements as $D$ 1 has in respect of *its*.

In the same way, the second diagram in Fig. 5 is interpreted as a picture. Of two isomorphic fields $F$ and $G$ one, say $F$, may always be considered as a picture of the other. If so, we call $F$ an *isomorphic picture of $G$*, the relation between $F$ and $G$ one of *isomorphic representation* and the key of isomorphism the *key of interpretation*.

---

[1] We might, for instance, regard the field as composed of

11 *objects:* the 5 letters, 4 arrows, and 2 circles.
3 *qualities:* the quality of being a letter, the quality of being an arrow, and the quality of being a circle.
1 *ternary relation:* that of one object *connecting* another with a third.
1 *binary relation:* that of one object *surrounding* another object.

(Only arrows can 'connect' and only circles 'surround', which shows that this system of elements determines an 'unhomogeneous' logical space in the sense of Chapter V, section 7.) I think there is a strong tendency to analyse $D$ 1 in this way, but this tendency must be suppressed if we are to understand how the diagram works as a picture.

[2] The reason for analysing $D$ 1 in terms of the elements mentioned in step (b) is that *these* elements occur on the left side of the key (C₁). That it must *not* be analysed in the way mentioned in the preceding footnote means that, for instance, the arrows do not appear as *objects* in this key. We can express this by saying that they are not significant *objects* in the picture, but function only as *characteristics* of the significant arrow-relation.

*It is essential to the concept of an isomorphic representation that the elements of the picture always stand for elements of their own category.* Only then is it possible for the picture to *show* the external structure of the prototype.

## 5. THE CONCEPT OF A PICTURE IN THE TRACTATUS

Many of the statements in the Tractatus can be given good interpretations if the words 'picture' (*Bild*) and 'representation' (*Abbildung*) are taken as referring to isomorphic pictures and representations. But there are some easily noticeable differences, too, between the concept of a picture in the Tractatus and our concept of an isomorphic picture.

One we have already touched upon. As stated above (p. 89) a picture, according to Wittgenstein's terminology, may be called either 'true' or 'false': 'The picture agrees with reality or not; it is right or wrong, true or false' (2.21), 'In the agreement or disagreement of its sense with reality, its truth or falsity consists' (2.222). But the words 'true' and 'false' cannot be used in this way in connection with the expression 'isomorphic picture'. (On the whole I think it is unnatural to speak about 'false' pictures.) Either a field $F$ does represent the field $G$ isomorphically according to a key $(C)$—or it does not. In the first case $F$ is, in the second it *is not*, an isomorphic picture of $G$. Thus to talk about 'false' isomorphic pictures is meaningless.

It follows that the concept of an isomorphic picture does not correspond logically to Wittgenstein's concept of a 'picture' but rather conforms to his concept of a 'true picture'. To bring our terminology in accordance with that of the Tractatus we must therefore think of a picture not as an isomorphic picture but as an articulate field of which the question of its being or not being an isomorphic picture can be *raised*. We obtain such a concept if we adopt the following definition:

(VI.1)  *An articulate field $F$ is called a picture (true or false) of the articulate field $G$ if there is a key of interpretation $(C)$ according to which the elements of $F$ are considered to stand for the elements of $G$.*
*The picture $F$ is said to be true or false according as it is an isomorphic picture of $G$ in respect of $(C)$ or not.*

Thus the criterion for F being a picture of G is the *existence of the key only*—the *isomorphism* is a criterion of the *truth* of the picture. (Cf. 2.223.)

This definition suffices for a good interpretation of the following statements:

2.13     Den Gegenständen entsprechen im Bilde die Elemente des Bildes.

2.131    Die Elemente des Bildes vertreten im Bild die Gegenstände.

2.14     Das Bild besteht darin, dass sich seine Elemente in bestimmter Art und Weise zu einander verhalten.

2.141    Das Bild ist eine Tatsache.

2.1513   Nach dieser Auffassung gehört also zum Bilde auch noch die abbildende Beziehung, die es zum Bild macht.

2.1514   Die abbildende Beziehung besteht aus den Zuordnungen der Elemente des Bildes und der Sachen.

For the interpretation of 2.13 we must remember that according to Wittgenstein's terminology not only objects are 'things' (*Gegenstände*) but also predicates. Thus it states that the elements of the prototype correspond to the elements of the picture. 2.131 should be rendered 'The elements of the picture deputize, in the picture, for the things' which I think gives an illuminating description of what is meant by the elements of the picture *standing for* the corresponding elements of the prototype.

2.141 requires comments of two kinds. 'A picture is a fact.' As formulated in this short and categorical manner it may seem obviously wrong. In everyday language pictures are certainly regarded as things rather than facts. It would perhaps therefore be preferable to make a distinction here between a 'picture as an object' and a 'picture as a fact'—corresponding to the distinction of Chapter II between 'the world as an object' and 'the world as a fact'. But in the same way as the concept of 'the world as a fact' was considered prior to the concept of 'the world as an object' we have to consider the concept of a picture as a fact prior to the concept of a picture as an object. What represents isomorphically is not an object but a *fact*. A picture as an object can be a picture *of* something only in so far as it is a complex object in an articulate field which is a picture as a fact. Unless otherwise stated we shall therefore always use the word 'picture' as meaning 'a picture as a fact'.

There is also another ambiguity to be settled here. Consider,

H

for instance, an articulate field $F$ that according to one key $(C)$ is a picture of a field $G$ and according to another key $(C')$ is a picture of another field $G'$. Shall we say in such a case that the *same* picture $F$ can be interpreted in two different ways or that there are two different pictures? According to 2.1513 we ought rather to adopt the latter view, and this seems also as a rule more convenient for our purpose. The articulate field $F$, as capable of different interpretations, we will call a *picture-field*, using the word *picture* as a name only for those picture-fields to which a fixed key of interpretation is attached. Using this terminology, however, it would be clearer to change the formulation of 2.141 as follows: 'A picture is an *interpreted* fact.' (The key of interpretation is in 2.1514 called the 'representing relation'—*abbildende Beziehung*.) On the other hand 2.14 perhaps refers to a *picture-field* rather than to a picture: 'A picture-field consists in its elements being combined[1] in a definite way' (cf. 2.031).

## 6. WHAT A PICTURE REPRESENTS AND WHAT IT DEPICTS OR PRESENTS

Consider now the first paragraph of 2.15:

> 2.15  Dass sich die Elemente des Bildes in bestimmter Art und Weise zu einander verhalten stellt vor, dass sich die Sachen so zu einander verhalten.
> . . . . . . . . . .

For the interpretation of this a distinction between the notions of *abbilden* and *vorstellen* is required. I have rendered *abbilden* above as 'represent' and *vorstellen* as 'depict'. If we adopt these translations we must pay attention to the following difference between their uses. A picture *represents* its prototype either truly or falsely, and this means that it represents the *same* prototype (by means of the key) whether or not it is true or false. If the picture is true, however, it not only represents the prototype, but also *depicts* it. But if it is false, it does *not* depict the prototype but depicts a possible state of affairs *other* than the real one.

And it is important to note that this is not to be understood as implying the existence of some 'imaginary fact' acting as a *prototype*

---

[1] Since the expression 'being combined' corresponds to the German expression *sich zu einander verhalten* the words 'with one another' of the English translation are superfluous and misleading.

of the false picture: the picture depicts the elements of the real prototype *as* standing in the way *shown* by its *own* external structure, and this may be so or not: 'That the elements of the picture are combined in a definite way depicts that the things are so combined.'

The same thought is expressed in 2.201–2.221 by use of the word *darstellen*, which may be rendered as 'present'. 'The picture *presents* what it presents, independently of its truth or falsehood, by means of its form of representation' (2.22, italics mine). 'The picture contains the possibility of the state of affairs which it presents' (2.203), which means: We learn to know that a state of affairs is *possible* from the fact that we can form a picture that *presents* it, that *depicts* it. To be presented or depicted in this way is, so to speak, the *mode of existence of merely possible states of affairs*.[1]

I shall sum up Wittgenstein's view on this subject in the following statement:

(VI.2)   *A picture is an interpreted fact that 'represents' a real prototype (truly or falsely). Its elements deputize for the elements of the prototype and it*

   (a) *'presents' ('depicts') these elements as combined in the way shown by its own external structure, and thus*

   (b) *shows the possibility of their being combined in such a way.*

Point (b) is of great importance in Wittgenstein's philosophy. It will be examined in more detail in the following discussion.

## 7. THE FORM OF REPRESENTATION

Many of the statements on the concept of a picture contain the expression 'form of representation' (*Form der Abbildung*). This is a vague concept, and it is difficult to see how it could be at one and the same time what it is said to be in 2.15, 2.151, and 2.17. But since its use covers important ideas it is necessary to understand its main import.

I shall start from 2.17. Here the 'form of representation' is defined as 'what a picture must have in common with reality in

---

[1] The rather 'technical' sense in which the word *darstellen* appears in this argument is not consistently maintained in the Tractatus. A corresponding observation holds true of most terms which are used in a 'technical' way in a certain context. This is not surprising in view of the character of Wittgenstein's literary style.

order to be capable of representing it after its manner—rightly or wrongly'. The 'form of representation', then, is determined by some kind of *similarity* between the picture and its prototype that exists *independently* of the truth or falsehood of the picture. This means that such a similarity cannot have any reference to the *external structure* of the fields concerned, but must be a characteristic which can be stated, if at all, simply on an examination of the *internal* properties of the elements and the key of interpretation:

(VI.3)  *The 'form of representation' is determined by an internal similarity between the systems of elements in the picture and the prototype.*

An internal similarity can consist either of a similarity in internal structure or of a similarity in content (or both). As stated above it is essential to the key of interpretation of an isomorphic representation that

(a) it should be a one-one correspondence,
(b) corresponding elements should be of the same category.

For a correspondence (C) between the elements of two articulate fields F and G to satisfy these conditions it is necessary that the systems of elements in F and G should have the *same categorial structure* (cf. above, p. 92). Conversely the fact that the systems of elements in F and G have the same categorial structure can be *established* only by bringing them into a correspondence which satisfies conditions (a) and (b). Thus (C)'s satisfying conditions (a) and (b) means that (C) is a correspondence by which the identity in categorial structure between the systems of elements in F and G can be established. We could therefore say that F and G have the same categorial structure *in respect of correspondence* (C) if these conditions are fulfilled. The fact that conditions (a) and (b) are fulfilled constitutes, if interpreted in this way, a similarity in internal structure between the systems of elements in the picture and the prototype, and this is actually the *only* kind of internal similarity between these systems that exists in *every* isomorphic representation. 'What the picture must have in common with reality' to be capable of representing it *isomorphically* is only the common categorial structure in respect of the key. We might therefore infer as follows:

(VI.4)  *The 'form of representation' of an isomorphic representation in general is the common categorial structure (in respect of the key of interpretation) of the systems of elements in the picture and the prototype.*

The reference to the key of interpretation in this formulation makes it more natural to call a common feature in the picture and the prototype the form of 'representation' than it would otherwise be.

If we presuppose the logical spaces of both picture $F$ and prototype $G$ to be homogeneous yes-and-no-spaces, the categorial structure of the elements can be said to coincide with their *internal* structure (cf. above p. 75). If we think only of yes-and-no spaces the expression 'categorial structure' seems therefore to be replaceable by the expression 'internal structure' in the above statement. But if we take into consideration the possibility that the logical space of $F$ or $G$ or both is unhomogeneous or has many-valued dimensions the expressions 'categorial structure' and 'internal structure' are certainly *not* interchangeable. This point is of importance for the interpretation of statements 2.171–2.19.

In 2.171 we are told that a picture can represent every reality whose form it has. As particular instances of this general rule Wittgenstein adds that a spatial picture can represent everything spatial, a picture in colour[1] everything coloured and so on. We may infer that being a spatial picture or a picture in colour is to be regarded as a characteristic of the form of representation. In 2.181 the concept of a 'logical picture' with a 'logical' form of representation is introduced. In 2.182 we read that *every* picture is *also* a 'logical' picture. For instance every spatial picture is also a logical one, though the converse is certainly not true. It follows that the 'logical' form of representation is the most general form of representation; any picture whatsoever must be a 'logical' picture and must have the 'logical' form of representation in common with what it represents (2.2).

From the point of view of our preceding analysis one might be tempted to interpret the 'logical form of representation' as the 'form of an isomorphic representation in general', as defined in

---

[1] Wittgenstein's *farbiges Bild* should be rendered 'picture in colour', not 'coloured picture'. There are 'coloured pictures' which are not 'pictures in colour'—as for instance a geological map in which the occurrence of, say, lime in the soil is marked by red. Such a 'coloured picture' could not be called a *farbiges Bild* in German.

(VI.4). And such an interpretation would be admissible if the logical spaces of all fields concerned were homogeneous yes-and-no spaces. But if we also take spaces with many-valued dimensions into consideration a more specified characterization of this concept seems to be required. In 2.151 Wittgenstein states that the 'form of representation is the possibility that the things are combined as are the elements of the picture'. But, as we shall see, this possibility does not always exist if the logical spaces of the picture and the prototype are different in internal structure. With regard to the possibility of spaces with many-valued dimensions we have therefore to presuppose that a 'logical' picture and its prototype have in common not only the *categorial structure* but also the rest of the *internal structure* of the systems of elements. If this interpretation is correct we may state:

(VI.5)    *The 'logical form of representation' is the internal structure of the systems of elements, which a 'logical' picture and its prototype must have in common in respect of the key.*

## 8. ADEQUATE AND INADEQUATE PICTURES

Since 'every picture is also a logical picture', an isomorphic picture cannot always be considered a 'picture' according to this interpretation of the Tractatus. For an interpreted field to be a 'picture' in the sense of the Tractatus, it is required not only that the elements of the picture should always stand for elements of the same category but also that they should always stand for elements of the same logical form. If there exist any logical connections between the elements of the prototype, the corresponding logical connections should exist between the elements of the picture, and conversely. Thus a 'logical representation' presupposes a greater amount of 'logical adequacy', so to speak, than does an isomorphic representation as such. With regard to this circumstance I shall call a 'logical' picture in the sense of (VI.5) a '(logically) *adequate* picture', and the 'logical form of representation' a (logically) *adequate* form of representation, with an *adequate* key of interpretation.

In order to understand the significance of the requirement of adequacy we have to consider the possible inconveniences resulting from the use of an inadequate form of representation. We may distinguish between two different kinds of inadequacy.

(1) There are logical connections between the elements of the prototype to which there are no corresponding connections in the picture. This difference in internal structure might be stated as a difference in 'logical freedom' between the corresponding elements, the elements of the picture having a *greater logical freedom* than the elements they stand for. An example of this possibility is given by our interpretation of diagram (i) of Fig. 5. The logical space of $D$ 1 may be considered a yes-and-no space: it is, for instance, possible to draw or not to draw an arrow between any given pair of letters independently of how the arrows are drawn between other pairs of letters. But the father-son relation does not possess the corresponding logical freedom, because it is asymmetrical and intransitive. This means that it is possible to draw diagrams which—according to key $(C_1)$ on p. 95—cannot be called simply 'false' pictures but must rather be characterized as 'impossible', because *they do not present any possible state of affairs.* The diagram in Fig. 6, for instance, is of this kind: According to key $(C_1)$ we ought to read from this diagram that Alan is his own father and that David is both the father and the son of Eric and so on. But this is certainly not a possible state of affairs.

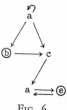

FIG. 6.

The inconvenience resulting from this kind of inadequacy, then, consists in the occurrence of 'impossible' pictures. This is an inconvenience of 'philosophical' and 'epistemological' rather than of 'scientific' interest. A scientist might find many pictures 'impossible' in the plain sense of being 'false' according to some general law of nature. And he will generally pay little attention to the fact that some pictures might be 'impossible' in a logical sense as well. To an epistemologist, however, this distinction is certainly important.[1]

Its philosophical importance may be illustrated by statements 2.224 and 2.225 of the Tractatus:

---

[1] There is an analogy between the notions of the 'adequacy' and 'truth' of a picture, the former consisting in an 'internal', the latter in an 'external' identity in structure in respect of a key. In some regards it would be convenient to call the relation between an adequate picture and its prototype an 'internal isomorphism' in contradistinction to ordinary isomorphism, which could then be called 'external isomorphism'. The concept of an 'internal isomorphism' might be defined in roughly the same way as ordinary isomorphism was defined on p. 93, the expression 'elementary state of affairs' being replaced by the expression 'logical connection'. I think scientists or mathematicians do not as a rule pay much attention to the question whether their isomorphisms are internal or external.

2.224   Aus dem Bild allein ist nicht zu erkennen, ob es wahr oder falsch ist.

2.225   Ein a priori wahres Bild gibt es nicht.

These statements can easily be accepted if by a picture is meant an *adequate* picture. An adequate picture always presents a possible state of affairs, and whether it is true or false can therefore be discovered only by a comparison of this state of affairs with the real one. From an *adequate* picture alone one cannot discover whether it is true or false (2.224). And there is no adequate picture which is true *a priori* (2.225).

If we admit that pictures can be pictures even if the key of interpretation is inadequate, statements 2.224 and 2.225 become more controversial. That the diagram in Fig. 6 is 'impossible' we can discover from the structure of the picture-field and the key of interpretation alone, without any reference to the real state of affairs. And since both the picture-field and the key of interpretation belong to the picture, it can be discovered, in this instance, from the picture alone that it is false.

However, we could 'save' the validity of 2.224 in respect of inadequate pictures by an argument of this kind. Even if inadequate pictures are called 'pictures' *if* they present a possible state of affairs, we need not allow 'impossible' pictures to be called 'pictures'. That a picture is 'impossible' does not mean that it presents an 'impossible state of affairs' but that it does not present any state of affairs at all. The reason why a picture is 'impossible' is that the picture-field *cannot* be interpreted by means of the key. And therefore an 'impossible' picture is, strictly speaking, not a picture at all. Diagram (i) in Fig. 5 is 'interpretable' by means of key ($C_1$) and therefore may be called a 'picture', though an inadequate one, but the diagram in Fig. 6 is not interpretable by means of this key and therefore is *not* a picture. And if in this way we assume that being a 'false picture' always presupposes interpretability by means of the key we cannot discover even from an inadequate picture alone that it is false.

But Wittgenstein certainly did not mean 2.224 to be true in this way. As 2.151 shows, he thought that the 'form of representation' *guarantees* the possibility of the elements of the prototype being combined as are the elements of the *picture-field*. There is no room left for 'impossible pictures'. And this means that the form of representation must be adequate.

As for 2.225, we can at least find *'a priori* true' *features* in an inadequate picture—for instance the fact that in diagram (i) in Fig. 5 no person is depicted as his own father.

(2) There are logical connections between the elements of the picture to which there are no corresponding connections in the prototype. In this case the elements of the picture possess a 'smaller logical freedom' than the elements which they stand for. If the inconveniences resulting from the first kind of inadequacy are mainly philosophical those resulting from this kind are 'scientific' as well, because the use of elements with too restricted a logical freedom makes some 'possible' states of affairs incapable of being presented in the picture. When in diagram (i) in Fig. 5, for instance, we mark fat persons red and tall persons blue we might 'from the picture alone' infer the 'impossibility' of a person's being at the same time fat and tall. And in such a case reality might happen to be 'paradoxical'.

To sum up: If we choose an inadequate key there are either 'pictures' which do not present a possible state of affairs or possible states of affairs that cannot be depicted by any picture. Thus, if the 'mode of existence' of a merely possible state of affairs should really consist in being presented by a picture—as we said in section 6—then we must presuppose that a 'picture' is to be understood to be an *adequate* picture.

And this is perhaps a good reason for saying that only 'adequate pictures' are 'logical pictures'. But it must be emphasized that the idea that *all* pictures are 'logical pictures' in this sense also leads to difficulties. We have so far regarded the acceptance of this idea as a mere matter of terminology. This means that for an interpreted articulate field $F$ to be *called* a true *picture* of an articulate field $G$ it is necessary that

(a) the key of interpretation should be adequate,
(b) the external structure of $F$ should be identical with that of $G$ in respect of the key.

Thus condition (a) is regarded as a necessary condition for $F$ to be a picture of $G$ at all, and (b) as a necessary condition for this picture to be true.

But when Wittgenstein thinks (a) to be a necessary condition for $F$ to be a picture of $G$ at all, he seems not to conceive of this necessity only as a consequence of the way in which the concept of a picture has been defined, but rather like this: If condition (a) is not satisfied the *question* whether condition (b) is satisfied or not *cannot be raised*. And therefore, if the picture is to be a picture at all, this presupposes that condition (a) is fulfilled.

That this is really what Wittgenstein means seems to be clear from the formulation of 2.18: 'What every picture, of whatever form, must have in common with reality to be capable of representing it at all—rightly or wrongly—is the logical form, that is, the form of reality.' We may therefore state as Wittgenstein's view:

(VI.6)   *Only if the key of interpretation is adequate can the question of whether an interpreted field is a true or false picture be raised.*
*Therefore every picture of reality—be it true or false—must have the internal structure of its elements in common with reality.*

To understand the import of this view we must remind ourselves of the fact that it is essential to an isomorphic representation for corresponding elements to be of the same category. Only if this is so can the picture *show* the external structure of the prototype— or even show an external structure which differs from it. For $F$ and $G$ to have the same external structure means that an elementary state of affairs exists or does not exist in $G$ according as the corresponding elementary state exists or does not exist in $F$. But *if the corresponding elements are not of the same category there are no corresponding elementary states of affairs.* And then certainly the question whether $F$ and $G$ have the same external structure or not cannot be raised.

If, as before, we assume that the key of interpretation is a one-one correspondence, the following statement holds true:

(VI.6′)   *Only if corresponding elements are of the same category can the question of whether an 'interpreted' field is a true or false picture be raised. Therefore every picture of reality—be it true or false—must have the categorial structure of the elements in common with reality.*

Thus the idea that every picture is a 'logical picture' implies that we are to accept proposition (VI.6) instead of the weaker proposition (VI.6′). But in fact (VI.6) is not valid, as the possibility of forming interpretable inadequate pictures shows. If in particular the logical freedom of the elements in the picture is greater than that of the elements in the prototype *every* possible state of affairs is presentable by an interpretable picture, and the fact that there are uninterpretable pictures as well does not prevent the interpretable ones from being capable of being either true or false.

Now the categorial structure determines the internal structure in a homogeneous yes-and-no space. Therefore (VI.6) says the same thing as (VI.6′) if we take for granted that all logical spaces which are involved are yes-and-no spaces—and this seems in fact to be the way in which Wittgenstein tends to think of logical pictures. But this circumstance does not make the distinction between (VI.6) and (VI.6′) less important to an analysis of the Tractatus. To be sure, *if* we assume all logical spaces to be homogeneous yes-and-no spaces, i.e. *if* we assume that there are no logical connections between the elements, and so on, then we have already presupposed that there cannot be other differences in internal structure between a picture and its prototype than differences in categorial structure, and then every isomorphic representation must be adequate. But why *should* we assume that all concerned logical spaces are homogeneous yes-and-no spaces? One possible reason is this. It is plausible to think that we can form a yes-and-no-space *picture* of any articulate field. Suppose now that one believes that every picture must be adequate. Then one might infer from such a possibility that the internal structure of the prototype must also correspond to a yes-and-no space. And from this again one could be led to believe that all picturing is ultimately founded on an analysability both of the picture and the reality it depicts in terms of a common logical form which corresponds to a yes-and-no space. And though I do not think that Wittgenstein thought—or at any rate *always* thought—in this way, I think it is as likely that he arrived at the conclusion that the logical space of reality must be a yes-and-no space *from* the assumption that all pictures must needs be adequate as the other way round. We will return to these considerations in Chapter X, section 5.

For the moment, however, we will disregard the difficulties arising from the idea that 'every picture is also a logical picture' and content ourselves with accepting this as the view taken in the Tractatus.

## 9. NATURALISTIC PICTURES

So far the 'internal similarity' constituting the form of representation has always been only *structural*. When we investigate the 'form of representation' characteristic of a spatial picture or a picture in colour we have to consider also similarities in *content* between the elements of the picture and the prototype. A picture in colour, for instance, is characterized by the circumstance that some of the corresponding elements in the picture and the prototype, viz. the colours, are *identical* or at least *similar in content*. Such a picture I shall call *naturalistic*. A spatial picture must also be naturalistic to some extent: in most spatial pictures some of the spatial relations of the picture stand for *themselves*.

It must be emphasized that naturalistic pictures are only a special kind of adequate pictures. It is often mistakenly believed that all pictures must be more or less 'naturalistic'. But neither an isomorphic nor an adequate picture presupposes anything but *structural* similarities: similarity in internal structure if it is to be a picture at all (of the kind in question), and identity in external structure if it is to be a true picture. And it must also be emphasized that similarity in structure cannot be described as implying that 'the same relations hold in the picture as in the prototype'. The 'relations' appearing as elements in a picture need not be 'similar' in content to the corresponding relations in the prototype. An adequate picture of a spatial prototype need not be spatial—if it is, it is at least partly naturalistic.

## 10. 'CONTENT', 'STRUCTURE' AND 'FORM'

In this context a terminological remark must be inserted. We have used the word 'content' in the preceding discussion to indicate an opposite of 'structure'. The word 'content' is, however, often used to indicate an opposite of 'form', and this is the way in which it is used in the Tractatus (cf. above, p. 79). But, as we have seen, the word 'form' occurs with many different meanings. We must always remember that we have to see from the context whether 'form' is to be understood as what we have called the 'logical form' of an individual element, or the 'internal structure' of a system of elements (e.g. the substance of the world) or the external structure of a state of affairs, or something else. The opposition 'form'–'content' is therefore highly ambiguous in the Tractatus.

The confusion arising from this is increased by the fact that the opposites 'form' and 'content' are also used in philosophical discourse to distinguish a picture-field from what it depicts or a linguistic expression from what it signifies, as for instance, if we are speaking of the 'content' of a picture or the 'descriptive content' of a sentence (the last mentioned expression we have used in Chapter III, and it will be used in the same way later in the book). It is, however, to be noted that the 'content' of a picture or the 'descriptive content' of a sentence has not only a 'content' in the sense of the present discussion but also a 'structure'.[1]

It is also to be noted that the opposition between 'structure' and 'content' does not mean that one could think of a 'content' in isolation from a 'structure' or conversely. Every element must have a 'logical form' which is a structural characteristic (cf. above, pp. 69 ff. and 79 ff.) as well as a content, though for instance, two elements of the same logical form may have different contents; and the same is true of a system of elements in respect of internal structure and content, or a state of affairs in respect of external structure and content.

## II. FICTITIOUS PICTURES

As mentioned above (p. 89), a picture is always treated in the Tractatus as having a *real* prototype, which it represents rightly or wrongly. However, it should be observed that the essential features of isomorphic representation are capable of being applied to 'fictitious' picturing as well,[2] and that fictitious picturing plays an important part in all theory building.

We have stated (p. 98) that we should not think of a false picture as one having an imaginary prototype which it depicts. To know what a picture depicts means to know the external structure of the picture-field and the key of interpretation, but it does not involve any knowledge of the prototype as a field.

The same view may be applied to fictitious pictures. If fictitious

---

[1] This must be taken into consideration in the interpretation of 3.13, where Wittgenstein, so far as I can see, uses the word 'content' both in the meaning of the descriptive content of a sentence and in the meaning of the 'content' of this descriptive content as opposed to its 'form', which here means its structure. Cf. below, Ch. VII, pp. 129 ff.
[2] Cf. *Phil. Inv.*, §§ 522 ff.

pictures are characterized as pictures with a 'fictitious prototype' this must be understood only as a *façon de parler*, the situation being in reality that there is no prototype at all.

This situation arises when we have an incomplete key of interpretation. And here two cases are of particular interest.

Firstly the key of interpretation may be incomplete in so far as the interpretation of the elementary *objects* is left out. That is, we think of the elementary objects of the picture merely as standing for *other* objects than themselves—these objects may be of some specified kind—without fixing any real objects as *the* objects for which they stand. As a matter of fact this is—strictly speaking—just the way in which we have interpreted diagram (i) in Fig. 5. The objects which according to the adopted key of interpretation were 'assigned' to the elementary objects of the diagram were only 'thought of' as real persons, but in reality they were not so. And this means that interpretations were in reality assigned to the predicative elements only; the interpretations of the elementary objects (the letters) were left out. Therefore the 'state of affairs' presented by such a picture is not a 'possible state of affairs' with a real system of elements—but a fictitious state of affairs. In order to obtain a key of interpretation according to which the picture really represents *reality*—rightly or wrongly—we must choose real persons as interpretations of the elementary objects—say the Aga Khan, Bulganin, Churchill, Dulles and Eden (in which case the diagram is certainly a false picture).

A fictitious picture of this kind may be either naturalistic or non-naturalistic. An illustration of a fairy tale may be considered a more or less naturalistic fictitious picture.

Secondly, the key of interpretation may also leave out the interpretations of the predicative elements. The interpretation of Fig. 4 in Chapter V (p. 70) may be considered to be of this kind. The 'key' of this interpretation was wholly fictitious: the letters were *thought* of as standing for some atomic objects, the circle-quality was *thought* of as standing for some atomic quality and the arrow-relation was *thought* of as standing for some atomic binary relation. Pictures of this kind might be said to present 'a pure structure', and this is the nearest one can come to the idea of a structure 'without' a content. When apprehending a diagram as an unspecified picture we 'abstract' from the particular *content* of the elements in the diagram and pay attention to their (relevant) structure only. An 'abstract system' in mathematics, for instance a finite series of natural numbers, could according to this view be interpreted as an alleged definite 'prototype' of a picture that in reality is given no definite interpretation at all. In certain respects, I think, this gives a better idea of the nature of natural numbers than does, for instance, their definition as classes of equivalent classes.

## 12. KEYS AND CLUES

From 'naturalistic' and 'fictitious' pictures it might seem easy to proceed to those kinds of pictures most common in ordinary life, as for instance photographs, landscape paintings or advertisement drawings. But there are some additional difficulties concerning the incorporation of such pictures into the range of modified isomorphic representation. On the one hand pictures of this kind seem to be pictures in the sense analysed in the preceding sections. We seem to have some more or less 'naturalistic' key of interpretation according to which such pictures are understood to present real, possible, or fictitious states of affairs. On the other hand, however, it is not easy to define this key. What, for instance, is the 'key' according to which the three-dimensional spatial relations between objects are 'read' from the relations perceived in a two-dimensional picture? Is it perhaps defined by means of the rules of perspective? But the rules of perspective do not uniquely determine the spatial relations to which the relations of the picture correspond; which can be seen simply from the fact that there is nothing in the rules of perspective to tell us that the 'prototype' of a picture in perspective is not itself two-dimensional.

I think the solution of this problem is to be sought along the following lines. We have stated above that a picture presents what it presents independently of its truth or falsehood. And this is certainly true if we adopt the definition of a picture given in (VI.1) and think of it as a field analysed in a definite way and interpreted according to a fixed key of interpretation. If, however, we take a 'picture' as meaning a field that can be analysed in different ways and given different interpretations the statement in question cannot be categorically maintained. And *prima facie*, I think, pictures of ordinary life are not pictures with fixed keys but fields to which different interpretations can be given. Certainly there are *some* rules given in advance, in accordance with which they are interpreted, as for instance rules of perspective or the rule that a picture in colour should be naturalistic. Such rules, however, do not generally function as a fixed *key* of interpretation but only as a *clue* to a possible interpretation. The spatial relations between the three-dimensional objects which different patches in the picture stand for are *guessed* at according to different conscious or unconscious devices. And it should be observed that our endeavour to find a 'reasonable' interpretation plays an important part in this activity. This endeavour affects both the analysis of the picture field and the choice of the key of interpretation. *A priori* many different articulations of the picture-field are possible' we choose, however, a structure that can be interpreted as a reasonable state of affairs—in certain cases the discovery of an interpretable articulation requires a considerable amount of effort. Thus the interpretation is perhaps not wholly independent of at least the believed 'truth' or 'falsehood' of the picture.

Wittgenstein does not seem to pay much attention to facts of this kind in the Tractatus. And I think some of the weak points in his treatment of the concept of 'substance' criticized above, and also some weak points in his treatment of language (to be considered later), are partly due to this omission.

13. PICTURE AND THOUGHT

As pointed out at the beginning of this chapter the circumstance that we form pictures of facts is of fundamental importance in Wittgenstein's philosophical system. That it is so is emphasized by main thesis 3 :

3  Das logische Bild der Tatsachen ist der Gedanke.

Thinking, then, is the formation of adequate—true or false—pictures of reality.

I suspect that Professor Ryle would oppose this view. Using arguments of the same type as his[1] we might object as follows: The explanation of thinking as 'picturing' implies the belief that, for instance, a thought of red flowers or green leaves is the formation of pictures in colour inside us, visible only by means of an 'inner' eye. And this idea is connected with the utterly false psychology in terms of a mind as a 'ghost in the machine'.

[1] See *The Concept of Mind*, Ch. VIII.

An objection of this kind, however, would imply a mis-understanding of Wittgenstein's view. Pictures of facts concerning red flowers or green leaves need not have the colours 'red' and 'green' as elements—as has been repeatedly stated above, there must only be a structural similarity between a picture and its prototype. We need only take this fact into consideration to give an account of 'thinking' as a sort of depicting which proceeds as easily on a completely physiological as on any other basis for psychology. From a physiological standpoint we might venture a description of the following kind: Not only thinking, but also perceiving, consists of the formation of an isomorphic 'neural' picture of reality, the elements of which are some entities belonging to the neural system as an articulate field. To perceive a field $G$ is then to 'have', as a neural response, a neural picture $F$ of $G$. Of $F$ we certainly cannot be aware, since being aware of $G$ consists in 'having' $F$. Now we can also 'imagine' a field $G$ without actually perceiving it, i.e. we can imagine $G$ as perceived. Such an imagination might consist in an autonomous generation of a neural state $F'$ which is in some respect similar to $F$ and which also forms an isomorphic picture of $G$. We certainly cannot be aware of $F'$, either, but are aware of the interpretation of it, which is described in terms of the state of affairs $G$ which, if perceived, would produce $F$ as a neural response. To 'imagine' $G$, then, is to form a 'mental picture' of it in this sense, we might call it a 'direct mental picture', of $G$. We can, however, also form an indirect mental picture of $G$ which consists in a 'direct mental picture' of a *picture*, say a diagrammatic picture, of $G$. A direct mental picture of $G$ we might also—in a metaphorical sense—call a 'naturalistic picture' of $G$, since the predicative elements of the picture in the form in which we become aware of it are the same as occur in a direct perception of $G$, whereas an indirect picture of $G$ may possibly be 'unnaturalistic'.

With the above cautions against misunderstandings we shall talk of 'naturalistic' and 'unnaturalistic' mental pictures. 'Thinking', then, according to thesis 3, consists of the formation of such mental pictures of reality—or perhaps also of the formation of pictures in a more 'public' material.[1]

A thorough analysis might expose many difficulties here. In the

---

[1] A similar idea was formulated in Hertz's *Mechanics*; see for instance § 428 (Dynamical Models: Observation 2; cf. the Tractatus, 4.04).

present investigation, however, we shall accept it as a description of something that might be considered true: all 'thinking' that is relevant to our inquiry is assumed to show the essential features of isomorphic representation.

The most important views connected with the conception of 'thought' as a picture are stated in sentences 2.203, 3.001, 3.02, and 3.03:

2.203   Das Bild enthält die Möglichkeit der Sachlage, die es darstellt.

3.001   "Ein Sachverhalt ist denkbar" heisst: Wir können uns ein Bild von ihm machen.

3.02   Der Gedanke enthält die Möglichkeit der Sachlage die er denkt. Was denkbar ist, ist auch möglich.

3.03   Wir können nichts Unlogisches denken, weil wir sonst unlogisch denken müssten.

These statements are related to the following question: *What is meant by an unreal state of affairs being 'possible'?* In reality things stand as they stand. We cannot combine the elements of reality into a *possible* state of affairs without making it *real*. In what sense, then, can we speak of a possible unreal state of affairs?

We have already touched on this problem in sections 6 and 8 of this chapter. We pointed out there that 'the mode of existence' of a merely possible state of affairs is that we can form a picture—or to be more exact—an adequate picture that presents it. We will develop this idea more fully here.

Consider the following example. In the diagram of Fig. 7 the letters are assumed to stand for two persons—say Alan and Brian—and the arrow relation for love. According to the diagram, then, Alan and Brian love one another but neither loves himself. This we shall assume to be the real state of affairs (at a certain time *t*); it forms an articulate field *G*, of which the diagram is a *true* picture. The elements of the prototype being combined as they are (at time *t*) they cannot be combined in any other way (at this point of time).

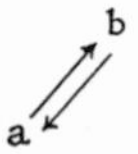

FIG. 7.

Consider now the picture field—it may be called *D*. As such the field *D* is also a piece of reality, a fact, and the elements of this field being combined as they are, they cannot be combined in any other way either. But when we consider the diagram as a *picture* there appears a sort of possibility of rearranging them as for instance in Fig. 8. We shall call this field $D'$.

The elements appearing in this diagram are, to be sure, *not* the same as the elements of $D$—because the letters of Fig. 8 are not the *same* objects as the corresponding letters of Fig. 7. But this does not prevent us from giving the elements of $D'$ the *same* interpretations as the corresponding elements of $D$. Interpreted in that way, $D'$ represents the same piece of reality as $D$, but depicts another state of affairs which is not the real state of affairs but only a possible one.

FIG. 8.

We are therefore capable of really *constructing* different fields which have (a) the predicative elements (b) the internal structure in common and which accordingly—provided that this internal structure is also that of the prototype field—can all be interpreted as true or false adequate pictures of the prototype. In this sense we are capable of *combining* the elements of the picture field in *any* way consistent with their internal structure. And since the key of interpretation is adequate every *actually* 'possible' combination of the picture elements *manifests* and forms a *criterion* of the *potential* 'possibility' of the corresponding combination of the elements of the prototype: 'the picture contains the possibility of the state of affairs that it presents', i.e. it defines it.

In the case under consideration we can form the following structurally different pictures:

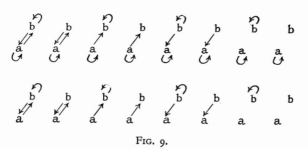

FIG. 9.

And these realized 'possibilities' of combining the picture elements define[1] the potential 'possibilities' of the relation of love in connection with Alan and Brian.[2]

---

[1] Cf. the last paragraph in 3.42.
[2] In regard to the last diagram of Fig. 9 it should be observed that the interpretation

What has been stated here about pictures in the form of printed diagrams also applies, according to the Tractatus, to mental pictures. To think is to form mental pictures; therefore ' "an elementary state of affairs is thinkable" means: we can form a (mental) picture of it' (3.001); therefore 'the thought contains the possibility of the state of affairs which it thinks', and 'what is thinkable is also possible' (3.02). It follows that what is not possible is not thinkable (3.03)— a picture depicting an impossible state of affairs adequately is *a contradictio in adiecto*.

Speaking of substance Wittgenstein states in 2.0212: 'It would then' (if the world had no substance) 'be impossible to form a picture of the world (true or false).' After the analysis of the concept of a picture we are better equipped to understand the import of this statement. To think is to form pictures. All understanding of the world is tied up with picturing. For it to be possible to form a picture of the world, however, the world must be analysed into elements. These elements constitute—according to Wittgenstein's view—the substance of the world.

---

presupposes an analysis of the picture-field in terms of three elements: the two letters and the arrow-relation. Thus it presents the state of affairs that Alan and Brian love neither each other nor themselves. In itself it could certainly be thought of as analysed in terms of an arbitrary number of qualities which are possessed by neither of the letters, or relations which do not hold beween them. This instance emphasizes the fact that an articulate field is determined only in respect of a given system of elements.

# VII

# THE SENTENCE AS A PICTURE

Wittgenstein begins his treatment of the relation between language and reality in statement 3.1:

3.1 Im Satz drückt sich der Gedanke sinnlich wahrnehmbar aus.

'In the sentence thought is expressed perceptible to the senses.' This means two things: first, what may be called thoughts can always be expressed in sentences, or more precisely—if we take number 4 into consideration—in *meaningful* sentences. Secondly, meaningful sentences conversely *are* thoughts, that is, thoughts expressed in a communicable way.

On the other hand, thought is characterized in 3 as a 'logical picture of facts' in the sense we have tried to analyse in the preceding chapter. It follows that *a meaningful sentence is a logical picture of facts.*

This conclusion might seem to involve a contradiction, because 'at first sight a sentence—say as it stands printed on paper—does not seem to be a picture of the reality of which it treats' (4.011). But actually there is no contradiction. A sentence *is* a picture of reality. This idea is expressly stated in 4.01 and developed in the subsequent statements. 4.01 runs:

4.01 Der Satz ist ein Bild der Wirklichkeit.
Der Satz ist ein Modell der Wirklichkeit, so wie wir sie uns denken.

That the word *Bild* in the first paragraph should be taken as 'picture' in the sense of 2.1 etc. is confirmed by the second paragraph, which may be compared to 2.12. It says that a sentence is a model of reality 'as we imagine it', that is, as we 'depict it in thought' (cf. Ch. VI, § 13). A meaningful sentence 'depicts' or 'presents' a possible state of affairs, because there is a representational relation between language and world of the same kind as between a gramophone record, a musical thought, a score, and the waves of sound. 'To all of them the logical structure is common' (4.014, cf. 4.0141–015).[1]

In the preceding chapter we have compared Wittgenstein's concept of a 'true logical picture' with the concept of an 'isomorphic picture'. We may infer that there is, according to Wittgenstein's view, at least an *analogy* between the relation between an 'isomorphic picture' and its prototype and the relation between a sentence and the reality with which it deals.

How close this analogy is will be investigated in the following discussion.

Before we go on to this, however, we must try to get an idea of the *problem* which the picture theory of sentence meaning is intended to solve.

## I. THE 'NAME THEORY' OF LINGUISTIC MEANING

As starting point for our analysis I take 3.144:

3.144   Sachlagen kann man beschreiben, nicht b e n e n n e n. (Namen gleichen Punkten, Sätze Pfeilen, sie haben Sinn.)

The simile between a sentence and an arrow used in the parenthesis we may leave out of consideration so far (cf. below, Ch. IX, § 7). There are two things to which we should direct our attention here: (1) Wittgenstein distinguishes between *naming* and *describing*, in that states of affairs can be described but not named. (2) This makes a difference between how *names* and *sentences* symbolize: only the latter have 'sense' (cf. 3.3).

In the *Philosophical Investigations* Wittgenstein starts his discussion with a quotation from Augustine to which he adds the following remark (§ 1):

---

[1] The representational relation in question is characterized in 4.014 as an 'internal' one. I think the word 'internal' is used here in a meaning that differs from that of 2.01231. Here it indicates only that the 'representational relation' is not an ordinary relation between *objects* but a relation of some different logical type. Cf. the third paragraph of 4.122.

These words, it seems to me, give us a particular picture of the essence of human language. It is this: the individual words in a language name objects—sentences are combinations of such names.——In this picture of language we find the roots of the following idea: Every word has a meaning. This meaning is correlated with the word. It is the object for which the word stands.

This remark can be considered polemical against the Tractatus—because in the Tractatus elementary sentences are considered 'combinations of names'.[1] But if one interprets it so, one must remember that there is at least a strong tendency toward a conception of language much more radically of this kind than that of the Tractatus. This is the idea that *all* words—not only words which occur in elementary sentences—are names, and that this is true also of all other significant expressions, including sentences: the essential function of language is one of naming. I shall call this idea the *Name Theory of Linguistic Meaning.*[2]

To testify that there is a strong tendency in the human mind toward such a conception of meaning one need not go back to Augustine. There are many instances of this tendency in much more recent philosophy and linguistics. But what is of interest in our present discussion is only the fact that the extreme 'realism' to which Russell seems to have adhered in the *Principles of Mathematics* appears to be founded on the idea that all kinds of linguistic expression are names of entities to which 'reality' of some kind must henceforth be ascribed,[3] and further that Frege regarded sentences as a kind of names.

Now Russell in 1905 attacked this idea as far as 'denoting phrases' are concerned (cf. above p. 64). According to Wittgenstein's view in the Tractatus we have to notice that it is wrong in the following ways:

[1] Cf. 2.01, 4.22 and 4.221. The word 'combination' here corresponds to the German word *Verbindung*, which I have translated as 'connection' when it appears in the Tractatus. Here, however, I think the translation 'combination' (in the English version of the *Philosophical Investigations*) is more appropriate.

[2] According to Bühler (*Sprachtheorie*, p. 28) an analysis of language as a means of communication must take into consideration, besides the *linguistic expression*, three further factors in the communication situation: (1) the *speaker* (writer), (2) the *listener* (reader), (3) the message conveyed. The linguistic expression is in relation to the speaker a *symptom*, in relation to the listener a *signal*, and in relation to the message conveyed a *symbol*. This tripartition implies a tripartition of linguistic meaning into three components which may be called symptom meaning, signal meaning, and symbol meaning. When we here talk of linguistic meaning it is, of course, only the symbol meaning, in this sense, that we are thinking of.

[3] *Principles of Mathematics*, § 47; and especially § 427, quoted by Urmson in *Philosophical Analysis*, p. 2.

(1) Symbols which refer to complexes are not names.
(2) Logical connectives are not names.
(3) Sentences are not names.

As we shall see, statement (1) leads to logical atomism. Statement (2) is connected with the theory of truth-functions and will be treated in the next chapter. Statement (3) is connected with the picture theory of sentence meaning. We may regard 3.144 as a more explicit formulation of it:

(VII.1)   *A sentence does not name a state of affairs but describes it. A sentence has not a denominatum but a sense.*

It should be emphasized that the difference between 'naming' and 'describing' introduced here does not correspond to Russell's distinction between things 'known by acquaintance' and things 'known by description' in *Problems of Philosophy* (Ch. V). Russell does not make any difference in *category* between what can be known by acquaintance and what can be known by description. But what can be named according to Wittgenstein is always a 'thing' in his sense, that is, an individual object or a predicate, whereas what is described always belongs to the *category of facts*. This distinction is essential to his theory.

2. THE CONCEPT OF A 'NAME'

As we have stated earlier, names are, according to the Tractatus, the linguistic counterparts of 'substance'. A name is always the name of an *atomic* thing, and an elementary sentence consists of names as an atomic state of affairs consists of atomic things.

However, this idea is a consequence of many different lines of thought, which should be kept apart.

There are four different aspects of the concept of a 'name' to be considered in this section. We arrive at the first by an examination of 3.203. It reads:

3.203   Der Name bedeutet den Gegenstand. Der Gegenstand ist seine Bedeutung. ("A" is dasselbe Zeichen wie "A").

The parenthesis we may leave out from consideration so far (see below, p. 147). The English version of the Tractatus translates the two first sentences thus: 'The name means the object. The object is its meaning.' The 'object' (*Gegenstand*) spoken of here is certainly the *denominatum* of the name. Hence 3.203 says that a name *means* its denominatum and that the denominatum *is its meaning*.

To this interpretation one might object that it is perhaps not correct to translate the German *bedeuten* as 'mean'. Frege made in a famous paper a distinction between *Bedeutung* and *Sinn* of a word or an expression. Mr. Black has rendered this differentiation in English as a distinction between 'reference' and 'sense'.[1] On the other hand the Tractatus, as we have seen, also distinguishes between *Bedeutung* and *Sinn*, so one could think that the correct translation of *bedeuten* is 'refer to' rather than 'mean'.

But I think this objection is unjustified. Wittgenstein's distinction between *Bedeutung* and *Sinn* does not at all correspond to Frege's. In a great many places Wittgenstein uses the word *bedeuten* as an equivalent of 'mean' (that is to say, in the same loose way as the word 'mean' is used). This, I think, is also the common German usage: the expression 'refers to' corresponds in ordinary usage to *bezieht sich auf* rather than *bedeutet*. But above all the point of 3.203 is lost if we do not translate *bedeuten* as 'mean'. What seems to be the main import of 3.203 is to stress a *difference* between names and other symbols. There are many different kinds of symbols and many different ways in which symbols can have meaning (cf. 3.261 and 3.321 ff.). Of names, however (and only of names), it is true that they *mean* things and that those things are their meanings.

As a matter of fact I think we may regard 3.203 as a kind of definition of the concept of a name. And to understand the import of this definition we must take the following circumstance into consideration. We have noticed earlier that the word *Gegenstand* in Wittgenstein's terminology means 'atomic thing'. And it seems obvious that it should be taken so here, too. The 'names' of which Wittgenstein speaks in 3.203 are the 'simple signs' (3.202) which occur in 'completely analysed sentences' (3.201). But *prima facie* I think we do well if we do not assume that a *Gegenstand* as spoken of in 3.203 must have any special formal properties. *Prima facie* we can take *Gegenstand* simply as the *Gegenstand des Benennens*, as 'the object of naming', that which the name names. If we do so we can paraphrase 3.203 as follows:

---

[1] Frege: *Translations*, p. 56.

(VII.2)   *A name is a symbol in language the function of which is to name an entity, called its denominatum. This is its meaning.*

To this definition of a name the later Wittgenstein would object that it implies a confusion between the bearer of a name and the meaning of it (*Ph. Inv.*, § 40). This is certainly so, and we shall discuss the import of the confusion later (pp. 138 ff.). At this stage, however, I think we may disregard the objection as merely termi-nological. In *some* sense we can say that 'to understand a name' is to know what it is a name of. And in this sense we can say that it 'means' its denominatum. We shall therefore as a complement to (VII.2) state:

(VII.3)   *To understand a name is to know what it names.*

This was the first aspect of the concept of a name. And so far as this is concerned we need not assume that the entity named could not be a fact or a state of affairs as well as an individual object or a predicate—this is something which proves to be so only on a closer analysis of the function of 'naming'. In the rest of this section, however, we shall take for granted that all names are names of objects and predicates. Our second aspect appears from 3.26:

3.26   Der Name ist durch keine Definition weiter zu zergliedern: er ist ein Urzeichen.

A name is a 'primitive sign' that cannot be analysed by definition. To make clear the connection between this characteristic of a name and its characterization by (VII.2) and (VII.3) we must take into consideration two ideas which Wittgenstein seems to adopt:

(a) that there is an absolute difference between *defined* symbols and *primitive* symbols,
(b) that defined symbols always signify *indirectly* whereas primitive symbols signify *directly*.

Both ideas are confused. The first of them seems to be implied by 3.25: 'There is one and only one complete analysis of a sentence', and the second sentence in 3.261: 'Two signs, one a primitive sign, and one defined by primitive signs cannot signify in the same way'. But only in a logical system—as for instance that of geometry—

is there a definite difference between 'defined' and 'primitive' concepts. And here too, *which* concepts are chosen as primitive and *which* are taken as defined is a matter of convention. In most systems of geometry the concept of a circle is considered defined, whereas the concept of a straight line is considered primitive, but there is nothing to prevent us from taking the concept of a circle as primitive and the concept of a straight line as defined. Hence there cannot be any absolute and intrinsic difference between defined and primitive symbols.[1]

The second idea is expressed in 3.261: 'Every defined sign signifies *via* those signs by which it is defined, and the definitions show the way. . . . Names *cannot* be analysed by definitions (nor any sign which alone and independently has meaning).' This could be expressed thus: Either a sign is a primitive sign, in which case it signifies *directly*, or it is a defined sign, and then it signifies *indirectly*, via the signs in terms of which it is defined. Names have meaning alone and independently and therefore signify directly. Hence they are primitive signs.

But suppose we have, for instance, a name '*a*', and that we introduce a new symbol '*b*' by the definition

$$b = a \quad \text{Def.}$$

From this definition we learn to know which object '*b*' means, and I cannot see any reason why '*b*' *after* this definition has been accepted, could not be considered a name, which has a meaning alone and independently.

This is a trivial example. But also if the definitions are more complicated there is no reason why a defined sign might not signify directly. At least the fact that a sign *can* be defined does not show that it does not signify directly (cf. below, Ch. X, §§ 5 and 6).

Logical atomism is strongly connected with the acceptance of ideas (a) and (b). As we have seen in Chapter V, section 2, Wittgenstein's conception of 'things' as 'logically atomic' is founded on the view that 'defined symbols' signify only *via* the 'primitive signs' in terms of which logical analysis shows them to be definable.

But as we have stated earlier (Ch. V, § 10), Wittgenstein does not consistently adhere to logical atomism. And in fact the problem which the picture theory of sentence meaning is intended to solve is

---

[1] On this argument cf. 5.42, where the fact that a crosswise definition of symbols is possible is regarded as a criterion of these symbols not being primitive.

as such independent both of the idea of an absolute difference between defined and primitive signs and of the idea that defined signs always signify indirectly. What matters is only the following circumstance:

We may distinguish between a sentence (if there are such sentences) that can *only* be understood by means of a *translation* of it into another sentence, and a sentence that *can* be understood as it stands, without being first translated. Of a sentence of the first kind we may say that it is understood indirectly, whereas a sentence of the other kind is understood directly. Now not *all* sentences can be of the former kind, for this would mean an infinite regress. We may therefore state:

> (VII.4)   *There must be sentences which are understood directly, without first being translated into other sentences.*

If a sentence is understood directly it is reasonable to say that its constituent parts also are understood directly. And it is further reasonable to think that names as characterized by (VII.2) and (VII.3) are understood directly. In *this* sense, but only in this, they might be called *primitive* signs. In the following discussion I shall, therefore, follow Wittgenstein in calling names 'primitive signs', but only in this changed sense:

> (VII.5)   *The constituent parts of sentences which are understood directly are also understood directly.*

> (VII.6)   *Names are understood directly and may be called primitive signs in this sense.*

It should once more be emphasized that this does *not* imply that defined signs could not be 'primitive' in this sense. Moreover I think that there is no absolute difference between what is understood directly and what is understood only indirectly. But for our present discussion it is of no importance that there should exist any symbols or sentences at all that can definitely be said to be understood only indirectly.

The third aspect of the concept of a name is Wittgenstein's idea that *complexes* cannot be named. This aspect is closely connected with the second. The reason for the view that complexes cannot be named is the idea that a symbol which refers to a complex can always be defined and therefore signifies indirectly. But, as we have seen, even if a symbol of a complex *can* be defined, it does not follow that it is not understood directly. Therefore there is no reason to think that a complex could not be 'named'. Moreover, there is no absolute difference between complexes and elements. Whether a thing appears as a complex or not is a question of how a field is analysed.

But the picture theory of sentence meaning is also independent of the idea that there is an absolute difference between complexes and 'atomic' things and that symbols of complexes always signify indirectly. This means that the picture theory of sentence meaning is *independent of logical atomism*. In order to show this we shall adopt the following view in our presentation of the picture theory:

(VII.7)    *There is no restriction as to the complexity of things that can occur as denominata of names.*

The fourth aspect of the concept of a name is this. In the Tractatus not only the denominatum of a name is regarded as simple but also the name itself: it is said to be a 'simple sign' in 3.202. On the other hand, however, Wittgenstein says in 3.3411 that 'no sort of composition is essential for a name'. We might perhaps interpret this thus: If a name is not a simple sign it always can be replaced by a simple sign (cf. 3.3441)—because what is essential to a name is only *what* thing it names but not how the name token is constructed.

Consider now a sentence that is understood directly. Such a sentence can either be compound or simple. If it is compound there must be simple sentences of which it is compounded, and since the sentence as a whole is understood directly this must also be true of those simple sentences. In order that any sentence at all should be understood directly there must therefore exist simple sentences that are understood directly.

Simple sentences which are understood directly Wittgenstein calls *elementary* sentences, and they are assumed to consist of names: 'It is obvious that in the analysis of sentences we must come to elementary sentences which consist of names in immediate connection (4.221). Whether a simple sentence which is understood directly must always consist of names may be doubted. For the moment, however, we shall adopt this view—but without the assumption that names must name atomic things.

According to the Tractatus an elementary sentence describes an atomic state of affairs. Since we have dropped the assumption that the denominata of names must be atomic, a simple sentence which is understood directly and consists of names need not describe an atomic state of affairs. But we may nevertheless assume that it describes a state of affairs which is *elementary* in the relative sense indicated in the preceding chapter (p. 90). This is a state of affairs in which a single predicate is attributed to a system of objects.

A simple sentence which is understood directly and consists of names I shall call a *semantical elementary sentence*.

We have stated that no sentence at all can be understood unless there are sentences that are understood directly. On the other hand no sentences can be understood directly unless there are simple sentences that are understood directly. We may therefore sum up the result of our analysis as follows:

(VII.8)    *In order that any sentence should be understood at all there must exist simple sentences which are understood directly. Those sentences are supposed to consist of names and are called 'semantical elementary sentences'.*

In the discussion of the picture theory of sentence meaning we may always replace 'elementary sentences' by 'semantical elementary sentences'.

Elementary sentences may symbolically be written in the form $fx$ or $\Phi(x, y)$ (or $xRy$) etc. (Cf. 4.24 and 3.1432.) When Wittgenstein says that sentences of this form consist of names he obviously means not only that letters like '$x$' or '$y$' are names of individual objects but also that the predicate letters '$f$' or '$\Phi$' or '$R$' are names of predicates. And though I think it is very confusing to call such predicate symbols 'names' I shall for the moment accept his terminology in this respect.

3. THE PROBLEM OF SENTENCE MEANING

What the picture theory of sentence meaning is primarily intended to explain is how (semantical) elementary sentences are understood. How other sentences are understood is explained by this theory only in so far as they are logically dependent on elementary sentences. When we speak of a 'sentence' in this section we should therefore mainly have only semantical elementary sentences in mind. I use the more general term because Wittgenstein does so.

I shall try to summarize the problem involved in understanding a sentence as follows:

(i) If the function of language is one of naming, to understand a sentence is to know what it is a name of. But what *is* a sentence a name of? A fact? But what is then a *false* sentence a name of? This is a much discussed problem.[1] I shall call it the problem of the false sentence.

Perhaps one could say that a false sentence is a name of a (possible) state of affairs. But how do we know *what* state of affairs a sentence names? We can ordinarily learn to know what entity a name names by pointing out the bearer of the name ostensively. But we cannot point out a non-existent state of affairs.

As we have stated in the preceding chapter (pp. 99 and 114 ff.) there is only one method of indicating a non-existent state of affairs. This is to make a picture of it. But how do we know *what* picture we should make of the 'denominatum' of a sentence?

(ii) This problem arises not only for false sentences but for true ones as well. In reality we understand a sentence in the same way whether it be true or false (cf. 4.024). In order that we should understand the different simple signs of which a sentence is composed, their meanings 'must be explained to us' (4.026) but this explanation does not as such explain *how* the *connection* of them called a sentence is to be understood. This we understand by ourselves, 'we understand the sense of the sentence-token, without having had it explained to us' (4.02). If we knew what a sentence refers to by having its reference pointed out we could only use a sentence for referring to facts already *known*, but in fact 'it is essential to a sentence, that it can communicate a *new* sense to us' (4.027) though the meanings of all its elements are 'old' (4.03)—that is, known before.

Consider for instance the sentence

(1)                    The moon is smaller than the earth

or written symbolically

(1′)                         *m S e.*

---

[1] See, for instance, Russell: *Problems of Philosophy*, Ch. XII, and Carnap: *Meaning and Necessity*, pp. 28 ff.

This sentence can be considered a semantical elementary sentence, in which 'the moon' ('*m*') and 'the earth' ('*e*') are names of *known* individual things, and 'is smaller than' ('*S*') is the 'name' of a *known* dyadic relation. But from the fact that the elements to which the names refer are known it does not follow that the meaning of the sentence (1) or (1′) is known. How then do we know this meaning?

(iii) This problem could also be stated in another way: The sentence (1) or (1′) consists of three names. As it stands it therefore looks like an *enumeration* of names. But how can an enumeration of names refer to a *fact*? (Cf. 3.142.) A fact is not an enumeration of things. 'How does the sentential connection come to be?' (4.221).

(iv) And finally: What *is* the use of 'names' in language? Linguistic activity does not consist in *naming* things. Names are used in isolation for communication only in quite primitive instances. A name has its essential function as a part of a sentence. 'Only a sentence has sense (*Sinn*); only in the context of a sentence has a name meaning' (3.3, cf. 3.144 and above pp. 118 ff.).

## 4. THE ANALOGY BETWEEN A SENTENCE AND A PICTURE

The picture theory of sentence meaning is intended to give a solution to these problems.

In order to understand how this comes about we should first notice that there is at least an *analogy* between a sentence—which must here be taken as a semantical elementary sentence—and a *picture* as defined in (VI.1).

The existence of such an analogy is stated in the following propositions (among others):

3.11    Wir benützen das sinnlich wahrnehmbare Zeichen (Laut- oder Schriftzeichen, etc.) des Satzes als Projektion der möglichen Sachlage.
       Die Projektionsmethode ist das Denken des Satz-Sinnes.

3.12    Das Zeichen, durch welches wir den Gedanken ausdrücken, nenne ich das Satzzeichen. Und der Satz ist das Satzzeichen in seiner projektiven Beziehung zur Welt.

3.14    Das Satzzeichen besteht darin, dass sich seine Elemente, die Wörter, in ihm auf bestimmte Art und Weise zu einander verhalten.
       Das Satzzeichen ist eine Tatsache. . . .

3.141    Der Satz ist kein Wörtergemisch. . . .
         Der Satz ist artikuliert.

3.2      Im Satze kann der Gedanke so ausgedrückt sein, dass den
         Gegenständen des Gedankens Elemente des Satzzeichens
         entsprechen.

3.201    Diese Elemente nenne ich "einfache Zeichen". . . .

3.202    Die im Satze angewandten einfachen Zeichen heissen Namen.

3.203    Der Name bedeutet den Gegenstand.   . . .

According to Chapter VI a picture is an interpreted fact, that is an articulate field $F$ the elements of which correspond to the elements of another articulate field $G$. Consider now a semantical elementary sentence, for instance the sentence (1′) of the preceding section. What is written there on the paper ('$m \, S \, e$') we call the *sentence-token* (*Satzzeichen*, cf. 3.12). This we may consider an articulate field (3.141), which is a *fact* (3.14).[1] The sentence itself, however, is not this articulate field in isolation, but the sentence-token regarded as a 'projection' (3.11–12) and this means that the elements of the sentence-token must be *interpreted* in order for it to become a sentence (cf. also 3.13). The elements of the sentence token are the 'words' (3.14). The words, however, are in (1′) the *names* ('$m$', '$S$' and '$e$'), and they have an 'interpretation' because they 'mean' *things* (3.2–203) which are elements of the articulate field described.

We have thus the following analogy between a sentence and a picture:

| | |
|---|---|
| The sentence-token | — the picture-field |
| The names | — the elements of the picture-field |
| That the names mean their denominata. | — the key of interpretation |
| The denominata of the names | — the elements of the prototype. |

On the other hand the problems of sentence meaning stated in the preceding section would be solved if we could assume that a sentence *is* a picture of reality. If the sentence is *itself* a picture, then it *itself* presents the state of affairs it describes. By means of the key of interpretation we can *read* from the sentence-token *what*

---

[1] Since a *Satzzeichen* is a 'fact' it is rather a unique 'token' than a 'type' of tokens. The same fact cannot occur in different places.

it depicts. We can read from itself its descriptive content. If this is called its sense, then the sentence itself '*shows* its sense'. It '*shows* how the things stand, *if* it is true' (4.022). It does so independently of whether it really is true or false (cf. 4.024). And so our first problem is solved. It appears to be only an illustration of features of isomorphic representation already familiar to us. (Cf. above, thesis (VI.2), p. 99, and the arguments leading to it.)

The same is true of the other problems. If a sentence is a picture we can communicate a new sense by means of elements the meanings of which are known, because the meanings of the elements determine only the *key* of isomorphism, whereas the sense is determined by how the elements are *arranged* in the picture field, i.e. the sentence-token (cf. 3.21). If a sentence is a picture it is not an enumeration of names but is in itself a *fact*, the structure of which shows the structure of the field described. And finally the function of names in language is clear; as elements of a picture they *deputize* in the sentence for the elements which they mean (3.22, cf. 2.131 and above p. 97).

It seems then that there is more than an analogy between a sentence and a picture. And indeed Wittgenstein, as we have seen, not only maintains that there is an analogy between a sentence and a picture but also claims that a sentence *is* a picture. But if this is so, we must be able to replace our 'analogy' by an exact definition.

5. THE FALSE AND THE TRUE KEY OF INTERPRETATION

And here we meet a difficulty. Consider once again the sentence (1) or (1'). According to the analogy between a sentence and a picture as it was given above the relation between names and their denominata corresponds to the key of interpretation. But the names, as we have conceived of them, are in (1') the letters '*m*', '*S*', and '*e*'. This means that the key of interpretation of (1'), considered as a picture, would read:

$$(K_1) \quad \begin{array}{l} \text{Name '}m\text{'} \;-\; \text{the moon} \\ \text{Name '}e\text{'} \;-\; \text{the earth} \\ \text{Name '}S\text{'} \;-\; \text{the smaller-than relation.} \end{array}$$

But now a 'key' like $(K_1)$ cannot function as a key of an isomorphic representation. For it does not fulfil an important requirement which such a key should always satisfy, namely that *corresponding* elements should always belong to the *same category*. The name '*S*' is an *object* whereas the corresponding element of the prototype is a *dyadic relation*.

In reality the elements '*m*', '*S*' and '*e*' *cannot* in themselves form a fact, because a fact cannot have as components only individual objects but must contain also a 'complementary' *predicative* component. (Cf. above, thesis (II.3), p. 28.) If we conceive of the sign '*m S e*' as a complex *object*, we could say that it consists of the objects '*m*', '*S*', and '*e*', but if we conceive of it as a fact, this fact must be *that* these signs are arranged in a certain way, i.e. that a certain triadic relation holds between them. This relation could, for instance, be described thus: 'the relation that holds between three objects, when the first is immediately to the left of the second and the second is immediately to the left of the third'. I shall call it the *triadic concatenation relation*. But if the sentence-token is analysed in such a way that the three names and the triadic concatenation relation appear as its elements, then it is a fact composed of *four* elements. And then it cannot be isomorphic with the fact that the moon is smaller than the earth, because this fact is analysed into three elements only.[1]

For it to be possible that (1) should be regarded as an isomorphic picture of what it describes, it must therefore be analysed in terms of three elements only, two individual objects and one dyadic relation. And this is indeed possible. But then we cannot take the symbol '*S*' as a *relevant object* (cf. p. 94 f.) of the sentence as a fact, but must regard it only as a *characteristic* of a dyadic relation— like the arrows in Fig. 5 (p. 91). The sentence-token as an un-analysed fact is a field that may be analysed in many ways into an articulate field, and only *one* of these ways is relevant for its interpretation as a picture of its descriptive content (cf. above, pp. 94 and 95, nn. 1 and 2). And this is the analysis of it in respect of the following elements:

Two objects:         the symbols '*m*' and '*e*';
One dyadic relation: the relation which holds between two objects when the first is to the left and the second to the right of the letter '*S*'.

The dyadic relation in question I shall call the '*S*'-relation.

---

[1] On this cf. Wisdom: 'Logical Constructions' (I), section V, and Daitz: 'The Picture Theory', p. 59.

If we now take as the key of interpretation the correspondence:

$(K_2)$
$$
\begin{aligned}
&\text{Name '}m\text{'} &&\text{— the moon}\\
&\text{Name '}e\text{'} &&\text{— the earth}\\
&\text{'}S\text{'-relation} &&\text{— the smaller-than relation,}
\end{aligned}
$$

then we have really an isomorphism between the sentence-token and the fact described by it. And only if we understand by a sentence a sentence-token that is interpreted in *this* way is a sentence really a *picture* of reality in the sense of (VI.1). Only then does it really depict and show what state of affairs it describes.[1]

I shall call $(K_1)$ the 'false' and $(K_2)$ the 'true' key of interpretation.

Did Wittgenstein found his picture theory of sentence meaning on a *false* or a *true* key?

Many of the statements quoted in the preceding section seem to indicate that Wittgenstein assumed a false rather than a true key of interpretation. On the other hand he says in 3.1432: 'We must not say, "The complex sign '$aRb$' says '$a$ stands in relation R to $b$' "; but we must say, "*That* '$a$' stands in a certain relation to '$b$' says that $aRb$" '. And this wording corresponds to a *true* key of interpretation (cf. 4.012), for it implies that the fact which is interpreted is analysed in terms of the elements '$a$' and '$b$' and the '$R$'-relation holding between them.[2]

So we may say that Wittgenstein oscillates between the assumption of a false and of a true key of interpretation. And I think the obscurity at this point is linked with an obscurity at another point to which we have called attention earlier (p. 63); I mean the obscurity which lies in calling predicates 'things' and regarding an atomic state of affairs as a 'connection' of things. *If* we analyse the sentence token (1') as a fact in terms of three objects '$m$', '$S$' and '$e$', and the triadic concatenation relation, and *if* we nevertheless want to say that the sentence depicts a state of affairs, then we must think of this state of affairs as composed of four elements, that is three 'things': the moon, the earth and the smaller-than relation, and one triadic relation 'connecting' them to a fact. And if we at the same

---

[1] I have put forward a picture theory of sentence meaning in this form previously, in 'Linguistic Structure' and the articles mentioned there, p. 157, n.3.

[2] It is a remarkable fact that 3.1432 is the only remnant in the Tractatus of a large group of statements which are repeatedly emphasized in Wittgenstein's earlier notes. Hints to a 'true' key of interpretation are, for instance, found in a fairly explicit form in his 'Notes on Logic', p. 237 and in particular in the Notes dictated to Moore.

time realize that the smaller-than relation is not a 'thing' in the same sense as are the earth and the moon, then it is natural to say that it is a 'thing' of a 'different logical form'.[1] And if we further realize that there is no genuine triadic relation to connect the 'things', then it is natural to talk of this imagined triadic relation only in a metaphorical way and say that the things 'hang in one another, like the links of a chain' (2.03).

But if this is how Wittgenstein thinks I believe it is convenient for the presentation of the remaining part of the Tractatus to *correct* him at this point. I think we can give a clearer account in that way not only of the picture theory of sentence meaning and related views on language but also of some of his central metaphysical views.

## 6. THE SENTENCE-TOKEN AS A FACT

I shall now give a somewhat fuller account of how the problem of sentence meaning is solved by means of a corrected picture theory.

When we talk of a 'sentence', here as before we are thinking of a semantical elementary sentence. According to 3.14 a sentence-token is a fact. In a corrected picture theory we cannot—as Wittgenstein thinks in 3.14—regard the *words* as the elements of this fact. As already stated the sentence-token as a fact is *prima facie* a field that may be analysed in different ways to form an articulate field. And there is *only one* analysis which is relevant to the understanding of the sentence as a picture. I shall call this analysis the *syntactically correct* analysis—that is, syntactically correct according to a 'logical syntax', which is related to but not identical with the syntax of

---

[1] In 2.0141 the (logical) form of a thing was defined as 'the possibility of its occurrence in atomic states of affairs'. According to our analysis above (Ch. V, § 5) this means that the logical form of a 'thing' (in respect of a yes-and-no space) is its category, because, for instance, a binary relation is characterized by the fact that it can be connected with *two* individual objects to an atomic state of affairs. Now there is an analysis of the concept of a 'symbol' in 3.31–3.317 which perhaps could be interpreted in this way: the (logical) form of a *symbol* is the way in which it can be connected with other symbols to form a sentence. Thus the logical form of the symbol '*S*' in (1′) is that it can be connected with two logical subjects to form a sentence. But then the 'logical form' of a symbol would appear as a syntactical quality of a linguistic object (that of being a characteristic of a dyadic relation). And this idea could induce one to believe that a dyadic relation, as for instance the smaller-than relation, is itself an object characterized by some kind of counterpart to a 'syntactical quality'.

However Wittgenstein's statements on this point are indeterminate and could also be interpreted in a way that conforms with a true rather than with a false key of interpretation. Cf. below, p. 136 n. and the discussion in Ch. X, § 4.

ordinary grammar.[1] By means of this analysis the sentence-token becomes an articulate field, the elements of which are as follows:

(a) The relevant *objects* of the field are one or more words or expressions which I shall call the '*logical subjects*' of the sentence-token. In (1′) the logical subjects are '*m*' and '*e*'.

(b) There is one relevant *predicate* of the field. This predicate has as many places as there are logical subjects. It is always derived from a relation between the logical subjects and one or more symbols which appear as 'characteristics' of the predicate. I shall call it the *logical predicate* of the sentence-token. In (1′) the logical predicate is the '*S*'-relation.

It should be noticed that the logical predicate of a sentence-token is a *predicate* in the 'philosophical' sense of the word (that is, a predicate belonging to the category of predicates) which the logical subjects possess. This circumstance determines the external structure of the sentence-token as a fact. In respect of those elements and in this way it is true that 'the sentence-token consists in the fact that its elements . . . are combined in it in a definite way' (3.14). But the elements are not 'the words'.

We shall illustrate this analysis by a few examples. We have taken the sentence (1′) as an instance of a sentence as a picture. But it should be noticed that we need not transform (1) into the form (1′) in order for it to be understood as a picture. The syntactical analysis of (1) gives as its elements:

*Logical subjects:* The expression 'the moon' and 'the earth'.
*Logical predicate:* The relation that holds between two expressions when the first is to the left and the second to the right of the expression 'is smaller than'.

The sentence-token as a fact is the fact that the expressions 'the moon' and 'the earth' are in this relation to one another.

Certainly it does not make any essential difference if we write (1) symbolically in the form

(1″)                              $S(m,e)$

instead of (1′). It is only a bit more difficult to describe the relation between '*m*' and '*e*' which appears here as the logical predicate.

---

[1] It is more in accordance with newer structuralistic approaches to grammar than with older ones.

In the sentence-token

(2)                              The earth is round

or written symbolically

(2')                                  R(*e*)

we have only one logical subject: 'the earth' ('*e*'). The predicate of (2) is 'to be immediately to the left of the expression "is round" '. In (2') it is 'to be surrounded by parentheses and put immediately to the right of letter "R" '.

I sum up:

(VII.9)   *A sentence-token is the fact that a certain linguistic predicate called the 'logical predicate' of the sentence-token, is attributed to certain symbols, called the 'logical subjects' of the sentence-token.*

We have so far considered only sentences the logical subjects of which could be regarded as proper names. But there is nothing to prevent us from applying the same syntactical analysis to sentences the logical subjects of which are what Russell calls 'definite descriptions'. In the sentence token

(3)                              The rose is red

the logical subject of the sentence-token is the expression 'the rose' and the logical predicate 'to be immediately to the left of the expression "is red" '. In

(4)              The boy is smaller than his younger sister

the logical subjects are 'the boy' and 'his younger sister' and the logical predicate is the same as in (1). And though Russell and probably also Wittgenstein would think otherwise, I think this analysis is essential to the way in which we understand those sentences.

## 7. WHAT NAMES ARE

'In the sentence the name deputizes for the thing' (3.22). As we have already stated (p. 130) this indicates an essential characteristic of the function of a *name* in language. A sentence-token becomes a *sentence* by means of an interpretation of its elements which makes the sentence-token as a fact into a picture. And the interpretation of the elements means that the names of which it is composed are given 'denominata'. The names 'deputize' for their denominata because the way in which they are combined in the sentence *shows* how their denominata are combined in the state of affairs described.

But in order that this could be regarded as true in relation to a correct key of interpretation we cannot take any *words* as 'names' of predicates. The only *words* (or expressions) in a sentence which can be said to deputize are the logical *subjects* of the sentence-token, which deputize for individual objects, but what deputizes for a predicate is the logical *predicate* of the sentence-token as defined above. And if we shall take 'names' as 'deputizing' symbols we must therefore state that expressions like 'is smaller than' in (1) or 'round' in (2) are not names.

Now I think it *is* very illuminating to define 'names' as 'deputizing symbols'. I shall do so, but at the same time state that there are two kinds of names:

(a) names of individual objects, which themselves belong to the category of individual objects,
(b) names of predicates, which themselves belong to the category of predicates and must have as many places as their denominata.[1]

According to this definition the *names* appearing in (1′) are '*m*', '*e*' and the '*S*'-relation. The names appearing in a semantical elementary sentence are its 'logical subjects' and its 'logical predicate'.

I introduce this terminology to make clear what could be called the *primary* function of names in linguistic communication. This is to appear as the elements of a sentence which is interpreted as a picture.

Names are elements of pictures. The relation between names and their denominata is purely conventional. The picture theory of sentence meaning does *not* imply that names themselves are pictures

---

[1] A hint that names of predicates are themselves predicates is given by Russell in 'Logical Atomism' (p. 338): 'Thus the proper symbol for "yellow" ... is not the single word "yellow", but the propositional function "*x* is yellow", where the structure of the symbol shows the position which the word "yellow" must have if it is to be significant'. Note that Russell was influenced by Wittgenstein when he wrote this article. Cf. Wittgenstein's Notes dictated to Moore and also Ramsey's review of the Tractatus, p. 275, where he correctly states an instance of a true key of interpretation. However, Ramsey adds confused objections to it.

of what they name.[1]  To be sure, you *could* use a picture (as an *object*) to name an object but at any rate this is inessential to the function of a name in a sentence.  Every picture *presupposes* a key of interpretation and the function of names is to furnish the sentence with such a key, which makes it possible to understand the sentence as a picture.  This is certainly Wittgenstein's view: 'A name stands for one thing, and another for another thing, and they are connected together.  And so the whole, like a *tableau vivant*, depicts an atomic state of affairs' (4.0311).[2]

Names and their denominata must be similar in logical form in that they belong to the same category.  But there need not, and, as a rule cannot, be any similarity in *content* between names and their denominata (cf. Ch. VI, §9).   Sentences cannot be *naturalistic* pictures of states of affairs; they are only *logical* pictures in Wittgenstein's sense (4.03).  Urmson's idea[3] that a language in which sentences depict naturalistically would be considered more 'perfect' than language as it is, does not correspond to Wittgenstein's view.

I sum up:

(VII.10)   *If what we call 'names' are the 'logical subjects' and the*
           *'logical predicate' of a semantical elementary sentence, then*
           *we can say that the essential function of names in language is*
           *to deputize in sentences for elements of reality.*

According to the Name Theory of Linguistic Meaning the essential function of language is one of naming.  From our discussion of the function of names we might conclude—and I believe this comes very near to Wittgenstein's view in the Tractatus—that the function of naming is subordinate to the function of describing, which is really the essential function of language:

---

[1] 'How can words have meaning?  You may answer that a word is, in a way, a picture, and that its meaning is what it pictures; and if words are put together to make a sentence, they can picture a more complex unit, a fact.  Let us call this the Picture Theory of Meaning' (Daitz: 'The Picture Theory of Meaning', p. 53).  This is an incorrect statement at least of Wittgenstein's picture theory of meaning, because the latter is a theory of sentence meaning, not of the meaning of words.  (The formulation of 4.016 is, however, indeed misleading in this respect.)  This and many others of Mrs. Daitz's misinterpretations of the Tractatus have been corrected by I. M. Copi ('Objects').  However, Mr. Copi, too, misinterprets the picture theory of sentence meaning in important respects.

[2] The simile of a *tableau vivant* strongly suggests the acceptance of a false key of interpretation.  Cf. 3.1431.

[3] *Philosophical Analysis*, p. 80.

(VII.11)   *The essential function of language is not one of naming but one of describing.*

The later Wittgenstein would surely oppose this view, too. We shall discuss one objection to it in Chapter IX.

Perhaps a reader may ask: If the word 'round' in (2) or the expression 'smaller than' in (1) are not names, then what do they mean? The answer to this question is that it is a product of an undue acceptance of the Name Theory of Linguistic Meaning. The 'meaning' (in the sense of the Tractatus) of a name is its denominatum and in *this* sense the word 'round' has no meaning in (2), because it has no denominatum. But in *another* sense the word 'round' has certainly 'meaning' and this is the sense in which the later Wittgenstein identifies the 'meaning' of a word with its *use* (*Phil. Inv.* § 43). The word 'round' has, to be sure, *different* uses, but one of them is to be employed (in combination with the word 'is') as a *characteristic* of a linguistic predicate which names roundness.[1] The same is true of most both adjectives and nouns.

Incidentally the mistake of believing that *nouns* always function as names seems to be the part of the Name Theory of Linguistic Meaning that has produced the most serious confusions of all. Nouns certainly function in some contexts like names or very nearly like names. This is when they are used in combination with the definite article as logical subjects in a sentence-token, like the noun 'rose' in (3) or 'boy' in (4). Therefore one might feel especially tempted to take nouns as names even when they occur as characteristics of predicates. Now the knowledge of what is named by a name of an *object* seems to presuppose that this object *exists*, that is, it seems to presuppose the *reality* of the denominatum. If one thinks that a noun is a name when it is used as a predicate symbol one is therefore tempted to think that an understanding of it presupposes that the predicate to which it refers must also be *real* in some sense. But the concept of 'reality' *does not apply at all* to

---

[1] Following Frege's terminology we might call the word 'round' in (2) 'incomplete' or 'unsaturated' as a *symbol*, since it does not name roundness but refers to it only as a 'part' of a linguistic quality naming roundness. But Frege went wrong when he transferred the 'unsaturatedness' of such a symbol to the quality or relation referred to by it, making 'unsaturatedness' a characteristic feature of what he called 'concepts' in contradistinctions to 'objects'. Roundness is, to be sure, 'unsaturated' in a way, since it is not 'independent' (2.0122, cf. above, p. 68); but this is an entirely different kind of 'unsaturatedness', which predicates have in common with objects, because predicates and objects are complementary (cf. p. 27f.).

predicates—at least not in the same sense as when one speaks of 'real' *objects*. Therefore there is a tendency either to hypostasize an 'idea' as the real thing which the noun names or otherwise to believe that one cannot understand a predicate symbol unless in some sense there *exist* objects that *have* this predicate.

But certainly I can know what predicate the word 'centaur' refers to without knowing any centaurs. To know a quality (and to be a centaur is a quality) is to know the *difference* between such objects as *have* the quality and such as do *not* have it. To know the quality 'red', for instance, is to know the difference between objects called 'red' and objects called 'not red'.[1] And I know pretty well *what* the difference is between things called 'centaurs' and things called 'non-centaurs'—this knowledge is a necessary condition for my knowledge that there exist no centaurs. Perhaps Wittgenstein is not quite free from mistaken views of this kind.[2]

According to Russell 'definite descriptions' are not names. This is probably also the view of Wittgenstein in the Tractatus, since sentences which contain 'definite descriptions' are thought to signify indirectly. But if we take names as deputizing symbols there is no reason for saying that definite descriptions cannot be names. If senrence (3), for instance, is used to describe a definite state of affairs, then the object to which the expression 'the rose' refers must be known. And this means that the expression deputizes in the sentence for this object, which may therefore be called its 'denominatum'. The same is true of the logical subjects of sentence (4).

But it is certainly misleading to say that the expression 'the rose' in such a statement 'means' its denominatum. As we have stated above (p. 122) we must distinguish between (a) 'meaning' in the sense of the Tractatus, according to which the meaning of a name is its denominatum, and (b) 'meaning' in the sense in which the later Wittgenstein identifies the meaning of a word or expression with its use. To make the difference clear I think it is suitable to refer to the distinction used by linguists following Saussure between '*language*' as a *system* and '*speech*', in which this system is used to form sentences.[3] The meaning in sense (b) belongs to language as a system, but the 'meaning' in sense (a) is not called 'meaning' but '*thing meant*' and is

---

[1] This view has been expounded in my earlier articles on the picture theory. See, for instance, 'Linguistic Structure', pp. 158 ff.

[2] On this argument cf. *The Blue Book*, p. 31, and *Phil. Inv.*, §§ 57–58.

[3] My argument here is a modification of arguments found in Sir Alan Gardiner's admirable book, *The Theory of Speech and Language*.

determined only in speech. The connection between 'language meaning' and 'thing meant' is given by the fact that language meaning gives a *clue* to the listener (or reader) for *finding out* the thing *meant* by the speaker (or writer).

We can say, then, that the *language meaning* of the expression 'the rose' is that it is *used* to name individual roses. And this is a clue for finding out what object is meant when the expression is *used* as a logical subject in a statement of the form (3).

Names with fixed denominata exist as a rule only in speech. And in any event denominata should not be introduced as 'meanings' into the language as a system. To ask for the language meaning of a word or expression is *not* to ask for an entity which it means. The significance of this observation for an appraisal of the ideas of the Tractatus will be analysed later (see in particular pp. 156 f.).

## 8. THE PROBLEM OF THE FALSE SENTENCE

Consider the two sentences

(1′)                              $m \, S \, e$

and

(5)                              $e \, S \, m.$

The first is true, the second false. According to the Name Theory of Linguistic Meaning the first names a fact. And the problem which we called 'the problem of the false sentence' is what the second names.

Now we have said that the function of 'names' is to deputize for things in sentences. According to this definition of a name we cannot say that a sentence 'names' a fact; we must say instead that it *describes* it. But still we may ask: What then does sentence (5) describe?

To answer this question we must recall the distinction we made in Chapter VI (§ 6) between the concepts 'represent' (*abbilden*) and 'depict' (*vorstellen*). According to Wittgenstein's terminology a picture *represents* the *same* prototype whether it be true or false, but a false picture does not 'depict' the real state of affairs but *another* possible state of affairs. This means that sentence (1′) and (5) as pictures *represent* the same fact, though (1′) represents it truly and (5) falsely. But they *depict* different states of affairs: (1′) depicts a real state of affairs whereas (5) depocts a state of affairs that is *merely possible*.

The answer to our question therefore depends on how we wish to use the word 'describe', and I think Wittgenstein has not made any definite choice here. If we take 'describe' in the sense of 'represent', then (5) 'describes' the fact that the moon is smaller than the earth, and describes it *falsely*, but if we take 'describe' in the sense of 'depict' then it describes a state of affairs which is merely possible.

If we take the latter view, as I think I should prefer here, we must realize, however, that this does not presuppose that the 'merely possible' state of affairs exist in some ideal world which we describe: what a sentence describes in the sense of depicting is *presented (darge-stellt)* by the sentence itself (4.031). The sentence *shows by its* own structure how the elements of its prototype should be combined in order for it to be true. And this (apart from the fact that we can also depict the same state of affairs by other kinds of pictures; cf. p. 114) is the *only* mode of existence of 'merely possible' states of affairs.

## 9. FICTITIOUS SENTENCES

According to Russell and probably also Wittgenstein definite descriptions are *never* names. However we have said in section 7 that it is natural to consider such phrases as names if they are used to refer to an existing object. It remains to investigate how, from such a point of view, one could cope with the problematic sentence

(6)                The present king of France is bald.

According to Russell it is *plainly false* (cf. above, p. 65). From the standpoint of a picture theory of sentence meaning as stated above it would be more natural to analyse sentence (6) in the following way.

The logical subject of the sentence-token is the phrase 'the present king of France'. The language meaning of this phrase is that it can be used to denote a person who is the only king of France. Now there is no such person. This means, that we have no key of interpretation according to which sentence (6) can be considered a picture that *represents* a fact either truly or falsely. It cannot be regarded as a picture of *reality* that could be characterized as true or false.

But this does not prevent us from regarding (6) as a picture in an extended sense. We can regard (6) as an instance of the first kind of what in Chapter VI we called 'fictitious pictures' (§ 11). We take the phrase 'the present king of France' as *fictitiously* deputizing for an object that is thought of as being the present king of France. But since this interpretation does not bring the picture into touch with reality the 'state of affairs' *presented* by the sentence as a picture is neither a real state of affairs nor a 'possible' state of affairs in the sense of the preceding chapter, but can be called a *fictitious* state of affairs. And since sentence (6) is 'fictitious' in this way, it can neither be called 'true' nor 'false'; it does not refer to reality. To my mind this analysis conforms with common sense.

This means that the phrase 'the present king of France' can hardly be called a 'name'. It is not the name of a fictitious object that exists somewhere but rather a symbol the naming function of which is fictitious.

## 10. SUMMARY

We have directed many criticisms against the form in which the picture theory of sentence meaning is presented in the Tractatus. But at one and the same time I hope to have shown that Wittgenstein's conception of a sentence as a picture is a fruitful idea in itself, and that it really gives us a solution to many problems about the functioning of language.

# VIII

# THE DESCRIPTIVE CONTENT
# OF COMPOUND SENTENCES

What Wittgenstein says in the statements surrounding the main theses 5 and 6 is to a great extent well known, or if not, concerns technicalities in the treatment of symbolic logic which fall outside the scope of this book. We shall content ourselves with pointing out a few special features in Wittgenstein's conception of logic, which are either interesting from the viewpoint of a general philosophy of language or important to his philosophical system.

In the preceding chapter we have shown how sentences could be regarded as pictures of facts. However, the picture theory of sentence meaning, as developed there, applies only to what we have called semantical elementary sentences. Now our semantical elementary sentences are in Wittgenstein's theory replaced by what he calls elementary sentences, that is sentences the elements of which are names of atomic things. Thus the picture theory in the sense of the preceding chapter would apply in his theory to elementary sentences only. But in effect Wittgenstein does not restrict the picture theory to elementary sentences. In 4.01 and other places he states that a sentence is a picture of reality without confining himself to sentences of any special kind. (The concept of an elementary sentence is introduced only in 4.21.) Now it is in one way very misleading to call sentences in general 'pictures'; actually, I think the most interesting aspect of the picture theory of sentence meaning is that it allows us to see in what ways sentences differ from pictures. But I will not discuss Wittgenstein's terminology in this respect here. Wittgenstein obviously thinks that any meaningful sentence could in *some* way be regarded as a picture and this is of importance to his metaphysics. We shall discuss the sense in which this could be so.

We remember that Wittgenstein seems to think that there are only three kinds of meaningful sentences: (a) elementary sentences, (b) logical compounds of elementary sentences, and (c) sentences which by means of definitions can be translated into sentences of kind (a) or (b).

A sentence of kind (c) is obviously considered a picture only in the sense that the translation of it is considered a picture. Since elementary sentences are 'depicting sentences' in the direct sense of the preceding chapter we may therefore say that there are two reasons why Wittgenstein thinks that all meaningful sentences can be regarded as pictures: (1) Every sentence can be translated into a logical compound of elementary sentences, and (2) logical compounds of depicting sentences can in some sense be regarded as depicting sentences too.

We shall direct our attention chiefly to the second of these reasons. As we have formulated it, it is as such independent of the idea that the only sentences which depict directly are the elementary sentences in Wittgenstein's sense. We may think of logical compounds of semantical elementary sentences and ask ourselves in what sense (if any) they could be regarded as pictures. This is our problem.

## I. HOW DO LOGICAL CONNECTIVES SIGNIFY?

To begin with, we may state a sense in which logical compounds are *not* pictures. Logical compounds of sentences can be formed by combining sentences with logical connectives such as 'and', 'or', etc. One could therefore be tempted to think that logical compounds of sentences are pictures in the sense that they depict states of affairs which are combinations of simpler states of affairs and some special entities called 'logical constants' much as elementary states of affairs are combinations of 'things'. This would mean that we consider logical connectives, like names, as a kind of 'deputizing symbols'. However, Wittgenstein emphatically disclaims such a view:

4.0312   Die Möglichkeit des Satzes beruht auf dem Prinzip der Vertretung von Gegenständen durch Zeichen.
Mein Grundgedanke ist, dass die "logischen Konstanten" nicht vertreten. Dass sich die L o g i k der Tatsachen nicht vertreten lässt.

Though Wittgenstein thinks that the possibility of sentences depends on the fact that signs deputize for things he states as a 'fundamental thought' that 'logical constants' (by which he obviously means 'logical connectives' here) do *not* deputize. In another place (5.4) he says that 'there are not any "logical things" or "logical constants" (in the sense of Frege and Russell)' (cf. 4.441). And this means the same as 4.0312: there are not any entities for which the logical connectives stand.

Referring to what we have called a true key of interpretation we have stated that predicate symbols like 'round' or 'smaller than' are not as such deputizing signs, it is only the predicates of which these symbols are 'characteristics' that are deputizing signs. We may therefore ask whether the logical connectives could be regarded as signifying in the same way as such characteristics. It is, however, obvious that Wittgenstein, even in so far as he accepted a 'true' key of interpretation, would have denied this: 'That ∨, ⊃, etc., are not relations in the sense of right and left, etc., is obvious,' he says in 5.42. And though I believe the reason for this opinion given in the same statement is confused, I think he is substantially right. Logical connectives are neither deputizing symbols themselves, nor characteristics of deputizing predicates. They are not 'names' in any sense of the word.

Incidentally this is true also for the words 'true' or 'false' (cf. the third paragraph in 4.063). In the sentence 'That the moon is smaller than the earth is true', the word 'true' does not refer to any predicate. The clause 'That the moon is smaller than the earth' does not name an object which has the quality of being true. The clause 'That the moon is smaller than the earth' describes a state of affairs and the sentence 'That the moon is smaller than the earth is true' says that this state of affairs exists, and therefore says the same as the sentence 'The moon is smaller than the earth'. The structure of the fact described by these two sentences is the same. Therefore the fact described by the sentence 'That the moon is smaller than the earth is true' cannot contain any element corresponding to the word 'true'.—I think Wittgenstein means that an analogous analysis shows that there cannot be any elements in facts corresponding to logical connectives.

But in that case, how do logical connectives signify? What is their 'meaning'? Wittgenstein's answer to this question is that the meaning of logical connectives is given by their truth-tables.

L

'A sentence is a truth-function of elementary sentences' (5). This means among other things that every logical compound is a truth-function of its constituents. This view may be disputed. But here we shall accept it. The descriptive content of a sentence which is a logical compound of semantical elementary sentences is given by the fact that it is a truth-function of these semantical elementary sentences. This circumstance also determines in what sense such a sentence can be regarded as a picture of what it describes.

## 2. COMPLETE DESCRIPTIONS AND PICTURES

Consider once again the diagram in Fig. 7 on page 114. According to the interpretation of it given there '*a*' and '*b*' denote two persons called Alan and Brian and the arrow relation stands for love. We shall now give a linguistic description of the fact presented by that picture. To this purpose we have to introduce two names for Alan and Brian—we may choose the letters '*a*' and '*b*' as in the diagram—and a linguistic relation that stands for the relation of love, say, the relation 'that holds between two objects when one is to the left and the other to the right of the letter *L*'; we shall in accordance with our former

FIG. 7.

terminology call this the '*L*'-relation. By means of these signs we can describe the fact represented by Fig. 7 in the following way:

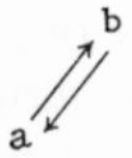

(1)                $\sim(a\,L\,a).\quad a\,L\,b.\quad b\,L\,a.\quad \sim(b\,L\,b).$

In a natural language description (1) may run in this way:

(2)     Alan does not love himself. Alan loves Brian. Brian loves Alan. Brian does not love himself.

But since the problem of how (2) shows its descriptive content is essentially the same as the corresponding problem for (1) (apart from the additional difficulty arising from the use of the pronoun 'himself' instead of 'Alan' or 'Brian' in the first and last sentence, the analysis of which would take us too far from our present subject) I shall confine myself to an analysis of (1).

We shall call (1) a *complete* description of the fact illustrated by Fig. 7 as it describes exactly the same thing as Fig. 7.

Can description (1) be understood as a picture? At least not in the same sense as that in which Fig. 7 is understood as a picture. The essential differences between the diagram and the description are the following: (a) While in the diagram only *one* object (the letter token '*a*') stands for Alan, there are in the description four *different* objects standing for Alan: the four tokens of type '*a*'. (The same is true of the symbol standing for Brian.) (b) While the fact that Alan does *not* love himself is shown in the diagram by the fact that letter '*a*' is *not* in the arrow-relation to itself, the same fact is indicated in the description by the fact that letter '*a*' *is* in the '*L*'-relation to itself combined with the fact that to the sentence-token having this structure is attached a negation mark (cf. 5.5151).

It should be noted that those differences between a description and a picture can both of them be regarded as consequences of the fact that linguistic descriptions are *one-dimensional* structures. One could not transform Fig. 7 into a one-dimensional structure without making changes of the kind indicated by (a) and (b).

The first difference means that the correspondence which is to function as a key of interpretation is not, as in a picture, a *one-one* correspondence. It is essential to an isomorphic representation that the key of interpretation is a one-one correspondence: for each element of the prototype stands one and only one element of the picture. But in the description four different elements (the different '*a*'s) stand for the *same* element of the prototype. The correspondence between the elements of a description and the elements of its prototype is a *many-one* correspondence.[1]

One could restore the one-one correspondence by a device of the following kind. To common sense it seems clear that the *same* object cannot appear in different places at the *same* time. But we could regard common sense as prejudiced in this respect, and say that the different '*a*'s are really the *same object*, appearing in four different places. Perhaps this is what Wittgenstein means when he says: ' "*A*" is the same sign as "*A*" ' (3.203).

But this device is actually artificial. I think it is clearer to regard the different '*a*'s as different objects and admit that the key of interpretation of a description is not a one-one correspondence. This means, however, that we must make a small correction in our

---

[1] This is true only in respect of the elements belonging to the category of *objects*. From the fact that many different '*L*'s appear in the description one should not mistakenly infer that the description contains different elements corresponding to love. The '*L*-relation* is the same, though it holds between different pairs of objects in the different elementary sentences.

statement that semantical elementary sentences always depict the state of affairs they describe in the sense of isomorphical depicting. For an elementary sentence of the form '*a L a*' the key of interpretation is a many-one correspondence.

This difference between a description and a picture is of minor importance. We can easily understand an articulate field as a picture even if we have to apply a many-one key of interpretation. The only thing we have to remember is that the structure of a (true) picture does not in such a case *show* the structure of the prototype as *directly* as an isomorphic picture. The picture is not here *identical* in structure with the prototype. For it to be so the different objects standing for the same object of the prototype must first be 'identified'.

The second difference is of more consequence. In a picture the circumstance that a system of objects has *not* a predicate is shown by the fact that the corresponding system of objects has *not* the corresponding predicate. That Alan does not love himself is shown in the picture by the fact that the object '*a*' is *not* in arrow-relation to itself. This method cannot be used in a linguistic description. In the linguistic description we show that Alan does not love himself by putting the letter '*a*' *in* '*L*'-relation to itself and adding a negation mark. To indicate a negative fact we produce a *false* picture and point out by the negation mark that it is to be understood as false. Wittgenstein says in 4.022: 'the sentence *shows* how things stand, *if* it is true. And it *says*, that they do so stand.' This is true of semantical elementary sentences. Of *negated* semantical elementary sentences we ought rather to say: The sentence *shows* how things stand, *if* it is false. And it says that they do *not* so stand.

Wittgenstein devotes many statements in the Tractatus to the problem of negation.[1] These statements contain different lines of thought, but in the present context we need pay attention only to the observation that the negation sign does not 'deputize' for anything. The affirmed and the negative sentence present as pictures the same state of affairs.[2] If we only take into consideration what sentences '*p*' and '$\sim p$' *depict* they say the same. And this shows 'that the sign "$\sim$" corresponds to nothing in the reality' (4.0621).

Our analysis of the difference between a complete linguistic

---

[1] See in particular 4.061–0641. Cf. also below, Ch. IX, §§ 7–8.
[2] Cf. also below, p. 171, n 2.

description and a picture leads to the following conclusion: A complete description like (1) is *not* a picture in the sense of isomorphic representation. But there are certain rules that can be characterized as *logical rules* of the description according to which the description can be *transformed* into a picture.

In connection with (1), these rules can be formulated as follows:

(i) Replace the different tokens of the types '*a*' and '*b*' appearing as logical *subjects* in (1) by a *single* object, one for each type.

In Fig. 7 all '*a*'s are replaced by the single object '*a*', and all '*b*'s by the single object '*b*'.

(ii) Replace the '*L*'-relation appearing as the only[1] logical *predicate* in (1) by some dyadic relation in this way: (a) If the sentence in which one object is in '*L*'-relation to another object is *affirmative* then the object replacing the first object is put into this relation to the object replacing the second object in the picture. (b) If the sentence in which one object is in '*L*'-relation to another object is *negative* then the object replacing the first object is *not* put into this relation to the object replacing the second object in the picture.

In Fig. 7 the '*L*'-relation is replaced by the arrow-relation. Since sentences '*a L b*' and '*b L a*' are affirmative in (1) '*a*' is put into arrow-relation to '*b*', and '*b*' is put into arrow-relation to '*a*' in Fig. 7. Since sentences '*a L a*' and '*b L b*' are negative in (1) neither '*a*' nor '*b*' is put into arrow-relation to itself in Fig. 7. Thus (1) is transformed into a picture-field which can be interpreted by means of the key of interpretation. And in this sense (1) can be said to depict *indirectly* the state of affairs it describes.

The fact that the negation mark as it appears in (1) can be regarded as an indication of how the description should be transformed into a picture gives, I think, a good illustration for the fact that the negation mark does not deputize for any element of reality. The picture into which (1) is transformed does not contain any negation mark. That a system of objects does *not* possess a predicate is shown by the fact that the system of deputizing objects does *not* possess the deputizing predicate. In a picture there is no need for any symbols indicating negation.

The peculiar way in which a description is constructed could be characterized thus: We first make pictures depicting *all elementary*

---

[1] Certainly there may also occur several different logical predicates in a complete description. Then each of them is to be replaced by a separate predicate in the picture-fields. The predicates in the picture must have as many places as the linguistic predicates they replace.

states of affairs which appear (positively or negatively) in the state of affairs $S$ to be described. Then we add a special device to indicate how these elementary states of affairs should be divided into 'positive' and 'negative' elementary states of affairs in respect to $S$. This enables us to construct a picture which presents $S$.

In (1) the division of the elementary states of affairs into positive and negative states of affairs is indicated by the occurrence of the negation mark. The division could, of course, be indicated also in other ways. One way is to attach a 'truth-value' to every elementary sentence as the following table shows:

(3)

| $a\,L\,a$ | $a\,L\,b$ | $b\,L\,a$ | $b\,L\,b$ |
|:---:|:---:|:---:|:---:|
| F | T | T | F |

There is a semantical difference between the description (1) and the table (3). A description in the form (1) consists of sentences in the indicative. And this means that it, according to its normal use, not only *describes* a possible state of affairs but also *asserts* this state of affairs to be the real one. Table (3), however, we should not normally understand as 'asserting' anything: it indicates a possible state of affairs, but does not assert this state of affairs to be the true one. It only indicates a *truth-possibility*, in Wittgenstein's terminology. (See 4.3 ff.) We could therefore call it 'purely descriptive'. The 'asserting function' of sentences in the indicative Wittgenstein does not grasp clearly in the Tractatus. We shall discuss it in the next chapter.

If we take (3) as purely descriptive it should be emphasized that the 'truth-values' in the table are to be understood in a would-be sense only. The truth-values indicate which elementary sentences *would* be true or false *if* the state of affairs described *were* existent. And this means that the use of the truth-values 'T(rue)' and 'F(alse)' is indeed misleading. Since in principle the state of affairs described is only *possible* and thus can be given to us only by means of a picture presenting it (cf. above, Ch. VI, § 13), the 'truth-values' appearing in table (3) are to be understood as prescriptions for the construction of a picture rather than as referring to what is the case. Therefore we should understand (3) as a division of semantical elementary sentences into 'positive' and 'negative' sentences (cf. above, p. 53) rather than a division into 'true' and 'false' sentences.

## 3. THE DESCRIPTIVE CONTENT OF COMPOUND SENTENCES

Consider now a sentence $P$ which is a truth-function of semantical elementary sentences. We will assume that the elementary sentences of which $P$ is a truth-function form a 'complete' system $(E)$ in relation to an articulate field $F$ in the sense that $(E)$ contains one and only one sentence depicting each elementary state of affairs belonging to $F$. Then every 'truth-possibility' of the sentences $(E)$ defines a complete description (true or false) of $F$,[1] which may be transformed into a picture. If the logical space around $F$ is a yes-and-no space the different pictures so obtained present all 'possible states of affairs' which can be formed of the elements of $F$. The system of those pictures may be called $Pt$.

That $P$ is a truth-function of the sentences $(E)$ means that every truth-possibility of these sentences determines a truth-value for $P$. Thus every complete description of $F$ or every picture in $Pt$ also determines a truth-value for $P$.

The truth-possibilities which verify $P$ Wittgenstein calls the *truth-grounds* of $P$ (5.101). Since the truth-grounds are complete descriptions which can be transformed into pictures, to $P$ corresponds a system of *alternative* pictures in $Pt$ presenting the different states of affairs the existence of which would verify $P$. And $P$ says that one of these states of affairs exists.

Thus we can say that the *descriptive content* of a compound sentence $P$ is presented by a system of alternative pictures presenting the states of affairs the existence of which are the truth-grounds of $P$. And in this way $P$ *shows* what is the case *if* $P$ is true. We may sum up the result of our analysis as follows:

(VIII.1)    *The logical rules governing the use of the logical signs indicate how a compound sentence $P$ can be transformed into a system of alternative pictures presenting the different states of affairs the existence of one of which verifies $P$. In this sense $P$ shows what is the case if $P$ is true.*

---

[1] Speaking of a picture we have distinguished between what it *represents* and what it *depicts* (or *presents*): a true and a false picture represent the same piece of reality but they depict different states of affairs. It is difficult to invent a corresponding terminology for complete linguistic descriptions. So I am bound to use the expression 'a description of' ambiguously. In one sense it refers to the piece of reality *represented* by the corresponding picture, in another to the state of affairs *depicted* by it. (Cf. above, p. 141.)

I shall illustrate this statement by an example. Consider the sentence

(4)                           $a \, L \, b \equiv b \, L \, a,$

which says that Alan loves Brian, if and only if, Brian loves Alan. As it stands there the truth-arguments of sentence (4) appears to be only the sentences '$a \, L \, b$' and '$b \, L \, a$'. But as we have pointed out before it can be regarded as a truth-function of all sentences '$a \, L \, a$', '$a \, L \, b$', '$b \, L \, a$', and '$b \, L \, b$' as well (cf. above, pp. 56 f.). If we form the truth tables of (4) in respect to these arguments the truth-grounds of it appear to be the truth-possibilities given in the following table:

| $a \, L \, a$ | $a \, L \, b$ | $b \, L \, a$ | $b \, L \, b$ |
| --- | --- | --- | --- |
| T | T | T | T |
| T | T | T | F |
| T | F | F | T |
| T | F | F | F |
| F | T | T | T |
| F | T | T | F |
| F | F | F | T |
| F | F | F | F |

These truth-possibilities are presented by pictures 1, 2, 7, 8, 9, 10, 15 and 16 of Fig. 9 (p. 115).

The logical signs indicate in combination with the logical rules how a sentence could be transformed into a system of alternative pictures. The pictures themselves do not contain any logical signs. Every picture presents only one state of affairs. In order to present a system of alternative states of affairs one must produce a system of alternative pictures. But what is meant by these pictures being *alternative*, i.e. presenting the alternative truth-grounds for a sentence, cannot be shown in a picture. We may sum up the part played in descriptive sentences by logical signs as follows:

(VIII.2)   *Logical signs indicate how a sentence is to be transformed into a system of alternative pictures but do not appear in the pictures themselves.*

The indication of how descriptive sentences are to be transformed into pictures is thus the essential function of the truth-functional logic. From this point of view one may note that the 'logic' of ordinary language is immensely complicated. Not only are the denominata of names in ordinary speech dependent on the speech context, but the logical rules according to which compound sentences of ordinary language might be transformed into pictures seem also to a great extent to be guessed at according to what appears as plausible. 'Colloquial language is a part of the human organism and is not less complicated than it.—From it, it is humanly impossible to gather immediately the logic of language' (4.002).

## 4. QUANTIFICATION

Obviously Wittgenstein thinks that sentences containing quantifiers should be treated according to his truth-functional scheme. The difficulty here is that we are to deal with truth-functions, the set of arguments of which may be infinite. This means, on the one hand, that the set of alternative pictures corresponding to a sentence may be infinite, and on the other hand, that the pictures themselves may be infinite, too.

To this difficulty Wittgenstein does not seem to pay any attention in the Tractatus. What is peculiar to his treatment of quantification is his interest in another problem, and this concerns the question of *how* the range of the variables is known (cf. 5.521 f.). I believe Wittgenstein's thought to this point could be described as follows:

Consider the sentence 'All men are mortal'. If we understand this sentence as a logical conjunction ranging over all men we take it as equivalent to the sentence: '*a* is mortal and *b* is mortal and . . .', where '*a*', '*b*', etc., are the names of all men. But in fact the latter sentence is *not* equivalent to the former, because in the latter sentence we have only stated of all men that they are mortal, but we have not stated, as in the former sentence, that the set of individuals, the mortality of which is stated, really comprises *all men* (and no others). The concept of 'all' therefore refers to the range of *arguments* (cf. 5.523) of a truth-function and is not explained by the nature of the truth-function alone. In fact the concept of 'all' appears not only in sentences of the form $(x)f(x)$, but is also 'concealed' (5.521) in sentences of the form $(Ex)f(x)$, because sentences of the latter form have also as truth-arguments *all* sentences of a certain kind.

However it is a well known fact of logic that every sentence which contains the terms 'all' or 'some' can be translated into a sentence in which the range of the quantifiers comprises all things in the whole of the 'Universe of Discourse'. This circumstance seems also to be essential to Wittgenstein's solution of his problem. If a variable of quantification ranges over *all things* (of a certain category) in the substance of the world, then the range of this variable is given. If, in other words, a sentence is regarded as a truth-function of *all* elementary sentences, then the range of the truth-arguments is given: 'If the objects are given, then therewith *all* objects are given.' 'If the elementary sentences are given, then therewith *all* elementary sentences are given.' (5.524.)

But, as we said, to the difficulty arising from the fact that the set of truth-arguments may be infinite Wittgenstein does not pay any attention in the Tractatus. We shall here follow him in this and consider what is said in (VIII.1) as valid also in regard to sentences which contain quantifiers. As the Universe of Discourse to which such quantifiers refer we may take the system of elements of an articulate field, and we will not exclude the possibility that this system is infinite.

## 5. IDENTITY

'Expressions of the form "$a = b$" are . . . only expedients in presentation: they assert nothing about the meaning[1] of the signs "$a$" and "$b$" ,' Wittgenstein says in 4.242. From our present point of view he is right at least in so far as the sign of identity is not a characteristic of a relation which *names* a relation of reality (cf. 5.5301). The sign of identity appears to be a 'logical sign' in the sense that it indicates how a sentence is to be *transformed* into a picture (or a system of alternative pictures) but does not appear in the picture itself.

In an isomorphic picture, identity between elements of the prototype is shown by *identity* between the corresponding elements of the picture and does not appear as an element of the picture. An expression of the form '$a = b$' indicates that tokens of types '$a$' and '$b$' are to be replaced by the *same* object, if sentences are transformed into pictures.

This means that equations are not elementary sentences; and since equations likewise cannot, according to Wittgenstein's view, be

---

[1] It should be remembered that by 'meaning' Wittgenstein understands the 'thing meant'.

defined as truth-functions of elementary sentences (5.5302[1]), he thought that the identity sign should be dispensed with altogether in a *Begriffsschrift* (5.53 ff.). But as a matter of fact I think this is due to a tendency to make linguistic expression more uniform than is at least necessary or convenient.[2]

## 6. THE GENERAL FORM OF A SENTENCE

So far we have tried to present the depicting nature of a sentence independently of the idea of logical atomism. Let us now reintroduce this idea. 'There is one and only one complete analysis of a sentence' (3.25). The conception of the relation between a 'perfect' language and the world involved in this statement may be summed up as follows:

There is a uniquely determined system of 'things', i.e. elements of the world, which form its 'substance'. Those elements are either individual objects or predicates with different numbers of places. Every predicate forms together with an appropriate number of individual objects an atomic state of affairs that can exist or not exist independently of the existence and non-existence of other atomic states of affairs. Every division of the atomic states of affairs into existent and non-existent states of affairs corresponds to a 'possible' world; the real world is determined by one such division.

In a 'perfect' language there is a unique name for every element of the world. The names of individual objects we may think of as 'simple symbols'. The names of predicates we may (in accordance with a true key of interpretation) think of as certain 'elementary' linguistic predicates. The fact that an elementary linguistic predicate belongs to an appropriate number of individual names is called an elementary sentence, which depicts and presents an atomic state of affairs. Every division of all elementary sentences into 'positive' and 'negative' sentences describes completely a possible world, and one such division gives a complete description of the real world. Every complete description of a possible world can be transformed into a picture presenting that possible world.

Every meaningful sentence can be translated into a sentence which is a truth-function of elementary sentences—and in this sense every meaningful sentence *is* a truth-function of elementary sentences.

---

[1] Cf. Waismann: 'Identität', and below, p. 219.
[2] As to the *possibility* of dispensing with the identity sign in symbolic logic, see Hintikka: 'Identity'.

Thus to be a truth-function of elementary sentences is the *general form* of a meaningful sentence (see main thesis 6).[1]

Every sentence which is a truth-function of elementary sentences can also be regarded as a truth-function of *all* elementary sentences. Thus the general form of a meaningful sentence implies that every meaningful sentence can be transformed into a system of *alternative* pictures of the world.[2] If one of those pictures is a true picture the sentence is true, otherwise it is false.

Wittgenstein's conception of the general form of a sentence can thus be said to imply that every meaningful sentence is essentially a depicting sentence, and that the elements of the world, to which the elements of the analysed sentence refer, are uniquely determined. Every meaningful sentence can be transformed into a system of alternative pictures the elements of which deputize for the elements of reality, which form the true substance of the world as a fact.

This is then the view that we may read from the main thesis 6 of the Tractatus. And of course we are enabled to say that this *is* the view of the Tractatus. But we must not forget all the reservations to this view which are found in different places in the book and to which we have tried to give attention in the preceding analysis.

The idea that every meaningful sentence can be understood as a truth-function of elementary sentences has been criticized in many ways in recent philosophical discussion. And I think it is wrong whether the elementary sentences are understood to be absolute elementary sentences or to be only semantical elementary sentences. Some arguments against this view will be discussed in the next two chapters.

What is interesting from a semantical point of view is not, however, the idea that *all* sentences are understood as truth-functions of elementary sentences but that *some* sentences are. There are sentences which can be understood as truth-functions of semantical elementary sentences, and such a sentence can be transformed into alternative pictures presenting the different states of affairs the existence of which verifies the sentence. Of such sentences I shall say that they are essentially depicting sentences. But there are other kinds of meaningful sentences as well.

---

[1] The particular way in which Wittgenstein thinks every truth-function of elementary sentences to be constructed need not concern us here. What interests us is only that the general form of a truth-function of elementary sentences is also the general form of a sentence.

[2] If the sentence is a truth-functional contradiction this system is, of course, vacuous.

IX

# DESCRIPTIVE CONTENT AND MOOD

Consider the following sentences:

(i)   You live here now.
(ii)  Live here now!
(iii) Do you live here now?

Sentences (i)–(iii) correspond to one another in this way: what is the case if (i) is true is also the case if (ii) is obeyed or if the correct answer to (iii) is yes. The three sentences have something in *common*, which R. M. Hare[1] calls the 'phrastic' of the sentence in contradistinction to a component distinguishing them, which he calls the 'neustic'. The 'phrastic' indicates the descriptive content of the sentence, i.e. the state of affairs described by them, which is the same in sentences (i)–(iii). What is different is the mood in which this state of affairs is presented: in (i) the mood is indicative, in (ii) imperative, and in (iii) interrogative.

The difference in mood between sentences (i)–(iii) means that they have *different sense*, at least if we understand by 'sense' what is ordinarily understood by it. Thus sentences may have different sense even though their descriptive content is the same. But if we admit this, then we must doubt the view taken in the Tractatus that the essential function of language is *descriptive* (see above, pp. 137 f.). The descriptive content of a sentence gives only a part of its sense.

The view of the Tractatus could be characterized as an *identification of the sense of a sentence with its descriptive content*. This identification seems most reasonable in respect of sentences in the indicative. Therefore there has been a tendency among logical empiricists to consider all sentences as disguised indicatives. This view seems also to be the only possible way of dealing with other moods than the indicative within the framework of the Tractatus. If we identify

---

[1] *The Language of Morals*, pp. 17 ff.

157

the sense of a sentence with its descriptive content, the difference in sense between e.g. (i), (ii) and (iii) must be explained as a *difference* in descriptive content. A 'complete analysis' of (ii) or (iii) must show that they do not correspond to the *same* truth-function of elementary sentences as (i). This idea might be carried out by interpreting (ii) and (iii) as statements about the state of the mind of the speaker. Sentence (ii) is then regarded as a description of the 'will' or 'intention' of the speaker, sentence (iii) as a description of his 'mental state of uncertainty' (cf. *Philosophical Investigations*, § 24).[1]

However it has rightly been pointed out in recent philosophical discussion that imperatives or questions are not statements of facts. To ask a question, for instance, differs from stating an uncertainty. The only natural analysis of sentences (i)–(iii) seems to show that they have indeed the same descriptive content. Thus the mood is an essential factor in the sense of a sentence, which cannot be included in its descriptive content.

It has been maintained that the later Wittgenstein rejected the picture theory of sentence meaning. If we take this theory to mean that it is an essential feature in language that there are sentences which depict their descriptive content, I cannot, however, see from what Wittgenstein says in the *Philosophical Investigations* that he *rejected* the picture theory. His remarks on the subject seem only to emphasize that the picture theory does not *explain* the essence of language to nearly so great an extent as he had believed in the Tractatus. So, for instance, the picture theory does not explain the modal function of a sentence.

Sentences (i)–(iii) can be regarded as semantical elementary sentences. They *show* their descriptive content in that they *depict* it. But what these sentences show as pictures cannot be identified with their sense—as Wittgenstein thinks in e.g. 4.031. There is an obvious difference between a sentence and a picture. A picture has as such no mood.

In order to clarify the significance of this point we will analyse the passage in the *Philosophical Investigations* most relevant to this subject. This is § 22, which reads (the letters in the margin I have added for reference):

---

[1] A more reasonable view is taken in the 'Notes on Logic', where we read (p. 234): 'Assertion is merely psychological. There are only unasserted propositions. Judgment, command, and question all stand on the same level; but all have in common the propositional form, and that alone interests us. What interests logic are only the unasserted propositions.' Cf. also Russell, *Principles of Mathematics*, §§ 38 and 478.

(a)    Frege's idea that every assertion contains an assumption, which is the thing that is asserted, really rests on the possibility found in our language of writing every statement in the form: 'It is asserted that such-and-such is the case.'—But 'that such-and-such is the case' is *not* a sentence in our language—it is not yet a

(b)    *move* in the language-game. And if I write, not 'It is asserted that . . .', but 'It is asserted: such and such is the case', the words 'It is asserted' simply become superfluous.

(c)    We might very well also write every statement in the form of a question followed by a 'Yes'; for instance: 'Is it raining? Yes!' Would this show that every statement contained a question?

Of course we have the right to use an assertion sign in contrast with a question-mark, for example, or if we want to distinguish an assertion from a fiction or an assumption. It is only a mistake if one thinks that the assertion consists of two actions, enter-

(d)    taining and asserting (assigning the truth-value, or something of the kind), and that in performing these actions we follow the propositional sign roughly as we sing from the musical score. Reading the written sentence loud or soft is indeed comparable with singing from a musical score, but *'meaning'* (thinking) the sentence that is read is not.

Frege's assertion sign marks the *beginning of the sentence*. Thus its function is like that of the full-stop. It distinguishes the whole period from a clause *within* the period. If I hear someone say

(e)    'it's raining' but do not know whether I have heard the beginning and end of a period, this sentence does not yet serve to tell me anything.

A remark at the bottom of page 11 obviously refers to this section:

Imagine a picture representing a boxer in a particular stance. Now, this picture can be used to tell someone how he should stand, should hold himself; or how he should not hold himself; or how a particular man did stand in such-and-such a place; and so on. One might (using the language of chemistry) call

(f)    this picture a sentence-radical.[1] This will be how Frege thought
(g)    of the 'assumption'.


## I. SENTENCE-RADICAL AND MODAL COMPONENT

I shall start my comments on these quotations with an examination of the chemical vocabulary to which Wittgenstein refers in

---

[1] In accordance with my earlier terminology I translate *Satzradikal* as 'sentence-radical' (the English version has 'proposition-radical'). I have made a few other changes in the translation of these passages.

passage (f). The term 'radical' is used in particular in organic chemistry. The formula of ordinary alcohol is given the form $C_2H_5(OH)$. This substance is regarded as a compound of two components: the 'ethyl group' $C_2H_5$-, and the 'hydroxyl group' –OH. Neither of these groups can exist in isolation; they can only exist as components in other chemical compounds and are therefore not chemical 'substances'. The reason for giving those groups separate names is the following circumstance: on the one hand for the ethyl group can be substituted other corresponding organic groups. We obtain in this way a series of *different* so called *alcohols*, for instance:

$$CH_3(OH) \text{ (methyl alcohol), } C_2H_5(OH) \text{ (ethyl alcohol), }$$
$$C_3H_7(OH) \text{ (propyl alcohol), etc.}$$

Here 'alcohol' is the name of substances of a *similar* chemical character, whereas the groups 'methyl', 'ethyl', etc., play in the first place (i.e. in respect to elementary chemical operations) the part only of the 'matter' to which this chemical character, or—as it also is called—chemical function, is attached. The hydroxyl group is therefore called a *'functional unity'*, whereas the methyl and ethyl groups, etc., are called *radicals*. On the other hand there are many different functional unities; beside the hydroxyl group we will mention the group $=O$, which is the characteristic of the class of substances called 'ethers', e.g.

$$(CH_3)_2O \text{ (methyl ether), } (C_2H_5)_2O \text{ (ethyl ether), }$$
$$(C_3H_7)_2O \text{ (propyl ether), etc.}$$

Wittgenstein's chemical vocabulary in passage (f) may thus be interpreted as follows: The *picture* of a boxer is a *sentence-radical*; it indicates, so to speak, the 'matter' of a sentence, but is not in itself a sentence, because for a sentence to be formed there is needed beside this matter a definite 'function' in which the picture is to be used: to show how someone should hold himself, or how he should not hold himself, etc.

In this context we may remind ourselves of 4.022: 'The sentence *shows* how things stand, *if* it is true. And it *says* that they do so stand'. This can be true only of an indicative sentence when it is used as an assertion (and though there are other uses of the indicative as well, we shall here discuss indicatives only as used to make assertions). If we in particular think of a semantical elementary sentence and take into account the picture theory of sentence meaning we could express the content of the statement in this way:

(IX.1)   *A sentence in the indicative depicts how things stand, if it is true. And it asserts that they do so stand.*

In effect 4.022 assigns two different tasks to a sentence: the task of *depicting* a state of affairs and the task of *asserting* that this state of affairs exists. And though Wittgenstein does not pay any attention to this circumstance in the Tractatus, the comparison of a sentence with an ordinary picture, like the above mentioned picture of a boxer, shows that these two factors must be separated also in indicatives: a *picture* does not in itself assert anything, it can be used for different purposes and is therefore not a 'sentence' but merely a sentence-radical. In order to form a sentence the sentence-radical is to be combined with a linguistic or extra-linguistic element which gives it a *function* in language when used as a means of communication, i.e. a function in what Wittgenstein calls the *language-game* (passage (b)).

The same distinction applies to compound sentences, which are 'depicting' sentences only in an extended sense. We may thus sum up the result of our analysis as follows: we must distinguish between two components in a sentence: the *sentence-radical* (i.e. the 'phrastic' in Hare's terminology), which shows the state of affairs (real or imagined) that the sentence describes, and the *functional* component (the 'neustic' in Hare's terminology), which indicates which function the *presentation* of this state of affairs has in the language-game. The state of affairs presented is the *descriptive content* of the sentence; the function is a semantical component which may be called its semantical *mood*. The sentence-radical thus indicates the descriptive content; the functional, or, as it also may be called, *modal* component indicates the mood. The modal component need not appear as a separate sign in the sentence; but it must be a characteristic that can in some way be noticed in the sentence when it is produced as a 'move in the language-game'.

M

The sentence-radical is not a 'sentence', because it is not as such a move in the language-game (passage (b)). And it is plausible to think that Frege had the descriptive content in mind when he spoke of an 'assumption' (passages (a) and (g)).[1]

## 2. MODAL OPERATORS

G. H. von Wright has introduced the notation '$OA$' to indicate that an 'act' $A$ is *obligatory*.[2] The obligatory he regards as one of what he calls the 'deontic modes'. By an 'act' he understands an 'act-property', i.e. a certain *kind* of individual acts, which he calls 'act-individuals'. His system of deontic logic could, however, be developed in the same way if we refer the sign '$O$' to act-individuals rather than to act-properties. I prefer to do so: if '$p$' is a certain individual act, then '$Op$' indicates that this individual act is obligatory. Now that an individual act is performed can be regarded as a state of affairs. Thus we can say that '$Op$' indicates that a certain state of affairs is obligatory. '$Op$' is then a sentence in the mood of obligatoriness.

What is now the logical status of the letter '$p$' appearing as a part of this notation? One could be tempted to answer that '$p$' is (an abbreviation for) a *sentence* describing the state of affairs which '$Op$' indicates as obligatory. But in view of our preceding analysis this answer is obviously wrong. Since the mood of sentence '$Op$' is indicated by the operator '$O$', which therefore can be considered the 'modal component' of the sentence, the expression '$p$' cannot have a mood of its own. The expression '$p$' can therefore only be a *sentence-radical*, not a sentence.

But if in a symbolic notation letter '$p$' is taken as a sentence-radical, not as a sentence, then the *assertion* of '$p$' cannot be written '$p$' (as we usually do). We must then introduce a separate modal operator, say '$I$', as a sign of the indicative mood. The same sentence-radical could in such a notation be used for the formation of sentences in different moods in the following way:

---

[1] Cf. Frege: *Translations*, p. 34. (The word *Annahme* is there rendered as 'supposition'.) The concept of an 'assumption' does not occur as an essential notion in Frege's writings. As Miss Anscombe has pointed out to me, Wittgenstein's attention seems to have been drawn to this notion by the fact that it plays an important part in Russell's account of Frege's views in the *Principles of Mathematics* (see p. 503 f.).

[2] 'Deontic Logic', p. 61. The basic deontic operator in von Wright's system is, however, not 'obligatory' but 'permitted'.

(1)·
$$
\begin{aligned}
Ip &= \text{You live here now.}\\
Op &= \text{It is obligatory for you to live here now.}\\
?p &= \text{Do you live here now?}\\
Np &= \text{It is necessary that you live here now.}\\
Vp &= \text{It is certain (verified) that you live here now, etc.}^{1}
\end{aligned}
$$

According to passage (b) the statement 'You live here now' could be given the form: 'It is asserted that you live here now'. However, I do not think this is correct. There is a difference in mood between asserting a thing, as one does when one says 'You live here now', and stating that this thing is asserted. The difference becomes manifest, I think, if one tries to form the negation of those statements. The negation of 'You live here now' runs 'You do not live here now', which symbolically could be written either as '$I(\sim p)$' or '$\sim Ip$'. This means that the following rule holds true for the indicative mood:

(2)
$$\sim I(p) \equiv I(\sim p).$$

But the negation of 'It is asserted that you live here now' is 'It is not asserted that you live here now', which is not the same as 'It is asserted that you do not live here now'. This feature in the logic of 'It is asserted that . . . ' it has in common with the logic of the operators '$O$', '$N$' and '$V$'. According to von Wright '$\sim Op$' means '$\sim p$ is permitted', whereas '$O(\sim p)$' means '$p$ is forbidden', and there is certainly a difference between those meanings. The corresponding is true of '$N$' and '$V$'.

The fact that (2) holds true for operator '$I$' makes it possible to use a notation of the following kind instead of (1). We take '$p$' as a *sentence* in the *indicative*, adding that the *sentence-radical* of a sentence in the indicative is formed by surrounding the sentence by parentheses. We adopt, that is, the rule: 'The sentence-radical belonging to the assertion '$p$' is signified by '$(p)$'. This means that the indicative mood can be indicated by leaving out the parentheses from the sentence-radical. Sentences (1) are in this notation given the form:

(3)
$$I(p) \text{ or } p, \quad O(p), \quad ?(p), \quad N(p), \quad V(p), \text{ etc.}$$

The notation '$p$' for '$I(p)$' would be ambiguous if rule (2) were not valid: '$\sim p$' stands for '$\sim I(p)$' as well as '$I(\sim p)$', but it is indifferent which.

¹ Cf. von Wright: *An Essay in Modal Logic*, p. 37.

This circumstance gives the indicative together with the interrogative mood a special position among the moods mentioned in (1) or (3). As a comment on passage (c) one could state: it would certainly be possible to take '$p$' as a sentence in the interrogative mood and always indicate the indicative mood by a separate operator. It would also be possible to take '$p$' as a sentence in the mood of obligatoriness and mark the indicative by a separate operator. But in that case one would have to introduce different notations for separating $\sim O(p)$ and $O(\sim p)$.

If we adopt notation (3) we have to realise that '$p$' is a sentence in the indicative only if it appears as a *separate* formula. This circumstance corresponds to what Wittgenstein says in passage (e) concerning 'it's raining'. In fact notation (3) corresponds more closely to ordinary language than (1). What in notation (3) is effected by surrounding a sentence with parentheses is in English effected by putting the word 'that' in front of it. Wittgenstein says in passage (b) that a that-clause is not a sentence in our language,[1] because it is not as such a move in the language-game. This means according to our previous analysis that a that-clause, like the expression '($p$)' in (3) and the picture of a boxer, functions only as a *sentence-radical.*[2] If we replace the use of parentheses by the use of the conjunction 'that' we could translate notation (3) as follows:

$$
\begin{array}{lll}
I(p) & = & \text{It is the case, that you live here now.} \\
p & = & \text{You live here now.} \\
O(p) & = & \text{It is obligatory, that you live here now.} \\
?(p) & = & \text{Is it the case, that you live here now?}
\end{array}
$$

(4) appears to the left of these lines.

## 3. THE SENTENCE-RADICAL AS A PICTURE

The use of a that-clause as a sentence-radical[3] is more natural, I think, than the use of verbal nouns of the type 'your living here now' suggested by Hare. For our purpose it has the additional advantage that we can apply our analysis of the picture theory of sentence meaning directly to sentence-radicals given in this form.

[1] In English it is not even called so, because grammarians distinguish between a 'sentence' and a 'clause'. The German *Satz*, however, is used of sentences as well as clauses.

[2] I do not claim that that-clauses always function as sentence-radicals. The conjunction 'that' is not always used in this way in English, nor are parentheses around sentences in symbolic logic. But other functions of that-clauses than this do not interest us in our present context.

[3] Cf. Lewis: *Knowledge and Valuation*, p. 49.

This is important because the main contention of the present argument could be formulated as follows:

(IX.2)  *The picture theory of sentence meaning applies to the sentence-radical only.*

This circumstance we have taken into consideration in the preceding chapters by pointing out that what a sentence *shows* and *presents* as a picture is its *descriptive content*. The descriptive content is the part of sentence meaning given by the sentence-radical.

Statement (IX.2) is to be understood to hold true not only of the picture theory of semantical elementary sentences as developed in Chapter VII, but also of the extended picture theory of compound sentences as developed in Chapter VIII. And in this connection one thing should be noticed. In section 2 of the present chapter we have used the negation sign for negating *sentences* in a determinate mood. This is, however, a peculiar use of the negation sign; in fact the semantical import of the negation sign and other logical connectives is not quite clear, when they appear in *front* of modal operators. Though this has not been expressly stated, the analysis of the logical connectives, as given in the preceding chapter, presupposes that the connectives *belong to the sentence-radical*. Also the use of negation in a complete description in the form (1) of Chapter VIII (p. 146) is to be understood in this way: it is convenient to think of the whole description as a sentence-radical, which may be produced in different moods.[1]

## 4. THE CONCEPT OF TRUTH IN THE SEMANTICS OF SENTENCE-RADICALS

Semanticists of the formal school have introduced the 'semantical' concept of *truth* as a fundamental concept of semantics. This idea seems also to be implicit in the use of the concept of a 'truth-function' as a fundamental concept in logic. However, sentences can significantly be said to be true or false only if they are in the indicative mood. In view of the fact that the descriptive content of a sentence is indicated by the sentence-radical, which may

---

[1] Cf. the passage in 'Notes on Logic' quoted above (p. 158 n.). What Wittgenstein here calls 'propositions' are obviously the sentence-radicals.

appear in other moods as well, we may therefore suspect that the concept of truth is not after all a fundamental concept in semantics so far as the descriptive content of sentences is concerned.

Now there is a sense in which 'true' and 'false' can be applied to sentence-radicals rather than to sentences. According to the terminology of the Tractatus pictures which have a real prototype are said to 'represent' this prototype either 'truly' or 'falsely' and thus to be either 'true' or 'false' pictures, as we have pointed out earlier. In this sense sentence-radicals which refer to reality can also be said to be either 'true' or 'false'; i.e. they are either 'true descriptions' or 'false descriptions'.

But even in this sense 'true' need not be introduced as a fundamental notion in the semantics of sentence-radicals. 'The sentence *shows* how things stand, *if* it is true.' If we consider this as referring to a sentence-radical and meaning that the sentence-radical shows how things stand, if it is a 'true' description, the concept of 'truth' may seem to appear as a fundamental concept in the explanation of the relation between a sentence-radical and its descriptive content. But the word 'true' appears here within an if-clause, which, if the sentence-radical is false, functions as a counter-factual hypothetical, the meaning of which is not clear. In fact the explanation can be given a form which does not contain a counter-factual hypothetical and does not make use of the concept of 'truth'.

As the argument of the preceding chapters shows, the concept of 'truth' is inessential in the analysis of the descriptive content of a sentence. The 'truth-functional' analysis of compound sentences shows how a sentence-radical is to be transformed into a system of alternative pictures. We can understand how this transformation is to be effected without any reference to reality: the 'truth-values' 'true' and 'false' mean only 'positive' and 'negative' in the picture-*field* (cf. above, p. 149); and the picture-fields can therefore be constructed without a knowledge of even the key of interpretation by means of which those picture-fields are understood as pictures. The 'logic' of the sentence-radical determines only the *structure* of the alternative picture-fields; it does not tell us anything about the content which is to be attached to this structure. When the key of interpretation is applied each of these picture-fields *presents* a state of affairs; then the analysed sentence-radical is brought into contact with reality, but the concept of 'truth' does not enter into the description of this process either. The different pictures depict the elements of the prototype *as* standing in the way shown by the structure of the picture-fields, and the sentence-radical describes the elements of the prototype *as* standing in one of these ways; thus its descriptive content is understood independently of what is the case in reality.

According to the 'correspondence theory of truth' a sentence is 'true' if it corresponds to reality. In view of the fact that 'truth' need not be taken as a fundamental concept in the semantics of sentence-radicals, this theory may really be regarded as giving a definition, and by no means a circular definition, of the concept of 'truth', as it is used when one says that a sentence-radical is a 'true' description. Since the descriptive content of a sentence-radical is defined independently of its truth or falsehood, we can define a sentence-radical as being a 'true' description if, and only if, one of the states of affairs belonging to its descriptive content is real. And this definition may be formulated: a description is 'true' if, and only if, it corresponds to reality.

## 5. THE SEMANTICS OF MOODS

Granted that the picture theory of sentence meaning explains how we understand the descriptive content of a sentence-radical, how do we understand the mood in which the picture is presented? Of what kind are the semantical rules according to which the sentence 'You live here now' is understood as a statement of a fact rather than as a question or command?[1] Or to put the question in another way: what does it *mean* for a sentence to be used as an assertion rather than in any other mood?

We have stated that the concept of 'truth' is not fundamental in the semantics of sentence-radicals. In the semantics of the indicative mood, however, I think it is fundamental in a way.

A sentence-radical may be a 'true' or 'false' description and can in this sense be called either 'true' or 'false'. But ordinarily we do not call sentence-radicals 'true' or 'false'. If someone utters the clause 'that you live here now' we should not maintain that what he said were either 'true' or 'false'. As a rule the attributes 'true' and 'false' are reserved to *sentences* in the *indicative*.

If we utter a that-clause what we have said is not regarded as

[1] It is understood so, that is, if the intonation does not show the contrary. Cf. next page.

true or as false. Why not? Following Wittgenstein in passage (b) we may answer: A that-clause is not as such a *move* in the language-game.

The idea of 'language-games' plays an important part in the *Philosophical Investigations*. I do not find the use of it in the beginning of the book as a basis for an examination of the semantics of separate words very fortunate. However, as a basis for the semantics of moods I think it is indeed clarifying. To understand the indicative mood is to understand that there is a 'correct' use of it, and the correct use of it can be characterized as a 'move' in a language-game the principle of which runs:

(IX.3)    *Produce a sentence in the indicative mood only if the sentence-radical is a true description.*

If a person $A$ utters sentence '$I(p)$' to a person $B$ he plays the language-game of the indicative mood correctly only if sentence-radical '$(p)$' is a true description, i.e. if the state of affairs described by '$(p)$' exists. This is therefore what $B$ believes, if he 'takes $A$ on his word'. And in this sense (IX.3) determines the 'meaning' of the indicative mood.

There are certainly also other language-games played with sentences which *grammatically* are in the indicative mood than that determined by rule (IX.3). In the following discussion I shall, however, reserve the term 'indicative mood' for the mood determined by rule (IX.3); other language-games played with grammatical indicatives I shall call uses of what are grammatically indicatives in what is 'semantically' a different mood.[1]

The word 'true' in rule (IX.3) refers to the concept of truth as applied to sentence-radicals. It follows that the concept of 'truth' as applied to sentences in the indicative is *different* from the concept of truth appearing in this rule. Thus the concept of truth as applied to sentences in the indicative may without circularity be *defined* in terms of this rule: A sentence in the indicative is said to be *true*, if it is used in accordance with rule (IX.3). And it is *this* concept of

---

[1] It must be emphasized that our analysis of 'moods' applies only to *sentences*, not to subordinate clauses; since subordinate clauses are never 'moves in the language-game'. If, for instance, different subordinate clauses in a sentence are in different grammatical moods, then, according to this line of analysis, the sentence as a whole must be interpreted as having a mixed semantical mood or something of the kind; it cannot be analysed as a compound of clauses in different semantical moods.

truth we are thinking of when we maintain that what a person says when he utters a that-clause cannot be regarded as true or false. The word 'true' in the meaning of 'in accordance with the rule of the indicative mood' cannot significantly be applied to an utterance which is not a move in the language-game of the indicative.

We might call the two concepts of truth 'modal truth' and 'descriptive truth'. The concept of truth appearing in the moral rule 'Always speak the truth' is the modal truth. The moral rule says that you must always play the language-game of the indicative mood correctly, not that you must always produce true sentence-radicals. Only the existence of rule (IX.3) makes it possible to deceive people by breaking it.

The corresponding rule for the imperative mood could be formulated as follows:

(IX.4)  *Make the sentence-radical true.*

This rule is a rule determining the 'correct' behaviour of the listener, not of the speaker as rule (IX.3). The language-game governed by it gives a command its semantical meaning. To say this does of course not imply that a person $A$ who utters a command to a person $B$ 'intends' $B$ to follow the command, nor that $B$ really follows it or tends to follow it. The game determines only what $B$ will do if he 'takes $A$ on his words'.

The rule of the language-game of the interrogative mood (as used in sentence (3)) might be stated in this way:

(IX.5)  *Answer 'yes' or 'no' according as the sentence-radical is a true description or not.*

One remark to rule (IX.3) is to be added. One could be tempted to replace the condition 'only if the sentence-radical is a true description' by 'only if you *know* (or *believe*) the sentence-radical is a true description'. But such a replacement is not correct. The use of a sentence in the indicative is correct or incorrect according as the sentence-radical is true or false, quite independently of whether the speaker is in 'good faith' when using it. The speaker's knowledge or belief in what he says shows only that he honestly *tries* to play the language-game correctly, not that he really does so.

## 6. THE ASSERTION SIGN

Let us return to our quotation from the *Philosophical Investigations*. Passage (d) evidently refers to number 4.442 in the Tractatus, where we read: 'Frege's assertion sign "⊢ " is logically altogether meaningless; in Frege (and Russell) it only shows that these authors hold as true the sentences marked in this way. "⊢ " belongs therefore to the sentences no more than does the number of the sentence. A sentence cannot possibly assert of itself that it is true'.[1]

'A sentence cannot possibly assert of itself that it is true.' The distinction between 'descriptive truth' and 'modal truth' shows an ambiguity in this statement. The reason why a sentence could not possibly assert its own truth is, I think, that this would involve some kind of vicious circle. And there is indeed a kind of vicious circle if we think that a sentence asserts its own modal truth (or that a sentence-radical contains its own descriptive truth). But the vicious circle is avoided if we think that a sentence in the indicative asserts the *descriptive* truth of its sentence-radical and that it is *modally* true if the sentence-radical is really descriptively true. Therefore the assertion sign is *not* meaningless if it is interpreted as a modal operator indicating the indicative mood, as Wittgenstein says in the first sentence of passage (d).

The formulation in passage (d) of what is really a mistake is complicated. According to the view taken in the preceding analysis there are two mistakes that might be hinted at in the passage: (i) It is meaningless to introduce an assertion sign, if what it is intended to refer to is already a *sentence* in the indicative, because if the sentence is really in the indicative, then it is already asserted. (ii) One should not believe that the assertion sign, if used as a modal operator, is a deputizing sign or in any other way belongs to the sentence as a picture in either the narrow or the extended sense.

## 7. SENSE AND DIRECTION

But the contrast in passage (d) between 'entertaining' (*Erwägen*) and 'asserting' (*Behaupten*) and the characterization of 'asserting' as 'assigning the truth-value, or something of the kind' seems to indicate that Wittgenstein has also a 'mistake' of a different kind in

[1] From the point of view of our present discussion it is interesting to note that this statement appears in almost the same formulation in 'Notes on Logic', and is there immediately followed by the passage quoted above (p. 158 n).

mind. And I believe his thought here is connected with his somewhat perplexing use of the concept *Sinn* in the Tractatus. Consider
the following passages:

3.144[1]    . . . . . . . . . .
          (Namen gleichen Punkten, Sätze Pfeilen, sie haben Sinn.)

4.064    Jeder Satz muss s c h o n einen Sinn haben; die Bejahung
         kann ihn ihm nicht geben, denn sie bejaht ja gerade den Sinn.
         Und dasselbe gilt von der Verneinung, etc.

5.2341    . . . . . . . . . .
          (Die Verneinung verkehrt den Sinn des Satzes.)

The quotation from 3.144 contains a pun on the word *Sinn*. The
passage is rendered in the English version as 'Names resemble
points; propositions resemble arrows, they have sense'. In order
to correspond to the German word *Sinn* the word 'sense' must be
understood here not only in its meaning of linguistic 'sense' but
also in the meaning of 'direction', given to it in mathematics. It is
in the latter meaning that having 'sense' constitutes a resemblance
between sentences and arrows. If we take the word 'sense' in its
linguistic meaning, we could express Wittgenstein's point in this
way: Sentences resemble arrows in that the sense (*Sinn*) of a sentence
is *directed* in contradistinction to the meaning (*Bedeutung*) of a name.[2]
In 4.064 *Sinn* must again be taken as 'direction' or 'directed sense':
the sentence must *already* have a *directed* sense: the affirmation cannot
give the sense its direction, because what is 'affirmed' is the sense
taken in the direction it has in itself. The same holds true of denial,
etc. It is, of course, also the *direction* of the sense which is reversed
by negation according to 5.2341.

Wittgenstein seems here to reject an idea which he feels a strong
temptation to hold. This is the thought that there must be some
'neutral kernel' which is common in affirmative and negative

---

[1] Cf. above, p. 118.

[2] According to the Tractatus only names have 'meaning' whereas sentences have
'sense' (see above, p. 118). In the 'Notes on Logic', however, a sentence is said to have
'meaning' as well as 'sense', the 'meaning' being the *fact* which the sentence corresponds
to or not, according as it is true or false, and the 'sense' being the state of affairs described
by the sentence. Thus the 'sense' is directed; it may either coincide with or be the
opposite to the 'meaning': 'Every proposition is essentially true-false. Thus a proposition has two poles (corresponding to case of its truth and case of its falsity). We call
this the *sense* of a proposition. The *meaning* of a proposition is the fact which actually
corresponds to it. The chief characteristic of my theory is: *p* has *the same meaning as
not-p*.' (P. 232.)

sentences and which is given a direction by being affirmed or denied. The temptation to think so may have different grounds of which one may consist in a confusion between the 'modal' and 'descriptive' concept of truth. In *one* sense a sentence in the indicative is given a direction only by its modal character (the 'affirmation' of the sentence-radical) because it is only by its modal character that an assertion states anything to be the case. But in another sense the sentence-radical has already a direction: it shows things as standing in one way and not in the opposite way. And the direction 'given' the sentence by being produced in the indicative mood is exactly the direction of the sentence-radical. If we interpret the first period in 4.064 as referring to this circumstance it could be restated in this way: The sentence-radical must already have a directed sense; the use of it in the indicative mood cannot give its sense a direction, because what is stated to be true by a sentence in the indicative is the directed sense of the sentence-radical. Wittgenstein seems to be thinking of this fact in passage (d) as well.

But when in 4.064 he adds that the same is true of the 'denial etc.', he seems rather to follow another line of thought and the same is true of 5.2341. If we take the negation sign as belonging to the sentence-*radical*, 5.2341 must refer to it and then seems to express a thought of the following kind: the sentence-radical '$(\sim aRb)$' can have a direction only if the picture '$aRb$' has a direction. The fact that a negated sentence-radical has a direction is founded on the fact that the unnegated clause to which it refers has already a direction, which the negation 'reverses'.[1]

Something similar can be said of the other logical connectives. This means that the fact that a sentence-radical has a direction is founded on the fact that the semantical elementary sentence-radicals of which it is a 'truth-function' are already 'directed'.

Why then are elementary sentence-radicals directed? I think this is due to the fact that their *predicates* have a directed meaning. We have earlier pointed out (p. 139) that to know a predicate is to know a *difference*. To know the quality 'red', for instance, is to know the difference between red objects and objects that are not red. But this characterization is in effect incomplete: to know the quality 'red' is to know this difference in a *directed* sense, because there are *two* qualities corresponding to the difference between red objects and objects that are not red: the quality 'red' and the quality

[1] Cf. 5.5151, especially the second paragraph.

'non-red'. Thus a linguistic quality which names redness has a *directed* 'meaning': it corresponds to 'red', not to 'non-red'. The directions of the denominata of predicate names are therefore the ultimate basis for the directions of sentence-radicals and, in consequence, sentences.[1] Thus Wittgenstein is wrong when he says in 3.144 that (all) names resemble 'points'. Names of *predicates* are more like 'arrows', because their 'meaning' is directed.

## 8. THE FUNDAMENTAL ROLE OF MODAL GAMES IN TEACHING THE USE OF LANGUAGE

'Can we not make ourselves understood by means of false sentences as hitherto with true ones, so long as we know that they are meant to be false?' Wittgenstein asks in 4.062. His answer is 'No': 'For a proposition is true, if what we assert by means of it is the case; and if by "$p$" we mean $\sim p$, and what we mean is the case, then "$p$" in the new conception is true and not false'.

What Wittgenstein intends to discuss could obviously in our terminology be restated as follows: Could we make ourselves understood if we replace the use of the indicative mood by a *modus negativus*, in the language-game of which rule (IX.3) is replaced by this rule: 'Produce a sentence in the negative mood only if its sentence-radical is a *false* description'?

In one sense this is quite possible. Of course we could make statements as comprehensibly by means of a language-game the rule of which is that we are always to produce false descriptions as by means of a language-game the rule of which is that we are always to produce true descriptions, if we only know *which* language-game we are playing.

Difficulties arise only when we ask *how* we could really *know* which language-game we are playing. Let us imagine a community in which all persons consistently said 'This is not red' when they meant that the thing spoken of was red, and 'This is red' when they meant that the thing spoken of was not red, and so on. There are at least two possibilities for explaining the difference between their language and ordinary English:

[1] A sentence is not only bi-polar (cf. the footnote to p. 171), but also directed, i.e. one of the poles is positive, the other negative. Both the *bi-polarity* and *direction* of a sentence are ultimately founded on the corresponding characteristics in predicates. And it must be emphasized that neither in respect of sentences, nor in respect of predicates does the directedness cancel the bi-polarity. Neither sentences, nor predicates have 'neutral kernels' of meaning. Cf. 5.5151, third paragraph, and above, pp. 56 and 147.

(a) Sentences that in English are used in the indicative are in their language used in the negative mood.

(b) Their semantical key differs from that of ordinary English in that they have 'reversed' the direction of all predicate names: in their language the word 'red' does not refer to the property called 'red' in English but to the property called 'not-red'.

How are we to decide which of these two explanations is the correct one? If the use of all moods is reversed consistently in the same way as the indicative (and if we in addition assume that the use of the two-place logical connectives and some other terms is not known *a priori*) I think it is in fact impossible to make such a decision. We could, at least roughly, characterize the situation thus: there is no difference in linguistic behaviour between two communities of which one reverses all moods and the other reverses the directions of the sentence-radicals. These two alternatives are only two different ways of describing the same linguistic behaviour.

In fact our *own* linguistic behaviour could also be described in two ways, either as it has been described above or by *reversing* all modal rules *and* at the same time *reversing* the semantical devices for the sentence-radicals in such a way as to give all sentence-radicals a reversed direction.

Why do we then tend to describe our language in the former rather than in the latter way? I will not discuss this here, but I would like to emphasize one thing: *That* we tend to describe it in the former way means among other things that we *presuppose* that the modal rule of assertions is the rule of the *indicative* mood, not the rule of the negative mood. And if this is so, then Wittgenstein's negative answer to his question is correct: a linguistic behaviour that *could* be described according to alternative (a) *would rather* be described according to alternative (b). But if we presuppose that the mood is unchanged, then, 'if by "$p$" we mean $\sim p$', what has been changed is the descriptive content of '$p$', and then the sentence-radical '$(p)$' (and, in consequence, the sentence '$p$') is true, if $\sim p$ is the case.

The fact that the mood and descriptive content of a sentence *could* be described negatively instead of positively is connected with another more important fact: we cannot *learn* the key of interpretation and other devices for understanding the descriptive content of a sentence without producing sentences in some *known* mood. Roughly speaking: we cannot learn how to make any pictures at all if we do not first learn how to make 'true' pictures. And though I think it is clearer not to use the concept of truth as a fundamental concept in a systematic *description* of the semantics of sentence-radicals, I believe that some notion of 'correctness' is in *this* sense fundamental in all semantics of sentences. Approval and disapproval are fundamental in all *teaching* of distinctions.

## 9. SUMMARY

We may distinguish between three different strata in the sense of a sentence:

(i) The *descriptive structure* of a sentence, i.e. the external structure of the alternative picture-fields into which the sentence-radical can be transformed. The descriptive structure of a sentence is determined by the external structure of the semantical elementary sentence-radicals (if 'correctly' analysed into logical predicate and logical subjects) of which its sentence-radical is considered a truth-function, and the logical rules governing the logical signs used in it.

(ii) The *descriptive content* of a sentence. The descriptive content is determined by the descriptive structure and the key of interpretation, by means of which the picture-fields are understood as pictures.

(iii) The *modal import* of a sentence, which is determined by the rules which govern its correct use in the language-game.

When I here speak of 'sentences' I think only of some special kind of sentence; I do not claim that this analysis is true of all that might be called 'sentences'. But I agree in so far with the earlier Wittgenstein that I think the kind of sentence analysable in this way forms a class of expressions the use of which is fundamental in human language.

'But how many kinds of sentence are there? Say assertion, question, and command?—There are *countless* kinds: countless different kinds of use of what we call "symbols", "words", "sentences" ' (*Philosophical Investigations*, § 23.) This means among other things that there are countless different moods in language and, in particular, that there are countless different moods in which a grammatical indicative may be used.

Perhaps there are. But in fact, I think, the 'language-game of the indicative' governed by rule (IX.3) is fundamental to most uses of the grammatical indicative. The use of the indicative mood in fiction, for instance, I should characterize rather as a 'feigned' playing of the indicative game than a 'fictive mood' founded on a language-game of its own. In the same way other uses of the grammatical indicative which seem to presuppose modal rules that differ from (IX.3) may be regarded as 'derived' uses answering to special demands which are as such not foreseen by the general rules of language.

# X

# INTERNAL STRUCTURE OF LANGUAGE AND REALITY

## 1. THE 'ONTOLOGICAL PICTURE THEORY' OF LANGUAGE

The picture theory of sentence meaning seems often to have been confused with a different 'picture theory of language' which concerns not the relation between a linguistic *description* and the reality described by it but the relation between language as a *system* and reality. According to the latter theory language, considered as the system used in sentence formation, is thought of as reflecting the 'logical' structure of reality. We might call this the 'ontological picture theory' in order to distinguish it from the 'descriptional' picture theory of sentence meaning.

Using the terminology introduced in Chapters V and VI we could characterize the difference between these theories roughly as follows: whereas the descriptional picture theory states that there is a similarity in *external* structure between a sentence and what it describes, the 'ontological' picture theory states that there is a similarity in *internal* structure between language and reality. Now by a 'picture' we have meant an articulate field which is identical in *external* structure with another articulate field. Thus the 'ontological' picture theory cannot, according to our terminology, be properly called a 'picture' theory at all; if we do so it can only be in a metaphorical way.

Now Wittgenstein advocates not only a descriptional but also an ontological picture theory in the Tractatus. In fact the two theories are interrelated. But they should not be confused. In this chapter we shall discuss the nature of their interrelation.

According to our analysis in the preceding chapter the descriptional picture theory applies to sentence-radicals rather than to sentences. As we have previously pointed out Wittgenstein does not take this point into consideration in the Tractatus. He thinks there of language as it is used in the language-game of science, i.e. as a tool for making true descriptions. And though the mood of this language must essentially be the indicative as defined above, I think we do Wittgenstein more justice if in the present discussion we somewhat vaguely call the mood of Wittgenstein's meaningful sentences 'descriptive' rather than 'indicative'. We will therefore state the relation between a sentence and a picture according to the Tractatus in the form of two assumptions: (i) Every meaningful sentence is descriptive. (ii) Every descriptive sentence is a picture either in the narrow or the extended sense.

Conditions (i) and (ii) could be said to characterize a certain type of language; I call language of this type *depicting language*.

## 2. WHAT CAN BE 'SHOWN' AND WHAT CAN BE 'SAID'

The difference between the descriptional and ontological picture theory is closely connected with the distinction made in the Tractatus between what can be 'shown' and what can be 'said'. Consider the following statements:

4.12    Der Satz kann die gesamte Wirklichkeit darstellen, aber er kann nicht das darstellen, was er mit der Wirklichkeit gemein haben muss, um sie darstellen zu können—die logische Form. . . .

4.121   Der Satz kann die logische Form nicht darstellen, sie spiegelt sich in ihm.
Was sich in der Sprache spiegelt, kann sie nicht darstellen.
Was s i c h in der Sprache ausdrückt, können w i r nicht durch sie ausdrücken.
Der Satz z e i g t die logische Form der Wirklichkeit.
Er weist sie auf.

4.1212  Was gezeigt werden k a n n, k a n n nicht gesagt werden.

We will start our analysis from 4.1212. What *can* be shown in language *cannot* be said, Wittgenstein states here. But this statement seems to be contradicted in 4.022, according to which a sentence *shows* how things stand, if it is true, *and says* that they do so stand. Obviously Wittgenstein uses the word 'show' (*zeigen*) in two different senses: in one sense of 'show' sentences *say* what they show, in another they *cannot say* what they 'show'. At least in the latter sense the word 'show' is, according to 4.121, synonymous with 'exhibit' (*aufweisen*). And what a sentence *exhibits* but cannot say is the 'logical form of reality'. According to 4.12 this is something that a sentence must have in common with reality to be *capable* of representing[1] it.

In order to understand these statements we must compare them with what is said in the corresponding statements on pictures, treated in Chapter VI, §§ 7 and 8. According to Wittgenstein every picture must be what we have called a (logically) 'adequate' picture, and this means that he adopts the following view: in order to be *capable* of representing a prototype either truly or falsely a picture must already have something in common with the prototype, and this is the 'logical form of representation', which consists in the identity in *internal structure* (in respect of the key) between the systems of elements in the picture and the prototype.

We can thus distinguish between two different kinds of 'showing' in regard to pictures. On the one hand a picture 'shows' by the *external* structure of the picture-field and by means of the key of interpretation a state of affairs that it *presents* or *depicts*, on the other hand it 'shows'—according to Wittgenstein—by the *internal* structure of its elements the internal structure of the elements of the prototype. And what it 'shows' in the latter sense it cannot 'show' in the former sense, because the possibility of 'showing' in the former sense *presupposes* that the elements of the prototype have the internal structure 'shown' in the latter sense. If we take the word 'show' in the latter sense we may therefore state (cf. 2.172):

(X.1)  *A picture can only 'show' or 'exhibit' the internal structure of reality but not depict it.*

The internal structure of the system of elements consists, according to our previous terminology, of the 'logical form' of the different elements. What a picture can only 'show' but not depict is thus the *logical form* of the elements of the prototype (4.12).

We have criticized in Chapter VI § 8 Wittgenstein's opinion that 'showing' of the external structure presupposes identity in internal

---

[1] The word *darstellen* we have earlier translated as 'present', using 'represent' as the English rendering of *abbilden*. Since, however, it would have been unnatural for Wittgenstein to use the word *abbilden* in 4.12, I think 'represent' is the correct translation of *darstellen* here. The technical difference which we have made between 'present' and 'represent' does not matter in this context.

structure. This means that we cannot approve of Wittgenstein's *reason* for accepting (X.1), but our criticism does not affect the validity of this thesis. In fact (X.1) follows immediately from the difference between 'external' and 'internal' structural properties. The structure depicted or presented by a picture belongs *per definitionem* to the external structure (cf. above, p. 93) of a state of affairs, and thus the internal structure of the elements in the proto-type or their logical form cannot be depicted but must, if at all, be shown in some other way. Moreover we have seen that 'depicting' really presupposes a partial showing of the internal structure, in that every isomorphic representation requires that the elements of the picture must belong to the same category as the elements they stand for and thus exhibit this category. We have also seen that it is natural to regard only adequate pictures as 'logical', and that therefore the elements of a picture really exhibit the logical form of the elements they stand for *if* the picture is 'logical'. Thus we seem to agree with Wittgenstein on the following points (cf. pp. 105 ff.):

(X.2)   *The elements of a picture always exhibit the category of the elements they stand for.*

(X.3)   *If a picture is a 'logical' picture, then its elements exhibit the logical form of the elements they stand for.*

The point in which we differ from Wittgenstein could with reference to these formulations be stated in this way: according to Wittgenstein every picture must necessarily be a 'logical' picture, and thus statement (X.3) implies the statement:

(X.4)   *The elements of a picture always exhibit the logical form of the elements they stand for.*

For our part, however, we cannot agree that every picture must be a 'logical' picture. Therefore we must state as an antithesis to (X.4) that a picture does not exhibit whether it is 'logical' or not: or, more explicitly, since by 'the elements of a picture' are understood the elements of the picture-*field* in (X. 4):

(X.4')   *The picture-field does not exhibit whether the picture is a 'logical' picture or not.*

In order to know whether a picture is 'logical' or not we must compare the logical form of the picture elements with the logical forms of the elements they stand for. Thus we cannot 'read' the logical forms of the elements of reality from those of the elements of the picture.

Let us now return to language. By means of (X.1) and (X.4) we can get an idea of what is meant by Wittgenstein's two uses of the word 'show' and the distinction between what can be 'shown' and what can be 'said'.

Showing of what can be 'shown' *and* said is an '*external*' *showing* whereas showing of what can only be 'shown', but *not* said is an '*internal*' *showing*.

A sentence *shows* by its *external* structure how things stand 'if it is true' and *says* that they do so *stand*. It *describes* reality as having the same external structure as the sentence itself.

But what a sentence 'shows' by its external structure must be distinguished from what it 'shows' by the *internal* structure of its elements. The elements of a sentence 'show' the logical form of the 'things' they name, and since all description presupposes, according to Wittgenstein's view, that the elements of reality have the internal structure 'shown' in this way by the elements of language, we must infer, on the one hand, that the internal structure of reality can only be 'shown' or 'exhibited' by language but not described by sentences, and on the other hand, that it is essential to the possibility of a linguistic description that the internal structure of language really *exhibits* the internal structure of the reality described in it. We thus arrive at the following theses:

(X.5)   *The internal structure of reality can only be shown or exhibited by language, not described in sentences.*

(X.6)   *The internal structure of language exhibits the internal structure of reality.*

Thesis (X.5) corresponds to (X.1) and (X.6) to (X.4). I have given these theses a vague form, speaking of 'reality' and 'language' instead of referring them to the elements of definite articulate fields and names of such elements. I have done so on purpose, because I have not wanted to give these theses the character of definite statements which can be said to be correct or incorrect in an unqualified sense, but rather to state two problems: *How far and in what sense are theses* (X.5) *and* (X.6) *really valid?* On the one hand a careless acceptance of them can certainly be the source of different kinds of philosophical mistakes. But on the other hand neither of them can be entirely false and therefore a careless rejection of them may be equally dangerous. These problems may be called the problems of the *ontological* picture theory.

Apart from this the vague form of theses (X.5) and (X.6) is convenient because it corresponds to Wittgenstein's thought to give them a wider application in respect to language than (X.1) and (X.4) in themselves would suggest. We have hitherto referred the terms 'internal properties' and 'logical form' only to 'things', i.e. to the elements of states of affairs. But Wittgenstein applies them to other entities as well, especially to facts, sentences, and so on. In 4.122 he defines an 'internal property' as a 'property of the structure'. This definition is confused, because a 'property of the structure' may be external as well as internal.[1] But I think it is convenient with regard to (X.5) and (X.6) and in concordance with Wittgenstein's main line of thought, if in the present context we extend the meaning of the terms in question as, for instance, the following example shows. Since we have called a difference in category between an object and a quality an 'internal' difference or a difference in 'logical form', it would be natural to characterize the difference in category between an object and a fact or a state of affairs in the same way. If we do so we may regard the circumstance that a sentence is itself a fact as a case in which (X.6) is valid: a 'sentence' exhibits by its own category the category of what it describes. And then we may also regard 'belonging to the category of facts' as an instance of what according to (X.5) can only be 'shown' but not described.

## 3. CORRESPONDING STATEMENTS ON
## LANGUAGE AND REALITY

From the assumptions that the internal structure of reality cannot be described in sentences and that all meaningful sentences are descriptive follows that all 'statements' on the internal structure of reality are in effect 'nonsensical'. If we call such statements 'onto-logical' we may thus state as a consequence of (X.5):

---

[1] This confusion is connected with Wittgenstein's tendency to identify the distinction 'internal-external' with the distinction 'structure-content'. Cf. above, p. 81, and Ch. VI, § 10.

(X.7) *'Ontological' statements are always nonsensical; what they 'state' can only be shown but not said.*

Now philosophical statements are often ontological, and therefore this idea appears to be an essential component of Wittgenstein's opinion that philosophical propositions are always nonsensical. Since, on the other hand, this seems to contain some form of absurdity, Carnap tried to modify it by his famous theory of philosophy as 'logical syntax of language'.[1] According to his view apparent 'metaphysical' statements are not exactly nonsensical but rather *disguised* 'syntactical' statements, i.e. they are statements in a 'material mode of speech' which, if reformulated in a 'formal mode of speech' have a clear descriptive content, though this content refers to *language*,[2] not to non-linguistic reality. Since an analysis of Carnap's view is illuminating in many respects we will examine his procedure in some detail.

Carnap applies the method of clarifying philosophical statements by 'translating' them into the formal mode of speech in a list of examples, among which numbers 29–32 are taken from the Tractatus. These statements are the following:[3]

| *Philosophical sentences* (Material mode of speech) | *Syntactical sentences* (Formal mode of speech) |
|---|---|
| 29a. The world is the totality of facts, not of things. | 29b. Science is a system of sentences, not of names. |
| 30a. A fact is a combination of objects (entities, things). | 30b. A sentence is a series of symbols. |
| 31a. If I know an object, then I also know all the possibilities of its occurrence in facts. | 31b. If the genus of a symbol is given, then all the possibilities of its occurrence in sentences are also given. |
| 32a. Identity is not a relation between objects. | 32b. The symbol of identity is not a descriptive symbol. |

Carnap adds that many other sentences of Wittgenstein's 'which at first appear obscure become clear when translated into the

---

[1] This idea was expounded in *The Logical Syntax of Language*, part V. As is well known, Carnap has since modified the opinions he embraced at the period when this book was written.

[2] It is essential to Carnap's view that the word 'formal' here means 'pertaining only to the linguistic expression'. Cf. Ch. VI, § 10.

[3] *Op. cit.*, p. 303. I quote the statements from the Tractatus in the form in which they are given in the English version of Carnap's book.

formal mode of speech'. And there is indeed a temptation to understand Wittgenstein's statements in this way. But is this correct?

Let us examine first 'translation' 29. The statement quoted as
29a is number 1.1. According to our analysis in Chapter II it presupposes that 'the world' is to be understood as 'the world as a fact'.
Thus statement 29a is logically connected with the statement:

(1)                     A fact is not a thing,

which according to Carnap's principle is to be considered a 'translation' of the statement:

(2)                     A sentence is not a name.

And statement (2) is to be regarded as expressing the clear 'meaning'
of 'pseudo-statement' (1).

Now it is certainly true that (1) and (2) *correspond* to each other
in a way. If we take 'fact' to mean in this context only an entity
that belongs to the *category* of facts, i.e. a state of affairs or a disjunction of states of affairs, etc., then we may state the following
correspondence between a depicting language and reality:

(3)      A sentence is the linguistic description of a fact.

(4)      A name is the linguistic counterpart of a thing.

And thus statement (2) states a differentiation on the linguistic
level which *corresponds* to the differentiation stated by (1) on the
'material' level.

But this does not mean that (1) states the same thing as (2). In
fact (1) is *neither* a translation of (2), *nor* is (2) clearer than (1). Why
this is so I shall now explain.

I shall start from the second point. Why should (2) have a 'clear'
meaning whereas (1) is a pseudo-statement? The reason is obviously
this: (1) is manifestedly an 'ontological' proposition, whereas (2) is
apparently only a classification of linguistic *objects* into different
classes and thus seems to have a plain descriptive meaning. Sentences
are expressions which are formed according to certain 'syntactical
rules' and thus differ in *shape* from names. And a statement on a
difference in shape is not an 'ontological' statement, but describes
the external properties of certain objects.

But if we take the distinction between 'sentences' and 'names' as being a classification of expressions according to their shape, then, according to Wittgenstein's view, statement (2) does not even *correspond* to (1). Statement (2) corresponds to (1) only if we adopt rules (3) and (4), but in a depicting language (3) and (4) can be valid only if a sentence is *itself* a fact and a name is *itself* a 'thing'.

If (2) is to correspond to (1), then by a 'sentence' we must understand a *sentence as a fact*, whereas by a 'name' we understand a 'thing', but then (2) expresses a difference in *category* as well as (1). Therefore, if (1) is a pseudo-statement, then (2) must also be a pseudo-statement; and if (1) is nonsensical then (2) is nonsensical as well.

It follows that (2) cannot be a 'translation' of (1) either. Proposition (2) makes a statement on the internal structure of *reality*; proposition (1) makes the corresponding statement on the internal structure of *language*; and thus these propositions state *different* things. The validity of one of two corresponding ontological statements does not *in itself* imply the validity of the other. To say that an ontological statement holds true for reality if, and only if, the corresponding statement holds true for language is actually only a different way of saying that the internal structure of language and reality is the *same*, i.e. that (X.6) is valid.

We thus arrive at the following conclusions:

(X.8) *'Ontological' statements about reality are not disguised ordinary statements about language. If one of two 'corresponding' statements about language and reality is ontological the other is also ontological.*

(X.9) *'Corresponding' ontological statements about language and reality certainly do not state the same thing; but (X.6) means that if one of two corresponding ontological statements is valid the other is also valid.*

Our question how far (X.6) is valid can thus also be formulated as the question how far the validity of one of two corresponding ontological statements really presupposes the validity of the other. And this is partly a problem of what we are to understand by 'corresponding' statements.

But in respect of 'translation' 29 this seems perfectly clear. If we take 'science' to mean 'science as a fact' the ontological statement on language corresponding to 29a might be given this form:

'Science is the totality of true sentences, not of names'. What is essential in this statement can be said to be contained in the formulation 29b. But it must be emphasized that this is so only if the expressions 'sentence' and 'science' are both taken as referring to linguistic entities of the category of facts. Thus 29b is an ontological statement as well as 29a, and the validity of statements 29a and 29b reflects a common feature in the internal structure of the world and the language of science.

What we have expressed in (X.8) and (X.9) is certainly in accordance with Wittgenstein's view in the Tractatus. And it is important to realize this not only in order to understand Wittgenstein's metaphysics, but also in order to get a correct idea of the whole structure of the Tractatus. When Wittgenstein starts his exposition with ontological statements about reality and only afterwards proceeds to the corresponding statements about language he is not playing at hide-and-seek with the reader. Wittgenstein's ontological statements about reality may in part be founded on an analysis of language, but this does not mean that they are in any sense translations of the corresponding statements about language. Corresponding ontological statements about language and reality have mutually independent import, and the fact that if an ontological statement is valid for reality the corresponding statement is valid for language and conversely is by no means trivial, but forms, according to Wittgenstein's view, a fundamental feature in the relation between language and reality.

### 4. LOGICAL SYNTAX

We proceed to 'translation' 30. Here the relation between the two statements is more complicated than in 29. Statement 30a is a rendering of number 2.01 in the Tractatus, which we have interpreted as meaning 'An atomic state of affairs is a connection of things'. But obviously Carnap takes a 'fact' here to mean any entity of the category of facts that may be described by a sentence. Let us, however, to make the 'translation' more reasonable, think of 30a as referring only to what we have called 'elementary states of affairs' and 30b as referring only to 'semantical elementary sentences'. Then there is indeed a temptation to think of 30a as a mere translation into a material mode of speech of 30b. On the one hand 30b is a descriptive statement in the ordinary sense, not an 'ontological' statement. On the other hand 30a seems to correspond to 30b in a way; i.e. 30a corresponds to 30b if we apply a *false* key of interpretation according to which the 'symbols' of which the sentence forms a series correspond to the 'things' of which the 'fact' is formed. Since 30a is 'ontological' and *not* true in the sense in which 30b is true, one can be tempted to think of 30b as expressing what is the proper meaning of 30a.

But as we have repeatedly pointed out 30b does not in fact correspond to any feature in the reality described by a sentence. The possibility of articulating a sentence as a series of 'symbols' (in Carnap's sense) is irrelevant for the understanding of it as a picture. For 30a to be a true ontological statement about an elementary state of affairs it must be interpreted as meaning that an elementary state of affairs is analysed into objects possessing a certain predicate, but then the corresponding proposition about a sentence states that it is analysed into linguistic objects possessing a linguistic predicate.

In respect to 31 the same difficulty arises. By the 'genus' of a symbol Carnap understands a syntactical property of this symbol defined by the rule that it can occur in sentences only in a certain way. Again 31b seems to be a plain *non-ontological* statement about linguistic objects and their possible interrelations according to certain rules, which seemingly corresponds to an *ontological* statement about reality. And again this view is in fact due to a misapprehension of the relation between language and reality. To begin with, 31b turns out to be *itself* an ontological statement if we pay attention to the circumstance that a sentence is an articulate fact. The 'genus' of a 'symbol' occurring in an elementary sentence is either that it is a logical subject or that it is a characteristic of the logical predicate of the sentence. Thus the definition of a difference in 'genus' presupposes the differentiation in category between sentence elements and this means that the 'genus' is a derived ontological concept.

But even as an ontological statement 31b does not correspond to statement 31a, since there are no elements in the reality described by sentences which correspond to the 'characteristics' of predicates. If we take 31a as referring to atomic states of affairs the corresponding statement on language runs in this way: If we know a 'name' (in the sense as we have spoken about 'names' in Ch. VII, § 7) then we know also the category to which it belongs and thus the way in which it can enter into an elementary sentence as a fact.

What Carnap states in 32b is roughly the same thing as we have stated (p. 154) by saying that the symbol of identity can be regarded as a 'logical' sign in that it only indicates how a sentence is to be transformed into a picture but does not appear in the picture itself. Thus 32b states a difference in internal structure between language and isomorphic pictures, and therefore also a difference in internal structure between language and reality. 32a states another aspect of the same difference.

In 31 as well as in 30 the translation theory is essentially founded on the application of a false key of interpretation leading to incorrect ontological statements which one tries to make 'correct' by interpreting them as disguised statements on language.

Now Wittgenstein is himself partly to be blamed for such mistakes in the interpretation of the Tractatus. As we have seen he tends to apply a false key of interpretation in his analysis of elementary sentences. Moreover mistakes of this kind are connected with an obscurity in the formulation of (X.6) which I think answers to a real obscurity in Wittgenstein's thinking.

In what way and to what extent does the internal structure of language exhibit the internal structure of reality? One aspect of this problem could be stated as follows: In what way and to what extent does the *categorial structure* of the system of elements of a *depicting language* exhibit the *categorial structure* of the system of elements of *reality*? Carnap's concept of the 'genus' of a symbol gives a starting point for an examination of this question.

Carnap's distinction between different genera of symbols corresponds to a distinction made by Wittgenstein between different 'forms' of symbols (cf. 3.31 ff.) with 'different *ways* of signification' or 'symbolizing' (3.321 ff.) What is called by Carnap a 'symbol' Wittgenstein calls a 'sign' (*Zeichen*), whereas to that which is called by Wittgenstein a 'symbol' belongs not only the 'sign' but also 'the way in which it signifies'. In short: Wittgensteinian 'symbol'= Carnapian 'symbol'[1]+Carnapian 'genus'. It follows that two *different* Wittgensteinian symbols can have the *sign* (which according to 3.32 is 'the part of the symbol perceptible by the senses') in *common* (3.321). Thus, for instance, 'in the sentence "Green is green"—where the first word is a proper name and the last an adjective—these words have not merely different meanings but they

---

[1] In this formulation I am disregarding the fact that a Carnapian 'symbol' is always 'simple' whereas a Wittgensteinian symbol may be compounded of other symbols.

are *different symbols*' (3.323). We see from this quotation that Wittgenstein's concept of a symbol, though it includes the 'way of symbolizing' of a sign, does not include its meaning. One and the same symbol might be used in different meanings.

For my present purpose I prefer to follow Carnap's rather than Wittgenstein's terminology.[1] A 'symbol' I shall take to mean a *type* of tokens as, for instance, the word 'green'. The difference between the two occurrences of 'green' in 'Green is green' I shall call a difference in 'genus' between two uses of the symbol 'green'. The 'genus' of a symbol can thus be characterized as a certain 'kind of symbolizing' which may be common to symbols with different meanings.

Symbols do not have a determinate 'genus' in ordinary language, as the example 'Green is green' shows. According to Wittgenstein this gives rise to 'the most fundamental confusions (of which the whole philosophy is full)' (3.324). 'In order to avoid these errors we must employ a symbolic language which excludes them', by not applying the same symbol in different genera and not applying symbols which symbolize in different ways in what to the eye appears as the same way. 'A symbolic language, that is to say, which obeys the rules of *logical* grammar—of logical syntax' (3.325). And Wittgenstein adds: 'The ideography of Frege and Russell is such a language, which, however, still does not exclude all errors.'

We see from this quotation that Wittgenstein introduces the idea of a 'logical syntax' as a kind of syntax which a 'perfect' language should possess *in opposition* to ordinary language, the syntax of which is not 'logical'. To possess a 'logical syntax' or not thus forms the difference between two *kinds* of language.

In Russell's introduction to the Tractatus we read (p. 7): 'In order to understand Mr. Wittgenstein's book, it is necessary to realize what is the problem with which he is concerned. In the part of his theory which deals with Symbolism he is concerned with the conditions which would have to be fulfilled by a logically perfect language.' This interpretation of the Tractatus seems to be confirmed by 3.325. However, the idea of a 'perfect' language reflecting the logical structure of the world has been much attacked in recent philosophy. Let us, therefore, examine the conception of 'logical syntax' as the syntax of a logically perfect language in some more detail.

---

[1] As to Wittgenstein's concept of a symbol, cf. above, p. 133 n.

What conditions should a language fulfil in order to have a logical syntax? According to 3.325 at least two conditions are considered necessary:

(i) Every symbol must have a definite genus.

(ii) Two symbols of different genera must not be used in what to the eye (*äusserlich*) appears as the same way.

In number 3.33 (cf. 3.317) an additional condition is stated:

(iii) Logical syntax 'must admit of being established without mention being thereby made of the *meaning* of a sign'.

Wittgenstein thinks that Russell's symbolism does not always fulfil this requirement: 'Russell's error' (in his *Theory of Types*) 'is shown by the fact that in drawing up his symbolic rules he has to speak about the things his signs mean' (3.331).

It is easy to outline a syntax which fulfils conditions (i) and (iii). In the present discussion we can restrict our analysis to such symbols as occur in semantical elementary sentences. We have then to take into consideration two kinds of genera: (a) names of individual objects, (b) characteristics of predicates with different numbers of places. We can without any reference to the meaning of symbols divide them into classes and prescribe that only the symbols of one class may be used as names of objects whereas only the symbols of another class may be used as characteristics of qualities, and so on. Stipulations of this kind are always adopted in symbolic logic.

Suppose now that conditions (i) and (iii) are fulfilled in this way. Does this mean that condition (ii) is also fulfilled? This depends on what we mean by being used in 'the same way to the eye'.

In 4.1211 Wittgenstein presents the following example of what language exhibits: 'Thus a sentence "*fa*" shows that in its sense the object *a* occurs . . .' But is this true? Is there any essential difference 'to the eye' between the ways in which the symbols '*f*' and '*a*' occur in '*fa*' showing that only the second can be understood as the name of an object? In one sense it is, because the difference between the symbols '*f*' and '*a*' is indeed not only a difference in meaning but also a difference in the way in which they occur in '*fa*'. But in another and important sense it is not: 'The sign determines a logical form only together with its use according to logical syntax (*seine logisch-syntaktische Verwendung*)', Wittgenstein says in 3.327; and this means that for the 'eye' to see any difference between these ways it must be accustomed to symbolic logic and 'know' the syntactical difference between the two symbols, thus 'knowing' that the fact '*fa*' *should* be analysed as a linguistic object '*a*' possessing the linguistic quality of 'being to the right of an "*f*" '. There is not, and cannot be, any *objective* feature in the field '*fa*' showing this to be the correct analysis of it. The *correctness* of this analysis is a matter of a *conventional* linguistic *rule*, and rules of this kind are an essential part of the 'logical syntax' of a symbolic language.

It follows that in one sense it is *impossible* even in a symbolic language *not* to use symbols of different genera in what 'to the eye' appears as 'the same way'. The 'eye' sees differences in genera *only* if it obeys the *rules* of logical syntax. But we need not be aware of the rules obeyed by the eye in this way. Therefore the construction of symbolic languages fulfilling certain conditions does not as such prevent us from making 'fundamental errors in philosophy'; and as the tendency to assume a false key of interpretation shows, such errors are really made in spite of the fact that we use a language fulfilling conditions (i) and (iii).

In order to avoid such errors we must be *aware* of the rules of 'logical syntax' obeyed in our language. But if this is so the essential difference between what is a 'rule of logical syntax' and what is not such a rule cannot be a difference between the syntactical rules *obeyed* in different languages, but must rather be a difference between two *kinds* of syntactical rules of one and the same language, i.e. between such syntactical rules as are called *logical* and such rules as are not so called, the former being relevant to the interpretation of the sentences in this language, the latter not. Thus the analysis of the sentence '*fa*' as an object '*a*' having the quality of being to the right of an '*f*' is a rule of *logical* syntax whereas the analysis of it as a series of symbols is not. In this sense of 'logical syntax', however, *every language* which can be used for description must have some kind of 'logical syntax'. There must be a logical syntax of natural languages as well as of symbolic languages. The fact that a language fulfils, for instance, condition (i) may make the rules of its logical syntax more conspicuous to a philosopher, but the rules obeyed cannot be said to be more 'logical' in one language than in another. (As for condition (iii) the situation is more complicated, since it seems to be possible to fulfil it to some extent in every language.) We may thus state:

(X.10)    *By 'logical syntax' is to be understood the rules of a logically correct syntactical analysis of the sentences in a language, not the 'syntax' of a logically correct language.*

But if this is so then 3.325 is incorrectly stated. And in fact Wittgenstein expresses a different opinion in other places in the Tractatus. As Ramsey objected in his review of the Tractatus (p. 270), Russell exaggerated Wittgenstein's concern with a logically perfect symbolism. Thus Wittgenstein states in 5.5563: 'All sentences of our colloquial language are actually, just as they are, logically completely in order.' And in 5.473 ff. he seems to adopt a line of thought which contradicts the necessity of condition (i) for a language to be 'logically correct'.

We read in 5.473: 'Everything which is possible in logic is also permitted. ("Socrates is identical" means nothing because there is no quality which is called "identical". The sentence is nonsensical because we have not made some arbitrary determination, not because the symbol is in itself unpermissible.)

This might be interpreted as follows: There is no need to say that 'Socrates is identical' is 'incorrect' according to logical syntax. In fact the logical syntax of English gives it a definite structure: 'Socrates' is the logical subject, and to be to the left of the words 'is identical' is the logical predicate. The sentence is nonsensical, *not* because logical syntax does not permit the use of the word 'identical' as a characteristic of a quality, but because we have not given the word 'identical' a meaning in *this* syntactical function. The fact that the word 'identical' has a meaning when it is used in *one* syntactical function does not provide it with a meaning when it is used in *another* syntactical function, because a different syntactical function presupposes a different *kind* of symbolizing. If we only remember *this* point (which is often overlooked by philosophers) philosophical errors can be avoided even in languages which do not fulfil condition (i).

That Wittgenstein means something of this kind is confirmed by 5.4733:

> 5.4733    Frege says: Every legitimately constructed sentence must have a sense; and I say: Every possible sentence is legitimately constructed, and if it has no sense this can only be because we have given no *meaning* to some of its constituent parts. (Even if we believe that we have done so.)
> Thus 'Socrates is identical' says nothing, because we have given *no* meaning to the word 'identical' as *adjective*. For when it occurs as the sign of equality it symbolizes in an entirely different way—the symbolizing relation is another—

therefore the symbol is in the two cases entirely different; the two symbols have the sign in common only by accident.

If our language does not fulfil condition (i) a *philosopher* must remember that the fact that a word has a meaning when used in one syntactical function does not provide it with a meaning when it is used in another syntactical function. But a person who *uses* this language in accordance with its logical syntax need not even 'remember' this, because it is *impossible* to give a word a meaning which does not fit its syntactical function. 'Socrates is identical' *cannot* be interpreted according to the ordinary meaning of 'identical'—its elements do not have the right categorial structure. 'We *cannot* give a sign the wrong sense' in this way (5.4732, italics mine) and therefore 'in a certain sense we cannot make mistakes in logic' (5.473)— our 'mistakes in logic' are philosophical mistakes as to how language functions, not mistakes in how logic is applied.

If 'logical syntax' is understood in this way it comprises the rules at which a philosopher arrives if he succeeds in giving a correct account of the rules actually applied when language is used as a means of description. The Name Theory of Linguistic Meaning is founded on a crude misapprehension of 'logical syntax' in this sense. And though Frege had taken a step in the right direction by distinguishing between symbols for objects and 'unsaturated' symbols for 'concepts' (cf. above, p. 138 n.), he, too, went wrong on Wittgenstein's view, when he did not realize that it is essential to logical syntax that a sentence-token should be considered as a fact, not as a thing. Frege conceived of a sentence-token as a thing, and as a consequence of this he regarded a sentence as a 'complex name' (3.143) and thus got a wrong idea of the function of sentences as well as of names.

If 'logical syntax' is taken in this sense we could express an important consequence of the picture theory of sentence meaning as follows (cf. X.2):

(X.11)   *If the sentence-token of a semantical elementary sentence is analysed in accordance with logical syntax, its elements exhibit the categorial structure of the elements they stand for.*

There is, however, one point which is to be observed in regard to 5.4733 in the same way as in regard to 4.1211 (cf. p. 190). It is true

o

that 'Socrates is identical' *cannot* be interpreted according to the ordinary meaning of 'identical' and that it *could* be interpreted *if* the word 'identical' were given a meaning as a characteristic of a quality (cf. above, p. 138). But one must not overlook the fact that what is 'true' in this way is true only relatively to the *rules* of logical syntax. And in themselves these rules are as *conventional* as the 'arbitrary determination' according to which the word 'identical' is, or is not, given a meaning as a characteristic of a quality. *Every* series of symbols is in fact a 'possible sentence' in the sense that it can be interpreted as a sentence by means of suitable conventions—in many different ways.

This observation is important for the following reason. If one says that the internal structure of language exhibits the internal structure of reality one can mean two different things by this. Either one can mean that there is an internal structure which is *common* to all languages and which every 'possible' language *must* possess as a consequence of a 'logical necessity', and that this internal '*a priori*' structure reflects the internal structure of reality in the sense that reality must possess this internal structure in order to be capable of being described in 'language', i.e. in any language whatsoever. Or one can mean that *every* language must possess an internal structure of its *own*, and that this internal structure reflects the internal structure of any piece of reality describable in *this* language.

Now I think both of these views are incorrect; but the first is more incorrect than the second, and Wittgenstein does not make a clear distinction between them. This means that he tends to think of what is 'possible in logic' in accordance with the first view—and this fact seems to play an essential part in his metaphysical argument. Moreover the critics of the 'picture theory of language' seem to take for granted that *this* is what the 'picture theory' intends to say. 'Language' *qua* language, or at least, every sufficiently 'perfect' language reflects the internal structure of all reality describable in sentences. And since this idea seems to contain some doubtful kind of linguistic metaphysics, one is tempted to infer that the underlying semantical theory must be wrong.

But the picture theory of sentence meaning does not in itself entail such metaphysical views. One should be careful in taking (X.11) as meaning that 'the categorial structure of Language' reflects the 'categorial structure of Reality'. The conventional character of logical syntax and the possibility of giving the *same* series of symbols *different* categorial structures according as the rules of logical syntax are chosen indicates that one cannot speak of such a thing as a categorial structure of '*language*' in general, but at most only of 'categorial structures' of different *languages*.

We can roughly characterize the situation in this way. There are two kinds of conventions governing the semantical use of a language $L$, which may be called 'rules of logical syntax' and 'logical or semantical rules' in the narrow sense. According to the rules of logical syntax the presentation of certain series of symbols in $L$—we may call such series *syntactical elementary sentences*—are to be apprehended as facts which are analysed in a *definite* way into a system of *syntactical objects* possessing a *syntactical predicate*. The system of all syntactical objects—we count here different tokens of the same type as occurrences of the 'same' syntactical object (cf. above, p. 147)—and all syntactical predicates occurring in any syntactical elementary sentences could be called the system of *syntactical elements* in $L$. The system of syntactical elements has a *definite* categorial structure, and this may be called the *categorial structure of* (the system of elements in) $L$. But independently of the rules of logical syntax there are no such things as 'elements' in a language and *a fortiori* no such thing as a 'categorial structure' of them. Thus we may state:

(X.12)   *Only relatively to the rules of logical syntax can a language possess a definite system of elements with a definite categorial structure.*

If we want to give some kind of 'list' of the syntactical elements in $L$ we encounter difficulties as to how to indicate the predicative elements. In practice we can proceed in this way. We indicate a predicative element by means of a 'matrix', i.e. a model of the syntactical elementary sentences in which it occurs as an element. Thus we can speak of the 'syntactical quality "$fx$"' meaning the *quality* which '$x$' has in '$fx$' (i.e. the quality of standing to the right of an '$f$'), and so on. By 'substituting' a syntactical *object*—say '$a$'—for '$x$' in this 'matrix' we attribute the quality '$fx$' to '$a$' and thus form a fact, i.e. the syntactical elementary sentence '$fa$'.

In regard to elementary sentences the part played by logical syntax is thus to define the *syntactical* elements and the *syntactical* elementary sentences in a language. Now *syntactical* elementary sentences are not in themselves *semantical* elementary sentences: in order to be so they must be interpreted. And the interpretation must in some way be determined by the semantical rules of L.

Let us assume that the semantical rules of L are of a very simple kind: to every syntactical element of L they attach a uniquely determined element of reality and thus establish a *one-one* correspondence between the elements of L and certain elements of reality; we may call this one-one correspondence the *semantical key* of L. In order to function as a key according to which the syntactical elementary sentences of L really *can* be interpreted the semantical key must be *appropriate* to the logical syntax of L—i.e. the elements of reality must have the same category as the corresponding syntactical elements. Thus the system of these elements must have the same categorial structure as the system of syntactical elements in L. We may therefore state:

(X.13)  *For the syntactical elementary sentences to be interpretable the semantical key must be appropriate to the logical syntax.*

(X.14)  *In order to be describable in a language L with a one-one semantical key reality must possess the categorial structure shown by the system of the syntactical elements in L.*

In this, but only in this, restricted sense, a depicting language L can be said to 'exhibit' the categorial structure of reality.

In the formulation of (X.14) the reference to a one-one semantical key is essential. However, the clue-theory of meaning (cf. above, p. 140) shows that this condition is not fulfilled in an ordinary language. So, for instance, there is not a one-one correspondence between the syntactical objects functioning as names of individuals and the objects they name. At the most some proper names may have a unique denominatum. But proper names are actually strangers in the system of language; as a rule the denominata of all 'names' in language vary according to the context.

Wittgenstein obviously thought that a 'perfect' symbolism should be founded on the principle that to every name corresponds a unique denominatum. This principle is also essentially presupposed in semantical systems as investigated by, for instance, Carnap.[1] But does the acceptance of this principle mean an 'improvement' of

[1] See, for instance, *Meaning and Necessity.*

language? In many respects it does not. Within the framework of a particular description the establishment of a one-one semantical key may be both possible and suitable. Moreover it must be remembered that *if* a given description is to be capable of being transformed into a system of alternative isomorphic pictures, there must at least exist *definite devices* according to which the system of elements used in this description can be transformed into a system of elements that are in one-one correspondence with the elements of the piece of reality described. But the idea of a depicting language is not tied up with the principle that the elements of a language are capable of being put into a one-one correspondence with the elements of reality *once for all*. If we have established such a correspondence once for all, then we have not, in effect, created a system capable of functioning as a 'language' in the ordinary sense, but only a systematic *notation*. Even in its descriptive capacity a 'language' presupposes a greater flexibility than that allowed for by a one-one semantical key.

The importance of this point is emphasized by the fact that what is described in language is always an articulate field with a *definite* external structure. But reality as a fact is—like series of symbols as facts—capable of being analysed in different ways. Before we can give any definite description of a piece of reality we must articulate this piece of reality in a certain way. What can be exhibited in language is the categorial structure of the elements of reality as *articulated* in a definite way, not the 'categorial structure of reality' in an absolute sense.

### 5. LOGICAL RULES

'Logical syntax' as we have treated it here comprises the rules of a logically correct syntactical analysis of sentences, the word 'syntactical' being taken in a way roughly agreeing with a grammarian's usage. But when Wittgenstein speaks of 'logical syntax' he—like Carnap—includes in it not only the syntactical analysis of sentences but also all that is usually regarded as belonging to 'formal logic' (cf. in particular 6.124). His idea is obviously that 'formal logic' is 'formal' in the same way as 'logical syntax' is 'formal'. For my part I prefer to make a definite distinction between 'logical syntax' and 'formal logic', the former being only a part of the latter.

In the preceding section we investigated the validity of (X.6) with regard to the 'categorial structure' of the elements of reality. In this section I shall proceed to the 'logical interrelations' between the predicative elements as treated in Chapter V, section 6. If we take 'internal structure' in an extended sense (cf. above, p. 182) we may also reckon as 'logical interrelations' belonging to the internal structure of reality the interrelations between a 'complex predicate' and the elements into which it is thought to be 'analysable', and so on. According to (X.6) all such interrelations are 'shown' in some way by the formal logic of language. We will now consider how far and in what way this can be true.

In the concept of 'formal logic' the notions 'formal' and 'logic' are both vague. The word 'formal' is, of course, to be understood here in the meaning of 'pertaining to the linguistic expression' (see above, Ch. VI, § 10), and 'formal logic' thus refers to a kind of 'logic' that can be established by the examination of linguistic expressions without reference to their 'meaning' or 'sense'. But it is not quite clear what the 'without' is to mean here.

It seems, however, obvious that logical connections belonging to the internal structure of reality—as for instance the fact that the qualities 'red' and 'blue' exclude each other—do not belong to *formal* logic. We must also assume that Wittgenstein does not—like Carnap—regard such interrelations as 'disguised' formal interrelations. That formal logic 'shows' the logical interrelations of reality means only that the existence or non-existence of logical connections in reality are shown by the existence or non-existence of, in some sense, 'corresponding' connections in formal logic.

It follows that the 'logical interrelations' of reality are 'logical' in a peculiar way. When we speak of 'logic' we usually think of some kind of 'rules' for a correct use of language. But the logical connection between two colours is not 'logical' in this sense. It has no reference to logical rules but is founded in the nature of those qualities themselves. We shall call such logical interrelations '*intrinsic* logical interrelations'. An intrinsic logical interrelation can consist of either the existence or the non-existence of an intrinsic logical connection.

Now we have stated in (X.3) that the elements of a 'logical', i.e. (logically) adequate, picture exhibit the logical form of the elements they stand for. This means, among other things, that the existence or non-existence of intrinsic logical connections between the predicative elements of the prototype is shown by the existence of the *same* intrinsic logical interrelations between the corresponding elements in the picture.

One might suppose that it is in this way that formal logic, too, is assumed to show the logical interrelations of reality; i.e. that (predicative) names 'show' by their own intrinsic logical interrelations the logical interrelations between the 'things' they stand for.

But what kind of intrinsic logical interrelations are there between names? Consider a symbolic language L with a definite logical syntax. Suppose that among the elements of L occur the syntactical qualities '$fx$' and '$gx$' and the syntactical object '$a$'. By attributing the qualities '$fx$' and '$gx$' to '$a$' we can form two facts, the sentences '$fa$' and '$ga$'; and the forming of one of these facts does not in itself make it impossible to form the other. The fact that a syntactical object possesses the syntactical quality '$fx$' does not *in itself* prevent the *same* object (in the sense, that is, in which we speak of the 'same' syntactical object) from possessing the quality '$gx$' or conversely. *Intrinsically* the syntactical qualities '$fx$' and '$gx$' can be said to be *logically independent*.

The same is true of all syntactical predicates. There are no intrinsic logical connections between syntactical predicates. All 'syntactical' elementary states of affairs are *mutually independent*. Therefore the internal structure of the system of names in a language must correspond to a yes-and-no space.

*If* the logical interrelations between the denominata of names is to be the *same* as the *intrinsic* logical relations between the names, then there can be no logical connections between the denominata of names. If formal logic 'shows' the logic of reality in *this* way, the internal structure of the elements of the reality described in a language *must necessarily correspond to a yes-and-no space*.

How far did this fact contribute to Wittgenstein's view that the internal structure of substance must correspond to a yes-and-no space? For my part I believe that it did so to a considerable extent. There are several statements in the Tractatus which can be regarded as indicating that formal logic shows what it shows by the intrinsic logical properties of 'symbols'. So, for instance, this seems to be implied by 6.124: '. . . We said that in the symbols which we use something is arbitrary, something not. In logic only the latter expresses: but this means that in logic it is not *we* who express, by means of signs, what we want; in logic the nature of inevitably necessary (*naturnotwendig*) signs itself expresses . . .'

We might construct a 'Wittgensteinian' argument of the following kind. Suppose that we introduce in a symbolic language the syntactical elements '$Rx$' and '$Bx$' to signify the qualities red and blue, and that '$a$' is the name of an object. Consider the sentence

(5)                          $Ra$ & $Ba$

The form of this sentence suggests that it could be understood as a depicting sentence presenting the state of affairs that $a$ possesses at one and the same time the qualities red and blue. Since the 'possibility' of a state of affairs means that it can be presented by a picture (see above, Ch. VI, §§ 6 and 13) the existence of sentence (5) would, if it were interpretable in the way suggested by its form, prove the possibility of this state of affairs. But now such a state of affairs is in fact logically impossible. Therefore the form of (5) does not correspond to thought (cf. 4.002). Sentence (5) cannot be analysed in *this* way in a depicting language, i.e. '$Ra$' and '$Ba$' cannot be elementary sentences, which are understood as pictures.

Since what (5) tries to say is logically impossible, a correct analysis of (5) must consist of a translation of it into a sentence which shows that it *cannot* be transformed into a picture, i.e. a translation of it into a contradiction in the truth-functional sense.[1] It follows that '$Rx$' and '$Bx$' are not names but 'signify indirectly', and thus refer to 'complexes' (cf. above, pp. 65, 76 and 124 f.). A corresponding analysis applies to every occurrence of logical *connections* between the 'meanings' of what at first appears as 'names'. All denominata of true names must therefore be mutually independent. And that this must be so is proved by an analysis of how a correct language works.

Now I do not believe this was *the* kind of argument by which Wittgenstein arrived at his doctrine of the logical independence of atomic predicates. On the whole I think the assumption that Wittgenstein was led to any of his fundamental views in the Tractatus by one determinate argument would not do justice to Wittgenstein's thinking. But since the picture theory of sentence meaning has been believed to imply this doctrine, and since an argument of the above kind seems to me to be the only one which could lead him from the one to the other, it is important to see how it is wrong.

---

[1] A truth-functional contradiction shows, that is, that the system of alternative picture-fields which correspond to it is vacuous. Cf. above, p. 156, n.2.

The error in it is founded on the assumption that every picture must be an adequate picture, i.e. that the adequacy of the key of interpretation is essential to the functioning of a picture. As we have seen this is not so (cf. above, Ch. VI, § 8, and in particular, theses (VI.6) and (VI.6')) and this means with regard to language that the picture theory of sentence meaning *allows* for the use of an inadequate semantical key. But if the key is inadequate—and here only an inadequacy of what we have called the 'first' kind (pp. 103 ff.) can occur[1]—then there are 'impossible' pictures, that is, picture-fields which cannot be interpreted as presenting a state of affairs by means of the key. Therefore the fact that (5) does not present a possible state of affairs does not prove that the analysis of it suggested by its form is incorrect, and consequently it does not prove, either, that '*Ra*' and '*Ba*' are not 'elementary' sentences, which are understood as pictures, or that '*Rx*' and '*Bx*' are not 'names', which can be understood directly as deputizing symbols. What the existence of contradictory sentences which are not contradictory in the truth-functional sense proves is simply *that* the semantical key is 'inadequate', i.e. *that* the denominata of names are *not* independent like the names themselves but logically connected.

We have stated in (X.4') that the elements of a picture-field cannot show whether the picture is 'logical' or not. It follows with regard to language that *no* kind of *intrinsic* formal properties of syntactical elements can show whether the semantical key is adequate or not, and thus no such properties show whether there are 'logical connections' between the denominata of names or not. In this sense 'formal logic' does not 'show' the logical interrelations in reality.

There is, however, another sense in which 'formal logic' *could* be said to 'show' the logical interrelations in the reality described in a language. According to Wittgenstein the fact *that* a certain sentence is a tautology or contradiction 'shows' the logical properties of the world (cf. 6.12, 6.124, 6.1202). Now Wittgenstein seems to think that this applies to 'tautologies' or 'contradictions' in the truth-functional sense, and this a closer examination shows to be a confused idea.[2] But with regard to contradictions like (5) the pro-

---

[1] This is so, because a yes-and-no structure means the greatest possible 'logical freedom' in internal structure.

[2] The rules of truth-functional logic 'show' how sentences are to be transformed into picture-fields, and thus tell us something about language, but they do not tell us anything about how these picture-fields are to be interpreted and therefore they show nothing about reality. Cf. above, pp. 149 ff., and 166.

posed kind of 'showing' is important. That (5) is a contradiction means that it does not 'show' externally a possible state of affairs. But *that* this is so 'shows' internally that the denominata of the names '*Rx*' and '*Bx*' exclude each other. The fact *that* sentence (5) is a contradiction can thus be said to form a 'logical connection' between the names '*Rx*' and '*Bx*', which 'shows' the existence of a logical connection between their denominata. Now one can know such 'logical interrelations' between names without knowing exactly *what* denominata they stand for. The totality of 'logical interrelations' of this kind could be called the '*logic of (predicative) names*' of a language. It comprises an indication of *all* sentences which are contradictions without being so in the truth-functional sense, and thus also of all sentences that are consistent. If 'formal logic' is understood to include the 'logic of names' in this sense, it could therefore be said to 'show' the logical interrelations in the reality described in a language.

But it is important that the logical interrelations in the logic of names are not 'logical interrelations' in the same sense as the logical interrelations they show. The 'logical interrelations' according to the logic of names are not *intrinsic* interrelations between predicative names but *rules* which partly determine the choice of the semantical key. Thus *conventional rules* again play an important part in what language 'shows', and these rules may be different in different languages.[1]

The possibility of treating the logic of names as a part of the 'formal logic' of a language is important from the following point of view. We have seen that the Tractatus defines 'thought' as a 'logical picture' (true or false) of reality. Now we could accept this idea in the way it is treated in Chapter VI (§ 13), even though we do not admit that every picture must be 'logical', and thus retain the important idea that the 'possibility' of a state of affairs simply means that it is 'thinkable'. But if 'thinking' is to form an *adequate* ('logical') picture of reality, then, in a way, the 'form' of a sentence like (5) does indeed not correspond to thought. The intrinsic yes-and-no structure of language 'disguises' thought, since thought

---

[1] It is to be noted that this is so even if all denominata of predicative names are mutually logically independent. A language in which *all* logical contradictions are contradictions in the truth-functional sense is not a language in which we have dispensed with the rules of a logic of names, but one in which the logic of names consists in the *rule* that only mutually independent predicates may be chosen as denominata of predicative names. Cf. above, p. 75.

operates, or at least, is capable of operating, with many-valued dimensions and other logical connections between predicates.

But what the intrinsic internal structure of language disguises is exhibited by the logical *rules* adopted in a language. If we know the rules of names in a language L, then we know which descriptions in L are consistent and thus present 'possible' states of affairs. In this way the logic of names determines a 'logical space' of consistent descriptions, which in its turn determines what could be called the 'internal structure' of the syntactical elements '*as defined* by the logic of names'. And since the rules of the logic of names are rules which restrict the choice of the semantical key, this *must* be 'adequate' relatively to the logic of names, and thus the logic of names, in which thought expresses itself in language, 'shows' the intrinsic logic of the system of elements to which thought refers.

To sum up: the picture theory of sentence meaning does not imply that sentences depict states of affairs *adequately*. Therefore reality need not have any special kind of internal structure in order to be describable in a depicting language. A language 'shows' the internal structure of the reality described in it only *relatively* to certain syntactical and logical *rules*, according to which this language is used.[1] And those rules can be chosen differently in different languages and also are actually chosen differently in the same language according to the context.

## 6. ELEMENTARY SENTENCES

Before we finish our analysis of (X.6) one aspect of the concept of elementary sentences in the Tractatus remains to be mentioned. We have thought of a depicting sentence as being a truth-function of semantical elementary sentences. This means that we have given semantical elementary sentences two functions in a depicting language. On the one hand the key of interpretation applies only to names; and names occur directly only in semantical elementary sentences. Thus the semantical elementary sentences are those sentences through which a depicting language is brought into *contact with reality*. I shall characterize this function of semantical elementary sentences by calling them *semantical primitive sentences*.

On the other hand the semantical elementary sentences are those

---

[1] A similar account could be given of the relation between language and a logically 'unhomogeneous' system of denominata, as treated in Ch. V, § 7.

sentences of which all other sentences are truth-functions. I shall characterize this function of semantical elementary sentences by calling them *logical basic sentences*.

Our conception of a depicting language is certainly in accordance with Wittgenstein's view so far—the difference being only that the elements of reality to which the names refer must according to Wittgenstein be the substance of the world, whereas we have thought of them as elements only of some articulate field which may vary according to the context.

But let us think of a physicist making a description of some phenomena. Does this conception of a depicting language correspond to the language he uses?

We might answer that a physicist uses *two* kinds of depicting language. There is one language used by him rather as a theoretical physicist—we may call it his *theoretical* language—the elements of which refer to such concepts as, say, atoms, electrons, neutrons, coordinates, etc. And there is another language used by him rather as an experimental physicist—we may call it his *experimental* language—the elements of which refer to his apparatus, i.e. to objects and predicates which can be in some sense indicated ostensively.

Now our conception of a depicting language seems to correspond fairly well to the physicist's *experimental* language. But in respect to his *theoretical* language there are at least two respects in which it is inappropriate:

(i) The elementary sentences of the theoretical language are, to be sure, logical *basic* sentences, but they are not semantical *primitive* sentences.

(ii) The elementary sentences of the theoretical language do not, at least not as a rule, occur explicitly in descriptions. All theoretical descriptions are general and contain explicitly only the *forms* of the elementary sentences of which they are truth-functions.

Feature (ii) is only one aspect of feature (i). That (i) is true is seen from the fact that it is the physicist's *experimental* language which brings his theories into contact with reality. What brings his *theoretical* language into contact with reality is therefore not the basic sentences of this language but the fact that his experimental and theoretical languages are logically connected. If there were no such connection there would be no contact between theoretical physics and reality.

This does not, however, mean that the physicist's theoretical language could not be regarded as a 'depicting' language, even if there were not such a connection. But it means that it is a depicting language rather in the sense in which we have spoken of *fictitious* pictures in Chapter VI, § 11 (cf. also Chapter VII, § 9). To be more exact its sentences correspond to what we called there pictures presenting a 'pure structure'. And they can be understood as depicting sentences of this kind without any reference to reality at all.

But now there *exists* a logical connection between the physicist's theoretical and experimental language. This connection we might imagine to be roughly of the following kind. The *elementary* sentences of the *experimental* language are in some way definable in terms of the elementary sentences of the theoretical language. I.e. if 'P' is an elementary sentence of the experimental language we can write:

(6)                        Df.   $P = F(p,q,..)$

where $F(p, q, ..$  ) means a truth-function of elementary sentences in the theoretical language.

According to such views as are called doctrines of 'logical constructions' the system of all defining equations of type (6) ought to be in some way solvable in respect to the elementary sentences $p,q, ..$ so as to make it possible to define all the physicist's theoretical statements in terms of his experimental sentences. I will not discuss here the idea of such a possibility as an *epistemological* theory. I only want to emphasize that such a possibility is in any case unimportant from a *semantical* point of view. Even if a conversion of definitions of type (6) *were* possible this does not explain how the physicist's theoretical language is understood. *Semantically* the sentences of this language are understood as fictitious descriptions, which are 'applied' to reality only by means of definitions of the type (6) or some other device of a similar kind.

In fact there is nothing to prevent us from constructing an intelligible depicting language which is brought into contact with reality only by means of definitions of type (6). The fact that Wittgenstein does not take this possibility into consideration in the Tractatus is one aspect of his tendency to identify the concept of a sign which 'signifies directly' with an 'indefinable sign' (cf. Ch. VII,

§ 2). Thus one of the main sources of Wittgenstein's logical atomism could be said to be his attempt to have elementary sentences functioning in three capacities which they cannot fulfil at one and the same time, i.e. (a) as semantical primitive sentences, (b) as logical basic sentences in science, (c) as a sort of epistemological basic sentences. And behind it all we can trace an overestimation of the importance of Russell's theory of descriptions.

## 7. VARIABLES AND THE THEORY OF TYPES

In theses (X.5) and (X.6) we formulated a negative and a positive statement on the relation between language and the internal structure of reality. In the preceding sections we have directed many criticisms against the positive statement. But as for the negative statement, it remains unaffected by these criticisms. And indeed, in a depicting language we *cannot describe* the internal structure of reality; if it is to be shown at all it must be shown in some other way. From the acceptance of this fact there is no escape. *Ontological statements can neither be translated into ordinary descriptive statements about language nor reformulated as depicting statements in any other way.*

In a depicting language ontological statements cannot be formulated. Wittgenstein illustrates this fact by some interesting examples. One is stated in 4.1272, where we read that 'the variable name "$x$" is the proper sign for the pseudo-concept *object*'. Now I do not think this is a very happy formulation; but what Wittgenstein means is obviously this. Suppose that we try to introduce a syntactical quality '$Ox$' into a depicting language as a 'name' of the 'quality' of being an object. We must remember that 'the syntactical quality "$Ox$" ' means the quality which symbol '$x$' possesses in '$Ox$'. If we substitute a name of an object, say '$a$' for '$x$' in the matrix '$Ox$' we attach this syntactical quality to the object '$a$' and thus form the sentence '$Oa$'. Now this sentence may *appear* to describe a as being an object, though it is in fact tautological and thus describes 'nothing'. But suppose that we try to say that a quality, say the quality 'red', which may be denoted by the syntactical quality '$fx$', is *not* an object. We might try to do this by forming the expression '$\sim Of$' or '$\sim Ofx$'. But both of these expressions are in fact nonsensical, because the expressions '$Of$' and '$Ofx$' are nonsensical.

We could explain why '$Of$' is nonsensical in this way: for '$Of$'

to be a sentence, it must, according to our logical syntax, be analysed into the syntactical *object* ' *f* ' and the syntactical predicate '*Ox*'. For such a syntactical sentence to have a sense, the symbol '*f*' must be the name of an *object*. But we have not given '*f*' any meaning as the name of an object, only as the characteristic of a name of a predicate (cf. above, p. 192).

Why '*Ofx*' is nonsensical we might rather explain thus: on the one hand what signifies in '*fx*' is the *syntactical quality* which '*x*' possesses in '*fx*', on the other hand '*Ofx*' can be a sentence only if '*fx*' is taken as a syntactical *object*. Thus logical syntax does not give this expression any structure as a sentence.

We might sum up this argument as follows:

(X.15)   *It is impossible to substitute a syntactical quality for a variable ranging over syntactical objects.*

We *cannot* substitute the name of a quality in the matrix '*Ox*', and therefore '*Ox*' *cannot* function as the 'name' of the 'quality' of being an object. The same difficulty arises whenever we try to interpret a syntactical predicate as standing for an 'internal' characteristic, or— to use Wittgenstein's terminology—'formal property'. Thus, for example, 'it would be as nonsensical to ascribe a formal property to a sentence as to deny it the formal property' (4.124).

What we have said in (X.15) could also be expressed in this way: a variable ranging over syntactical objects is *itself* a syntactical object. And we cannot substitute other entities than objects for syntactical objects. The corresponding statement holds true of variables for predicates. Thus the category of a variable 'shows' the category of the syntactical entities substitutable for it.

It follows that a syntactical quality can *never* be substituted for the variable of its own matrix. It is *impossible* to attach a syntactical quality to itself. And this logical fact is according to Wittgenstein 'the whole theory of types' (3.331–3.333).

We shall not discuss here how far this fact can really be said to be the 'whole' theory of types. But at least it must be regarded as an important aspect of this theory.

## 8. PHILOSOPHY AS AN ACTIVITY

Since Wittgenstein thinks all language properly so called to be depicting language it is consistent enough that he should regard all philosophical statements as nonsensical. But the use of this terminology is certainly not only a matter of consistency. Wittgenstein would not have said that all philosophical statements were nonsensical if this had not fitted into his general philosophical outlook. We may express it in this way. Wittgenstein does not call nondepicting sentences nonsensical merely *because* he thinks all language properly so called is depicting, but the *converse* is equally true. The distinction between 'depicting' and 'non-depicting' sentences conforms well to the distinction he wants to make between 'sense' and 'nonsense'.

From this point of view it is interesting to consider the question how far we could do *without* non-depicting sentences. What inconveniences would result, if all language *were* really depicting language?

Wittgenstein's answer to this question would probably follow this line:

As for the *external* structure of reality, we can describe it in a depicting language. Thus non-depicting sentences are unnecessary in genuine descriptions of the world. Our need for a non-depicting language can therefore be said to be of three kinds:

(i) To make statements as to how language works.

(ii) To make statements on the *internal* structure of reality or language. But as soon as we know how language works it *shows* its own internal structure and in consequence also the internal structure of reality. We need not *describe* it.

(iii) To make statements on what can be neither 'shown' nor 'said'. But if we understand how language works we see that such statements are nonsensical in a remarkable degree. They result from questions which misuse logical syntax in the same way as the question 'whether the Good is more or less identical than the Beautiful'. Thus 'it is no wonder that the deepest problems are properly speaking *not* problems' (4.003); and it is important to one's general outlook to realize that this is so.

There remain the statements of the first kind, and these form the domain of semantical analysis. But in fact non-depicting statements of this kind have only a preparatory function; they become superfluous when we have understood how language works. Thus we can say that the *need* for non-depicting sentences of this kind vanishes as soon as we learn to see clearly what they try to state. 'The purpose of philosophy is the logical clarification of thoughts.

Philosophy is not a theory but an activity. A philosophical work consists essentially of elucidations. The result of philosophy is not a number of philosophical statements, but to make sentences[1] clear. Philosophy should make clear and delimit sharply the thoughts which are otherwise, as it were, opaque and blurred' (4.112). And since the philosophical activity confirms that philosophical statements are not genuine 'statements', we must not believe them to be so: therefore it is important that he who understands the statements of the Tractatus 'finally recognizes them as nonsensical' (6.54).

It should be observed that the classification of non-depicting sentences used in this argument is not explicitly stated in the Tractatus; but I think it is useful, if we try to understand how far such an argument can be considered correct. Moreover I think it is in effect implicitly made in Wittgenstein's philosophy. We shall return to it in the next chapter.

Now it is plausible to think that a community *could* do without non-depicting statements to a great extent. If we take into consideration the conventional component in the concept of internal structure we might say that we need not *describe* the internal structure of reality or language: we simply *choose* a certain internal structure as a framework for descriptions of a certain kind. And since we can *use* a language correctly without being aware of how it works there is no basic need either for a *description* of how language works.

But could we in any sense do *philosophy* in a depicting language? I shall not undertake any detailed analysis of this question. From a semantical point of view there are two questions of great interest which are related to it. If philosophical statements are in effect no 'statements' at all, is there any other way in which we could communicate our philosophical opinions? And apart from this: philosophical statements could not even have a preparatory function, if we did not understand them in *some* way. What is this way?

## 9. THE LOGICAL MOOD

In order to elucidate the first of these questions we will examine the problem of 'logical sentences'.

Since all logical sentences are tautologies, all logical sentences say the *same* thing, that is, nothing. This is Wittgenstein's opinion

---

[1] I have translated one of the two occurrences of the word *Sätze* in this proposition as 'statements', the other as 'sentences'.

P

(5.43), and on the one hand it seems to follow inevitably from the definition of a 'logical sentence'. But on the other hand it seems to be absurd in some way.

One could try to solve the dilemma in this way: we must distinguish between a first order sentence '$p$' and the metastatement '$p$ is a tautology'. That the first order statement says nothing does not imply, or at least, *need* not imply that the metastatement says nothing. To be sure, the metastatement is a non-depicting sentence, because it states something 'internal' either about reality or about language; and it cannot be reformulated as a 'depicting sentence'; but it can nevertheless have a 'descriptive content' according to some other kind of interpretation. If therefore a 'logical sentence' is interpreted as a disguised metastatement it need not say 'nothing' after all.

But in fact we can account for the felt difference in 'meaning' between different 'tautologies' without assuming that they have a 'disguised content'.

Consider the tautologies

(7)                     It is raining or it is not raining,

and

(8)                     If it is raining it is raining.

Though we have the feeling that (7) and (8) differ in 'meaning' I think nobody would deny that neither of them gives any information about the weather, and that their descriptive content is empty at least in *this* sense (cf. 4.461). If these sentences are used to give information about the weather they really say the same, that is, nothing. Since we nevertheless conceive of them as having different 'meaning', we must feel that they are *not* used for giving information about the weather but to some different purpose. And the fact that we ask here for the purpose for which a sentence is used suggests that the felt difference in 'meaning' between sentences (7) and (8) is connected with their *modal* import rather than with their descriptive content.

And indeed, if we examine the defining rule of the indicative mood in Chapter IX, we see that it can be used to direct the listener's attention to a 'logical fact' as well as to an external fact of reality. The necessary condition for a sentence to be modally true is that the sentence-radical is descriptively true. Now this condition is certainly fulfilled if the sentence-radical is a tautology. To utter sentence (7) or (8) in the indicative is therefore a correct move in the modal game. But since the purpose of this move cannot be to direct the listener's attention to an external fact it must be to direct his attention to the logical fact *that* the sentence-radical is tautological. But if this is the purpose of the move then it is of course not indifferent which of the two tautologies one utters. Therefore we feel a difference in 'meaning' between them.

Whether it is a good terminology to say that (7) and (8) really *have* a different 'modal import' when they are used in the indicative mood I will not discuss here.

In ordinary language we often use indicatives without being clear whether they are intended to give information about external or logical facts. In the logician's language-game, however, this difference is perfectly clear. Actually a logician does not use tautologies in the indicative mood, but rather in what could be called a 'logical mood', the defining rule of which could be stated thus:

(X.16)     *Do not produce a sentence in the logical mood unless it is a logical truth, i.e. unless its descriptive content is empty.*

And if used in the logical mood sentences (7) and (8) must *definitely* be taken to have different modal sense, though their descriptive content is the same.

By applying the logical mood to a tautology in the logic of names one can inform a listener of a feature in the internal structure of reality. This shows that the introduction of different moods in a depicting language can serve as a substitute for at least some kinds of philosophical statements.

## 10. SYNTACTICAL METAPHORS

But not all non-depicting statements can be dispensed with in this way. And even if they were there remains the fact that non-depicting sentences *can* be understood, and that there must be some way in which they are understood.

I said earlier that the most interesting feature in the picture theory of sentence meaning is the fact that it allows for stating which is the way sentences differ from pictures. One such way is shown by the possibility of non-depicting statements. Such statements are found

P*

not only in philosophy but also, for instance, in mathematics. Thus the concept of an isomorphism is a mathematical concept, but it is obviously defined in a non-depicting language. So non-depicting language *can* be perfectly clear.

But this does not imply that the picture-theory of sentence meaning must be wrong. It must be wrong *only* if we believe that it really accounts as such for *all* kinds of meaning of sentences.

In fact the picture theory of sentence meaning can be regarded as *fundamental* also to an understanding of how non-depicting language works. The semantics of non-depicting language is an interesting subject which cannot be treated at all in this book. But to illustrate the fundamental character of the picture theory we shall examine one example. Consider the statement:

(9)                    Red is not an object.

We have seen in section 7 why this statement cannot be formulated in a depicting language. Does not the fact that we have formulated it here make this observation unimportant? But *do* we really understand sentence (9)? A traditional objection to it is that it forms some kind of contradiction in terms. In order to say that red is not an object one must presuppose that red *is* an object; but at the same time one denies this to be so. And this objection means exactly an application of the semantics of *depicting* language to a non-depicting sentence. Red is a quality and to be an object is a categorial characteristic, but the syntactical structure of (9) suggests according to the semantics of depicting language that the subject is an *object* and that the predicate is a *quality*. Therefore we are misled by the syntactical form[1] of the statement and have difficulties in grasping its meaning.

Perhaps we could indicate the logical status of sentence (9) by characterizing it as a *syntactical metaphor*. Its sense does not have the form suggested by its logical syntax, but nevertheless this syntax seems to be the best syntax we can give it.[2]

If we adopt this terminology we could state that *all philosophical statements are syntactical metaphors*. And though this statement is

---

[1] Cf. Frege's analysis of sentences like (9), according to which 'the concept *horse* is not a concept' but an object. (*Translations*, p. 46 f.).

[2] What I call 'syntactical metaphors' seems to be much the same thing as is called by Professor Ryle 'systematically' misleading expressions. See his paper for further examples.

itself metaphorical in many ways, I think it does more justice to the real difficulties arising from the use of philosophical statements than the statement that all philosophical statements are nonsensical.

If we regard isomorphic representation as a standard form of picturing there are also metaphorical 'pictures'. Fig. 3 considered as a 'picture' of the logical space is of this kind. Its function is actually to vizualize a metaphorical way of speaking.

## II. SEMANTICS AND METAPHYSICS

J. O. Urmson has paid due attention to the difference between the Wittgensteinian view that language reflects the internal structure of reality and the 'positivistic theory' that ontological statements are disguised statements on language.[1] But I think he is wrong in calling the former view metaphysical and the latter anti-metaphysical. To be sure, logical atomism can be said to be admittedly metaphysical philosophy, whereas the 'positivistic theory' pretends to be anti-metaphysical. Moreover the word 'metaphysical' can of course mean different things. But actually the 'positivistic theory' may be called 'metaphysical' in a traditional sense, because it shares the logical prejudices of old metaphysical doctrines. The 'positivistic theory' is one form of the view that there are not any 'genuine entities' to be spoken of besides *objects*, and that all statements on predicates are in fact disguised statements on objects (cf. above, pp. 183 ff.). And the idea that all 'genuine entities' are in fact 'objects' is the common mistake underlying traditional 'realistic' as well as 'nominalistic' views. If this book could make clear that we must not discard the distinction between the categories, and that predicates are *as* genuine components of reality as are objects, its author would regard this as an important achievement.

Now the view that predicates are as genuine components of reality as are objects could in its turn be called a 'metaphysical doctrine'. But in effect this would be misleading, since it suggests that this view implies more than it really does. Our distinctions are logical and semantical, and they do not justify any *a priori* views as to the structure of reality. At least I believe it is a good methodological device to look for the flaw whenever we are tempted to form 'metaphysical' views for logical or semantical reasons—or conversely.

[1] *Philosophical Analysis*, Ch. 8.

# XI

# WITTGENSTEIN AS A KANTIAN PHILOSOPHER

In the preceding chapters we have mainly directed our attention to the author of the *Tractatus* as a logician and a semanticist. In this final chapter we will give a short analysis of Wittgenstein's philosophical system.

In so far as Wittgenstein adhered to 'logical atomism' he could be characterized as a metaphysician of a rather Anglo-Saxon type. But I believe this sort of metaphysics to be in fact of only secondary importance in his philosophical system, which is, on the whole, more related to German metaphysics, and in particular to the metaphysics of Kant.

Wittgenstein rejected the possibility of any synthetic propositions *a priori*. Since the basic task of Kant's *Critique of Pure Reason* was to show how synthetic propositions *a priori* are possible, we might infer that Wittgenstein—like the logical positivists—was strongly anti-Kantian. But this is not so—at least it is not undisputably so. Unlike the logical positivists Wittgenstein was in essential respects a Kantian philosopher; his anti-Kantianism meant only that he—like other Kantians—transformed the system of Kant and thus created a Kantianism of a peculiar kind.

This is not to be understood to mean that Wittgenstein had been directly influenced by Kant's writings.[1] One did not need to have read Kant to be influenced by a more or less clearly stated Kantianism; it belonged to the intellectual atmosphere in the German speaking world. Moreover we know that Wittgenstein read and appreciated Schopenhauer,[2] who was in his way a Kantian of a

---

[1] According to von Wright ('Wittgenstein', p. 543) Wittgenstein said that he could get only 'occasional glimpses of understanding' from Spinoza, Hume, and Kant.

[2] See von Wright, *l.c.*, p. 530. Concerning the influence of Kantianism on Wittgenstein, cf. also above, p. 87 n.

peculiar kind. In what sense Wittgenstein was so I shall now try to explain.

## I. KANTIAN PHILOSOPHY

I shall begin with emphasizing one particular feature in Kantian philosophy. Kant's question 'How are synthetic judgements *a priori* possible?' was, to be sure, a basic question in the *Critique of Pure Reason*, but his interest in this question was not only an interest in an epistemological problem as such. His investigation of the *a priori* had a purpose which was still more fundamental to his philosophical outlook. This was to make a dichotomy between what belongs to the genuine province of 'theoretical reason' and what does not belong to it. The error in Leibniz-Wolffian metaphysics, which Kant called 'dogmatic', was that it applied the forms of theoretical reason to questions which do not belong to the province of theoretical knowledge—as questions about God, the immortal soul, the universe as a whole, the free will, morals, and so on. All those questions belong to the province of 'practical reason' and can be answered only by methods proper to it. We can thus state as a fundamental line in Kantian thought the *dichotomy* between questions belonging to the provinces of *theoretical* and *practical* reason.[1] The same distinction—though certainly interpreted in a different, more mystical, way—is found in the very title of Schopenhauer's main work *The World as Will and Idea*, where the 'World as Will' corresponds to the province of practical reason and the 'World as Idea' to the province of theoretical reason.

Starting from this distinction we can indicate as the main purpose of Kant's basic question that it serves as a basis for fixing the *limits* of the province of theoretical reason. 'How are synthetic judgements *a priori* possible?' Kant's famous 'Copernican revolution', which gave him the answer to this question, consisted in the 'discovery' that there are two components in human experience *qua* human experience. One component emanates from our *sensations*, and this is empirical and *a posteriori*, but there is also a component emanating from our *theoretical reason*, and this is *a priori*. The latter component consists of two parts. Our 'sensations' (*Empfindung*) are not yet 'perceptions' (*Wahrnehmung*); in order to give rise to a

---

[1] This dichotomy was in fact already made in the *Dreams of a Visionary Explained by Dreams of Metaphysics*, which has been regarded as the first of the works from Kant's 'critical' period, and can thus be said to form a starting-point of his critical philosophy.

perception a sensation must be *interpreted* within the framework of space and time; thus space and time constitute the *a priori form of perception*.[1] And our perceptions are still not 'experiences'; in order to be so they must be subjected to the conceptual framework of experience, which—together with the form of perception—constitutes the *a priori form of experience*. The fact that all our experiences must have the *a priori* form of experience is the source of a number of synthetic judgements *a priori*: the form of perception is the source of the mathematical propositions, the conceptual framework of experience is the source of the propositions of 'pure science'—as, for instance, the law of causality. Such statements are not analytic, but they are nevertheless true *a priori*, because they are *prior* to all experience *qua* experience: they are prescribed to nature in so far as nature is capable of being experienced at all by *theoretical reason*.

An investigation of our theoretical reason shows the *limits* of all possible experience and thus also what kind of questions lies outside this limit. Such an investigation Kant calls a *transcendental deduction*—it shows the limits of our theoretical reason. And what is 'transcendental' in this sense must be distinguished from what is *transcendent*,[2] that is, what transcends this limit. To the domain of the transcendent belongs also the *Ding an sich*, i.e., a 'thing' which exists independently of the form of experience. Schopenhauer assumed that the mind has access to the *Ding an sich* through the intuition of the will, which rends the 'Veil of Maya' by which theoretical reason covers reality. But this was a definitely non-Kantian turn of Kantianism. To Kant himself any kind of 'knowledge' was a matter of theoretical reason; principles of practical reason cannot be known by any special faculty of intuition but only *postulated* as necessary conditions for the existence of a moral world order.

The *method* used by Kant in his transcendental deductions, and in particular in his deduction of the form of perception is of interest if we wish to compare his views with the philosophy of Wittgenstein. Anything that can be perceived by a human mind must be submitted to the laws of (Euclidean) geometry, Kant argues. But

---

[1] I use the term 'Form of Perception' (*Form der Wahrnehmung*) for what Kant calls either *Form der Anschauung* or *Form der Sinulichkeit*, in order to indicate the analogy between this concept and the Kantian concept 'Form of Experience' (*Form der Erfahrung*) mentioned below.

[2] The distinction between the terms 'transcendental', which refers to the limits of theoretical knowledge, and 'transcendent', which refers to what falls outside this limit, is hinted at in the *Critique of Pure Reason*, but not consistently upheld. It is, however, clarifying to use the terms in this way.

how can he know this to be so? The method he actually uses for arriving at this knowledge is an analysis of what he calls our *Anschauung*. The word *Anschauung* is usually translated as 'intuition', but from our present point of view this is a very bad translation. Rather one ought to render the word as 'imagination', because the *a priori* character of the geometrical theorems is guaranteed by the fact that we can prove them by means of *reine Anschauung*, i.e. 'pure imagination' without any reference to sensations. This idea could, however, be expressed thus: we cannot even *imagine* a world in which the theorems of geometry were not valid, and since the real world, in so far as it is capable of being perceived, must be an *imaginable* world, the theorems of geometry must necessarily hold true in the real world. A world which is 'possible' in terms of our theoretical reason must be an *imaginable* world. Thus an investigation of what is imaginable to us shows what is *a priori* true with regard to perception. In the same way an investigation of what is *intelligible* to theoretical reason in other respects gives us additional *a priori* knowledge of the world of experience.

What I call Kantian philosophy could thus be summed up in the following theses:

(a) The *task* of *theoretical* philosophy is to make transcendental deductions concerning the limits of theoretical discourse, not to speculate over what transcends this limit and thus cannot be theoretically known.

(b) A world is a possible world of experience only if it is 'possible' to theoretical reason, i.e. if it is imaginable and intelligible.

(c) Our experience has a 'form' which is founded in theoretical reason and a 'content' which is based on our sensations.

(d) True synthetical propositions are *a priori* if they refer only to the *form* of experience, *a posteriori* if they refer also to the content.

(e) Thus there exist synthetic propositions *a priori* (e.g. mathematical statements, the law of causality).

(f) There are also 'transcendent' propositions (e.g. propositions on God, the immortal soul, the universe as a whole, free will, morals, etc.). Such propositions cannot be *known* to be true by theoretical knowledge, but only 'postulated' by practical reason (*Kant*) or intuited by the will (*Schopenhauer*).

The establishment of such propositions belongs to the task of *practical* philosophy.

(g) The *Ding an sich* is transcendent.

## 2. WITTGENSTEIN'S TRANSCENDENTAL DEDUCTIONS

If formulated in this, to be sure rather Wittgensteinian, way our theses of Kantianism need only to be modified in one respect in order to be transformed into the main points of Wittgenstein's philosophical system.

I start from thesis (b). As it stands there it could be accepted by Wittgenstein. But we have to realize that what is 'imaginable' and 'intelligible' is what is 'thinkable' and that 'thought' is the 'logical picture of reality', which means that what is 'thinkable' is that which we can present by a logical picture, or in other words, that which can be *described* in a depicting language. And since Wittgenstein assumes all language to be depicting language, it follows that what is in (b) characterized as 'imaginable' and 'intelligible' is identical with what can be *described in meaningful language*.

Thus to be possible to theoretical reason corresponds in Wittgenstein's philosophy to possibility in terms of what is describable in meaningful language. This is the essential modification of the Kantian view which gives rise to all differences between Wittgenstein and Kant. The *task* of (theoretical) philosophy is for Wittgenstein as for Kant to indicate the limits of theoretical discourse. But since what belongs to theoretical discourse is what can be 'said' at all in language, the investigation of this limit is the investigation of the 'logic' of language, which shows the 'logic of the world'. 'Logic is not a theory but a reflexion of the world,' Wittgenstein says in 6.13, and adds: 'Logic is transcendental', which can be interpreted in this way: *What Kant's transcendental deductions are intended to perform: this is performed by the logical analysis of language.*

And this is the way in which thesis (a) is transformed in Wittgenstein's system. 'Philosophy limits the domain of scientific discourse' (4.113). 'It has to limit the thinkable and thereby the unthinkable. It has to limit the unthinkable from within through the thinkable. It will indicate the unsayable by clearly presenting the sayable' (4.114–115).

Wittgenstein moves the limits of theoretical reason to the limits of language. Whereas Kant thought 'possible to theoretical reason' to be a more *narrow* concept than 'logically possible', these two concepts are *identical* according to Wittgenstein. Therefore, what Kant calls the 'form of experience' is the common form of all logically possible worlds, that is, the 'logical form of substance' or 'internal structure of substance', which—if we take logical atomism for granted—is shown by the internal structure of language revealed by logical analysis. Thus thesis (c) holds true in this sense in Wittgenstein's system—though we must include in the 'content' spoken of here also the external structure of reality (cf. Ch. VI, § 10).

Since the logical form of substance is prior to all experience it could be said to be *a priori* (cf. above, Ch. V, § 10). Thus Wittgenstein like Kant could regard statements on the 'form' as *a priori*, if there only *were* any such statements. But since the 'logical form' is the form of language there cannot be any meaningful sentences *on* the 'form'. Therefore (d) must be replaced by the thesis that the '*a priori*' form of reality can only be *exhibited* by language but not expressed by sentences. It follows that thesis (e) is false. That a sentence is 'synthetical' means that its negation is logically possible, and thus a world in which the negation holds true is thinkable.

But what about mathematical statements? 'Mathematics', Wittgenstein argues, 'is a logical method' (6.2); its sentences 'are equations, and therefore pseudo-statements' (6.2) (cf. Ch. VIII, §5), i.e. they 'express no thoughts' (6.21). Perhaps we could interpret this as meaning that the mathematical statements are 'tautologies' in the sense that their descriptive content is empty, though they are not tautologies in the truth-functional sense,[1] and thus they 'show' the logic of the world. And to the question whether we need *Anschauung* for the solution of mathematical problems it must be answered that language itself here supplies the necessary *Anschauung* (6.233).

As for the law of causality there is only one kind of laws *a priori*, and these are the logical laws (6.3, 6.31). The 'law of causality' is not a 'law' but the form of a law (6.32)—that is, an empirical law can be called a 'law of causality' if it is of a certain type (6.321). That there *are* laws of this kind is *a priori* true only in so far as we can form hypotheses of this form in language (6.3211 f.). What a 'law of causality' ought to say if it is to be true *a priori* is that 'there are

---

[1] I.e., equations may be regarded as tautologies in sense (a) of p. 76, though they are not so in sense (b). According to Ramsey (*Foundations of Mathematics*, p. 17) this was Wittgenstein's view, whereas Ramsey himself tried to show that all mathematical propositions are tautologies also in sense (b). Cf. also Waismann: 'Identität', p. 63.

natural laws' (6.36) in the sense that we can give our hypotheses of 'connections' in nature the form of general laws—and Kantianism is right in so far as this logical form is the only form under which *connections* in nature are thinkable (6.361)—but this can in effect only be 'shown' but not 'said' (6.36). And since what is 'shown' here by language is 'shown' by all description of 'natural connections' what the 'law of causality' is intended to exclude cannot be described (6.362)[1].

To sum up: it is essential to Wittgenstein's outlook that logical analysis of language as he conceives of it is a kind of 'transcendental deduction' in Kant's sense, the aim of which is to indicate the *a priori* form of experience which is 'shown' by all meaningful language and therefore cannot be 'said'. From this point of view the Tractatus could be called a 'Critique of Pure Language'[2]: 'The book will . . . draw a limit to thinking, or rather—not to thinking, but to the expression of thoughts; for, in order to draw a limit to thinking we should have to be able to think both sides of this limit (we should therefore have to be able to think what cannot be thought).—The limit can, therefore, only be drawn in language and what lies on the other side of the limit will be simply nonsense' (Preface).

## 3. TRANSCENDENTAL LINGUALISM

Kantianism has been called 'Critical Idealism' or 'Transcendental Idealism'. This terminology emphasizes the fact that Kantianism is an 'idealistic' philosophy in the restricted sense that the *form* of experience, but *only* the form is imposed on the world of experience by the structure of the human mind. In a way the form of experience can therefore be said to be 'subjective', but 'subjective' only in a 'metaphysical' or 'transcendental' sense, since the 'subject', the 'ego', as we ordinarily conceive of it, is not this 'metaphysical' or 'transcendental' subject but an object *in* the world of experience, that is, an object in a world which already has the 'form' prescribed by the mind of the metaphysical subject. With regard to this terminology Wittgenstein's philosophical system could be called 'Critical Lingualism' or 'Transcendental Lingualism' or even 'Lingualistic Idealism'. For Wittgenstein, too, the form of experience is 'subjective' in the transcendental sense, the metaphysical subject

---

[1] I think this argument is confused in a way which answers to a corresponding confusion in Kant's thinking.

[2] I owe this expression to Mr. P. Geach.

being the 'subject' which uses and understands language, and which must be distinguished from the empirical subject, which is part of the world describable in language. Therefore, '*the limits of my language* mean the limits of my world' (5.6). The limits of the world of the metaphysical subject, or rather, the limits of the metaphysical subject's 'logical space' of possible worlds, is determined by the limits of his language.

The real world of science is the world as describable in meaningful language, and this is, in a sense, '*my* world:'

5.62   ........
> Was der Solipsismus nämlich m e i n t, ist ganz richtig, nur lässt es sich nicht s a g e n, sondern es zeigt sich.
> Dass die Welt m e i n e Welt ist, das zeigt sich darin, dass die Grenzen d e r Sprache (der Sprache, die allein ich verstehe) die Grenzen m e i n e r Welt bedeuten.

Like Russell[1] I take the word *allein* in the second paragraph as referring to the relative pronoun *die*,[2] and think the passage could be translated as follows: 'That the world is *my* world, shows itself in the fact that the limits of *Language* (which is the only language I understand) mean the limits of *my* world.' The parenthesis can be interpreted in this way: since the limits of language are the transcendental limits of the world and since Language is *my* language (the only language which I understand) the limits of Language are the limits of *my* world. The Ego to which the word 'my' refers here is the metaphysical subject, which in a sense, does not exist (5.631), because it is transcendental, it 'does not belong to the world but it is a limit of the world' (5.632)—it is like the eye in relation to the field of sight; the eye cannot see itself (5.633–6331). And the metaphysical subject is to be distinguished from the empirical ego: in the book 'The world as I found it' there is an ego which must be described, but of the metaphysical ego there could be no mention in this book (5.631). The world is my world if the word 'my' refers to the metaphysical ego, and that this is so implies that 'solipsism'[3] can

---

[1] See his introduction to the Tractatus, p. 18.

[2] Cf. Hintikka: 'On Wittgenstein's "Solipsism",' p. 88. Wittgenstein's formulation is, to be sure, ambiguous, but I suppose that Wittgenstein, if he had meant '*the* language, which I alone understand' (Urmson: *Philosophical Analysis*, p. 135), would have written *die nur ich verstehe*. Moreover a thought of this kind is unparalleled in the Tractatus and would not fit into the context. On the interpretation of what Wittgenstein wants to say here, cf. also Rhees' argument in his review of Cornforth, pp. 388 f.

[3] According to Hintikka Wittgenstein does not mean by 'solipsism' what is ordinarily meant by it. I think he is right at least in so far as Wittgenstein ought to have used the word 'idealism' rather than 'solipsism', because what he calls 'solipsism' is exactly his

be considered true in a sense; that is, what solipsism *intends* to say is quite correct, but—since we cannot speak of the metaphysical ego— this cannot be *said*. That the metaphysical ego is transcendental implies also 'that solipsism strictly carried out coincides with pure realism. The Ego in solipsism shrinks to an extensionless point and there remains the reality co-ordinated with it' (5.64).

### 4. NONSENSE

The limit to thinking drawn by Wittgenstein's transcendental deductions can, as we have seen, properly be drawn only in language. We cannot think what is unthinkable, but we can form linguistic expressions which do not express thoughts, since they are simply nonsensical. Thus the limit between what in Kantian terms belongs, and belongs not to theoretical reason is shown by the logical distinction between sense and nonsense.

It follows that problems which according to Kant are unsolvable by theoretical reason cannot even be raised; 'the deepest problems are properly speaking not *problems*' (4.003, italics mine). 'For an answer which cannot be expressed the question too cannot be expressed.—The *riddle* does not exist' (6.5).

There are no 'transcendent' statements, because what they try to say cannot be said. But this does not mean that our Kantian thesis (f) is wholly wrong. 'There is, however, the inexpressible', Wittgenstein admits in 6.522. 'This *shows* itself; it is the mystical.' Thus there is indeed a domain of 'practical reason', but this lies outside what is expressible in language. God belongs to this domain: 'God does not reveal himself *in* the world' (6.432). Ethics lies also beyond language. One cannot (as Kant did) speak of the 'will' as the subject of ethics, because the 'will' of which one can *speak* 'is only of interest to psychology' (6.423).[1] 'It is clear that ethics cannot be expressed. Ethics is transcendental' (6.421)—I think Wittgenstein would rather have said 'Ethics is transcendent' if he had adopted the above distinction between 'transcendental' and 'transcendent'.[2]

---

linguistic turn of Kantian idealism. Urmson seems to understand 'solipsism' as the doctrine that there are no other minds instead of the doctrine that there is no external world, but this peculiar meaning of 'solipsism' can hardly have been known to Wittgenstein when he wrote the Tractatus; it is in fact unknown to all philosophical dictionaries I have consulted.

[1] This implies also that the Problem of Free Will cannot be treated in the spirit of Kant. Wittgenstein hints at his attitude to this problem in 5.1362.

[2] In the world describable in language there are no (objective) values, since all sentences are 'of equal value' (6.4).

As for the immortality of the soul, 'the solution of the riddle of life in space and time lies *outside* space and time' (6.4312).

In a logical empiricist's vocabulary 'nonsensicality' means something purely negative. Wittgenstein's identification of the inexpressible with the mystical seems to show that to him 'nonsensicality' has a rather positive ring. The German word *Unaussprechlich* means not only 'inexpressible' but also 'ineffable'. Thus the identification in 6.522 of *das Unaussprechliche* with the mystical could be interpreted as a statement of the old thought that the mystical is ineffable.

The inexpressible in this sense '*shows* itself'. In Chapter X, section 8, we made a distinction between two kinds of things that cannot be said: that which can be shown in language but not said, and that which can be neither shown nor said in language. The mystical belongs, I think, to the latter kind of inexpressible things. It does not reflect itself in *language*. How does it then express itself? I believe this is to be understood as a matter of *feeling*. One 'experiences' the mystical as a form of emotional experience which in German would be called *Erlebnis* in contradistinction to ordinary fact-stating 'experience' that is called *Erfahrung*. '*Die Anschauung der Welt sub specie aeterni ist ihre Anschauung als—begrenztes—Ganzes*' (6.45). I think this ought to be translated in this way: 'The contemplation of the world *sub specie aeterni* is the intuition of it as a—limited—whole'. And Wittgenstein adds: 'The *feeling* of the world as a limited whole is the *mystical* feeling' (italics mine). One could perhaps characterize this feeling as an emotional experience of the world from what one feels as God's point of view. This has nothing to do with 'facts' describable in language: 'The facts belong all to the task (*Aufgabe*) and not to its performance (*Lösung*)'—that is, to the inexpressible problem, not to its solution (6.4321).

This argument leads us to the idea of the transcendent *Ding an sich* (thesis (g)). The 'things' of Wittgenstein's logical atomism belong to the framework of a world description, and could therefore be called 'transcendental'—and this would actually conform with one aspect of Kant's own view. But the *Ding an sich* which is thought of as existing independently of the form of experience is not this transcendental thing, but appears in Kantianism, and in particular in Schopenhauer's philosophy, as a symbol for the unreachable transcendent. And I think there is a reminiscence of this idea in the Tractatus.

In the second chapter I asked myself why Wittgenstein gives his first thesis in the Tractatus the form of an answer to the question *what* the world is. I believe this form is connected with the old philosophical feeling that a *what*, if it could be answered, would bring us into a mystical contact with the world whereas an answer to a *how* only takes the form of an impassive description. 'Logic *precedes* every *Erfahrung*—that something is *so*', and therefore 'it is before the How', but it is 'not before the What' (5.552). '*How* the world is, is completely indifferent for what is higher' (6.432). 'Not *how* the world is, is the mystical, but *that* it is' (6.44).

We have criticized Wittgenstein's logical atomism in many respects. Does this criticism essentially affect his Kantian metaphysics? Even if we admit that logical atomism is wrong, even if we admit that there are many ways of saying things, and that the idea of a 'depicting' language can be extended in many directions, cannot the distinction between what, on the one hand, can be said or shown in language, and what, on the other hand, lies entirely outside language always be reconstructed, though the basis for this distinction must be more complicated than that assumed by logical atomism?

It is difficult to give a definite answer to this question. But I share the opinion of many others that a distinction of this kind does not in any case answer to the demands made on it in the Tractatus. So, for instance, the difference between ethical judgements and scientific statements is not a difference between a transcendent reality and a reality of science, but a difference between two kinds of problems corresponding to different moods of language. What is of lasting value in the Tractatus is not the philosophical system which is its alleged result, but the views proposed in the different steps of the argument 'leading' to it, that is, of the ladder which according to 6.54 is to be thrown away after one had climbed up on it.

In fact the inconsistencies in the Tractatus are in the main inconsistencies between the philosophical system and the investigations performed in the different steps. And in view of this fact the following point in Wittgenstein's attitude to nonsense is of interest. Since Wittgenstein believed our deepest problems to lie beyond language one could expect him to extend his conception of 'philosophy as an activity' in such a way as to comprise practices of an Indian kind for the attainment of a contact with the mystical Ineffable. That his philosophy did not take this turn is significant.

If my second-hand impression of Wittgenstein's personality is correct he did not in fact have any strong inclination to mysticism; at least it was counterbalanced by an opposite tendency. Logical positivists did not simply invert Wittgenstein's attitude to nonsensicality, because it is in fact ambiguous in the Tractatus. On the one hand the 'inexpressible', as we have seen, has a positive ring, but on the other hand Wittgenstein seems to share the positivistic tendency to regard it as nonsense which does not deserve our attention.

In 6.52 we read: 'We feel that even if *all possible* scientific questions be answered, the problems of life have still not been touched at all.' This conforms with the positive evaluation of the inexpressible. But the positive evaluation becomes dubious when Wittgenstein adds in 6.52 and 6.521: 'To be sure, there is then no question left, and just this is the answer.—The solution of the problem of life is seen in the vanishing of the problem.' And when he states in 6.53 that the *only* correct method in philosophy is to demonstrate to anyone who 'wishes to say something metaphysical that he had not given any meaning to certain of the signs in his sentences', then we have a definite feeling that what is inexpressible is just nonsense and nothing else. Wittgenstein says not merely 'The riddle is inexpressible', but 'The riddle does not *exist*'.

'Whereof one cannot speak, thereon one must be silent.' As a matter of fact this is *not* a reverence for the ineffable. It could rather be characterized as the expression of a way of escape. When Wittgenstein determined to be silent he turned away from philosophy and tried to enter an active life. The philosophical activity neither meant to him an amusing occupation of the mind, nor was it a means for establishing some independent doctrine of life or reality; it was a passion from which he could never free himself. He did not feel himself as a captive of Language which bars the contact with what is ineffable; but he felt himself indeed as a captive—in philosophy. And therefore the essential aim of philosophy was to find a way out from itself.

I have stated earlier that the 'nonsensicality' of all philosophical statements according to the Tractatus did not imply that philosophy as an activity is aimless. But I think one ought to add to this that an essential aim of the philosophical activity in the Tractatus actually was to *make* philosophy aimless. The 'definitiveness' of the truth of the thoughts expressed in the book thus meant that Wittgenstein considered this aim to be reached—at least for his own part.

Later he changed his mind in this respect. But he made no essential change in his attitude toward the aim of philosophy. The main error in the Tractatus in this was the endeavour to find a once-for-all remedy for the philosophical disease. Wittgenstein discovered that one could find means of interrupting the philosophical activity when one wants to, without finding a method for stopping it altogether. Or to quote his own words in the *Philosophical Investigations*, § 133:

> . . . For the clarity that we are aiming at is indeed *complete* clarity. But this simply means that the philosophical problems should *completely* disappear.
> The real discovery is the one that makes me capable of interrupting doing philosophy when I want to.—The one that gives philosophy peace, so that it is no longer tormented by questions which bring *itself* in question.—We demonstrate a method, by examples; and the series of examples can be broken off. Problems are solved (difficulties eliminated), not a *single* problem.
> There is not *one* philosophical method; but there are indeed methods, like different therapies.

This passage, in its formulation strangely intermediate between the statement of a personal predicament and the establishment of a rule for general acceptance, can be regarded as a pathetic expression of Wittgenstein's struggle with the problems of philosophy. And it gives us an idea of the form in which the belief in the nonsensicality of philosophical statements is retained in the thought of the later Wittgenstein.

'All philosophy is "Critique of language"' (4.0031). For my part I do not believe this thesis to be an exhaustive characterization even of what ought to be the aim of philosophical analysis. But in so far as philosophy is critique of language it is an investigation which must be carried out step by step like investigations in science. This does not mean that philosophical investigations are 'empirical'— their result is indeed 'clarity' rather than 'knowledge' in a scientific sense: 'The word "philosophy" must mean something which stands above or below, but not beside the natural sciences' (4.111). But we cannot content ourselves with considering the results of philosophical analysis as inexpressible. We have to find means of expressing them, and expressing them with increasing clarity, unless the philosophical activity is to remain an eternal vicious circle.

# REFERENCES

# REFERENCES

Bühler, K.: *Sprachtheorie*. Jena, 1934.
Carnap, R.: *The Logical Syntax of Language*. London, 1937.
—— *Meaning and Necessity*. Chicago, 1947.
Copi, I. M.: 'Objects, Properties, and Relations in the *Tractatus*', *Mind*, N.S. LXVII, 1958.
Daitz, E.: 'The Picture Theory of Language' (1953) reprinted in Flew, *Conceptual Analysis*.
Flew, A. G. N., ed.: *Logic and Language*, (I), Oxford, 1952; (II), Oxford, 1953.
—— *Essays in Conceptual Analysis*. London, 1956.
Frege, G.: *Translations from the Philosophical Writings of Gottlob Frege*, by P. Geach and M. Black. Oxford, 1952.
Gardiner, A.: *The Theory of Speech and Language*. Oxford, 1932.
Hare, R. M.: *The Language of Morals*. Oxford, 1952.
Hertz, H.: *The Principles of Mechanics*, translated by D. E. Jones and J. T. Walley. London & New York, 1899.
Hintikka, J.: 'Identity, Variables, and Impredicative Definitions', *The Journal of Symbolic Logic*, XXI, 1956.
—— 'On Wittgenstein's "Solipsism" ', *Mind*, N.S. LXVII, 1958.
Langer, S. K.: *Philosophy in a New Key* (1942), Mentor ed. New York, 1948.
—— *Feeling and Form*. New York, 1953.
Lewis, C. I.: *An Analysis of Knowledge and Valuation*. La Salle, 1946.
Petrus Hispanus: *Summulae Logicales*, ed. I. M. Bocheński. Fribourg, 1947.
Ramsey, F. P.: 'The Foundations of Mathematics' (1925) and 'Critical Notice of L. Wittgenstein's *Tractatus Logico-Philosophicus*' (1923), reprinted in *The Foundations of Mathematics*, London, 1950.
Reenpää, Y.: 'Wahrnehmen und Denken', *Theoria*, XI, 1945.
Rhees, R.: Review of Cornforth: 'Science Versus Idealism', *Mind*, N.S. LVI, 1947.
Russell, B.: *The Principles of Mathematics*. Cambridge, 1903.
—— *The Problems of Philosophy*. London, 1912.
—— 'On Denoting' (1905) and 'Logical Atomism' (1924), reprinted in *Logic and Knowledge*, London, 1956.
Ryle, G.: *The Concept of Mind*. London, 1949.
—— 'Syntactically Misleading Expressions' (1931–32), reprinted in Flew, *Logic and Language* (I).

Q                              229

STENIUS, E.: *Tankens gryning* (The Dawn of Thought). Helsingfors, 1953.
—— 'Linguistic Structure and the Structure of Experience', *Theoria*, XX, 1954.
URMSON, J. O.: *Philosophical Analysis*. Oxford, 1956.
WAISMANN, F.: 'Logische Analyse der Wahrscheinlichkeitsbegriffe', *Erkenntnis*, I, 1930–31.
—— 'Uber den Begriff der Identität', *Erkenntnis*, VI, 1936.
—— 'Was ist Logische Analyse?' *The Journal of Unified Science* (*Erkenntnis*), VIII, 1939-40.
WEILER, G.: 'On Fritz Mauthner's Critique of Language', *Mind*, N.S. LXVII, 1958.
WHITEHEAD, A. N., and RUSSELL, B.: *Principia Mathematica*, I. Cambridge, 1910.
WISDOM, J. O.: 'Logical Constructions' (I), *Mind*, N.S. XL, 1931.
WITTGENSTEIN, L.: *Tractatus Logico-Philosophicus*. London, 1922. Sixth impression with a few corrections and an index, 1955.
—— *Philosophical Investigations*. Oxford, 1953.
—— 'Some Remarks on Logical Form', *Proceedings of the Aristotelian Society*, suppl. vol. IX, 1929.
—— 'Notes on Logic' (1913), published in a slightly corrupt version in *The Journal of Philosophy*, LIV, 1957.
—— *The Blue & Brown Books*. Oxford, 1958.
VON WRIGHT, G. H.: *An Essay in Modal Logic*. Amsterdam, 1951.
—— 'Deontic Logic' (1951), reprinted in *Logical Studies*. London, 1957.
—— 'Ludwig Wittgenstein, a Biographical Sketch', *The Philosophical Review*, LXIV, 1955.

# INDEX

# INDEX

## (i) General

(Italics refer to chapter and section)

*Abbilden, Abbildung* (represent, representation) 89, 91, 96, 98, 140, 179 n.
*Abbildende Beziehung* (representing relation) 98
Analysis
　logical 65, 76; *VII.2*; 144, 155, 158, 183, 198, 200, 208, 220
　complete, of a sentence 65
　121 f., 125, 155, 158 (cf. 205)
　philosophical 208, 220, 226 (cf. 183, 213)
Anaxagoras, 18-20
*Annahme* (assumption) 162 n.
*Anschauung* (intuition, imagination) 217, 219
Anscombe 162 n.
*A priori* (cf. Framework, Logical Space) 10; *V.10*; 104 f., 112, 194 (cf. 197, 203), 213; *XI.1,2*
Aristotle 18-21
Assertion (cf. Mood, Modal) 158 n., 159, 174 f.
　depicting and asserting 150
　and description 157 f., 161 f., 166-70
　notation for 161-4, 170
　assertion sign 159, 170
Assumption 159, 162
*Aufweisen* (exhibit), 179

*Bedeuten, Bedeutung* (mean, meaning), 121, 171
*Begriffsschrift* (ideography, cf. 'perfect language') 155
*Bestehen* (exist) 30-2
*Bild* (picture) 96, 117
Black 121
Bühler 119 n. 2

Carnap 34, 57, 127 n., 183-9, 196-8
Categories (cf. Form, logical) 20-2, 182; *X.3*; 207, 213
　of names see Names
　of Wittgensteinian 'things' *V.1.5*; 132 f.

Causal nexus 59 f. (cf. 220)
Causality, law of 216 f., 219 f.
Chain, simile of 63, 133
Characteristic of a predicate 95 n., 2, 131, 133 n., 134, 145, 154
　not a name 138, 145
　'genus' of 187, 190
　'meaning' of 138 (cf. 192, 194, 207)
Circumstance 30 f., 33
Clarity 209, 226
Clue see Key
Clue Theory of meaning 140, 196
Colour concepts 42, 47, 72, 76; *V.7*; 80, 198, 200 f.
Combination see Connection
Complementarity see Objects
Complexes 28, 64 f., 76, 120, 124 f., 198, 200
Concatenation 63, 132
　concatenation relation 131-3
Configuration 80
Connections
　of 'things' 61-3, 119 n., 128, 132 f.
　causal 220 (cf. 59 f.)
　logical see Logical
Content see Form, Structure
　descriptive see Descriptive
　external and internal 81
Copi 137 n.
Critique of Language 220, 226

Daitz 131 n., 137 n.
*Darstellen* (present) 11, 99, 141, 179 n.
Definition 65, 122-5, 144 (cf. 200 f.), 205
Denominatum 120-2, 138-40 (cf. 142)
Depict, 88; *VI.6*; 118, 132, 140 f., 151 n., 158
Deputize, 63, 97, 130; *VII.7*; 144 f., 148 f., 170, 201
Describe see Naming and describing; Descriptions
Descriptions
　complete 41, 43, 49; *VIII.2*; 155, 165
　definite, 64 f., 135, 139, 141 f., 206

Descriptive content of a sentence 30, 109, 157, 161, 165, 175
  of compound sentences *VIII.165*
  of elementary sentences 33 f., 37
  of 'logical sentences', 210
  and mood *IX*
  of semantical elementary sentences *VII*
  and sense see Sense
  determined by the sentence-radical, 161 f., 165–7, 175
  depicted by the sentence-token *VII.4, 5*; 139; *VIII.3*; 161; *IX.3*
Dimensions (cf. Logical Space) *IV.1*
  different for different points *IV.9*
  discrete 45
  many-valued *IV.3*; 58; *V.6*
  number of, infinite 58 f.
  two-valued *IV.3*
  yes-and-no 46
*Ding* (thing) 22, 26 n., 61
*Ding an sich* (cf. Thing in itself) 216, 218, 223
Direction *IX.7,8*
Dualism 79

Ego, empirical and metaphysical 221 f.
Einstein 83 n. 2, 86
*Elementarsatz* (elementary sentence) 12
Elements
  of an articulate field 90 *and passim*
  atomic see 'Things'
  of a fact 24 f., 27
  of language, syntactical 195 f., 199 ff.
  of a picture-field 94–6
  of a sentence-token *VII.4*; *VII.6*
  of the world (cf. 'Thing', Substance) 27 f.
*Empfindung*, Kantian term, (sensation) 215 f.
*Erfahrung* and *Erlebnis* (experience) 223 f.
Events 83 n. 2
Exhibit (cf. Show, internally) 179 f., 219
Experience 223 f.
  possible (Kant) 216
Expressions see Signs
External-internal, distinction between (cf. Content, Predicate, Show, Structure) 68 f., 71 f., 76; *V.8*; 82 f., 179–82

Facts
  as a 'task' 223
  atomic (cf. atomic states of affairs) 29, 35–7
  category of 20, 22–6, 32, 61 f., 120, 184
  negative and positive 35 f., 46–8, 53
  priority of *II. 3–5*
  simple 47 f.

Facts (*Continued*)—
  and (atomic) states of affairs (cf. *Sachverhalt, Sachlage*) 30, 33; *III.4,5*
False see True
  false sentence, problem of 127, 130; *VII.8*
Faraday 27
Field 90
  articulate (cf. Picture-field, Sentence-token) *VI.2*; 115 n. 2
  of perception *II.4*
  world field *II.5*
Form (cf. Structure, internal; Framework)
  apriority of 217, 219
  and content 79–81; *VI.10*; 183 n., 217, 219
  Kantian concept of 87; *XI.1*
  of experience 216 f., 219
  of perception 216 f.
  logical 67–9, 73, 75–80, 133, 179 f., 182
  and categories *V.5*; 73–5, 182
  of an expression or a symbol (cf. Genus) 68, 133 n.
  and internal qualities 69, 72 f.; *V.8*
  of reality see Structure, internal
  of representation 99; *VI.7*
  (logically) adequate (=logical) 101 f.; *VI.8*
  and structure *VI.10*
  of substance see Structure, internal 71, 219 (cf. 179)
  of 'things' 67, see Form, logical
*Form der Abbildung* (form of representation) 99
  *der Anschauung, Sinnlichkeit, Wahrnehmung* (form of perception), 216 n.
  *der Erfahrung* (form of experience) 216 n.
Framework for a (scientific) description, priority of 50, 52, 83; *V.10*; 104 f., 194, 197, 203, 209, 216 (cf. 219, 224)
Free will 215, 217, 222 n.
Frege 119, 121, 138 n., 145, 159, 162 n., 170, 180, 192 f., 212 n. 2
Functional component 160 f.

Gardiner 139 n.
Geach 220 n. 2
*Gegenstand* ('thing') 61, 72, 97, 121
Genus of a symbol 187–91
God 215, 217, 222 f.

Hare 157, 161, 164
Hertz 41, 83 n., 87, 113 n.
Hintikka 155 n. 2, 221 n.
Hume's thesis *IV.9*; 82
Husserl 31 n. 2

Idealism (lingualistic) 220, 221 n.
Identity *VIII.5*; 183, 188, 219 n.
Ideography (symbolic language; cf. 'perfect language') 189, 191
Imaginable 217 f.
Imagination 217
Immortality 215, 217, 223
Induction 83
Ineffable 223–5
Inexpressible *XI.4*
Intelligible 217 f.
Internal and external see External
Interpretation see Key
Isomorphism (cf. Representation) *VI.3* 212
  defined 93
  internal 103 n. (cf. 83)

Kant 87, 214–8, 222–4
Kantianism 214; *XI.1,2*; 223 f.
Key
  of interpretation 93, 101
    adequate 102
    and clue *VI.12*; 140, 196 (cf. 153)
    incomplete *VI.11*
    many-one 147 f.
    reasonable 92
    semantical 174, 196, 201
  of a sentence 129 f.; *VII.7*
    false and true 132 f., 137 n. 2, 187 f., 191
  of an isomorphism 93, 95

Language
  depicting 178, 188, 196 f., 200, 203–12, 218, 224
  essential function of, 128, 137 f., 157
  and languages 194 f. (cf. 220 f.)
  language meaning and thing meant 140 f.
  non-depicting *X.8–10*
  perfect, see Perfect language
  possible 199
  and reality, *X*; see Structure, categorial, internal
    corresponding statements on *X.3*; 198
  symbolic see Ideography
  as a system vs. speech 139 (cf. 176), 177
  and systematic notations, 199
  and thought 6, 117, 202 f., 218, 220
Language of Physics, theoretical and experimental 204 f.
Language-games 159, 161; *IX.5*; 173–6, 211
Leibniz-Wolffian metaphysics, 215
Lewis 164

Life, problems of, 222, 225 f.
Limit
  of experience 216
  of language 13, 220; *XI.3*; 225
  of theoretical reason 215 f., 218, 222
  of thinking *etc.* 13; *X.1–3*; 222
  of 'my' world *XI.3*
Lingualism, transcendental *XI. 3*
Logic 218, 224
  formal 197–9, 202
  of (predicative) names 202 f., 211
  sentences of, 13, 76, 204; *X.9* (cf. 218)
  truth-functional 152, 200–2 (cf. 76)
Logical
  atomism 64–6, 84 f., 120; *VII.2*; *VIII.6* (cf. 194 f., 199 ff.), 206, 213 f., 219, 223 f.
  connections 40, 74–6; *VI.8*; *X.5*
    intrinsic *X.5*
  connectives (cf. Logical signs) 120; *VIII.1*; 165, 174
  constants 144 f.
  constructions, doctrine of, 205
  contradictions 57, 156
    truth-functional vs. contradictions in the logic of names, 200–02
  form, see Form
  freedom 102–5, 201 n.
  independence, of atomic states of affairs (cf. Logical connections) *III.3*; 37; *IV.1–4,9*; 76, 199 f.
  interrelations 75; *X.5*
    intrinsic 198–203
    negative and positive 75
  mood *X.9*
  picture see Pictures, logical
  position *IV.8*
  predicates see Predicates
  rules see Rules
  signs (cf. Logical connectives) 151–4, 175
  space (cf. Dimensions) 114 f.; *IV*; 90
    as a framework for description 50, 52, 66, 83; *V.10*; 197, 203 (cf. 219, 224)
    and geometrical 43, 54
    homogeneous 71; *V.6*; 77 f.
    and internal structure 71–9
    many-valued *IV.3*; *V.6*; 78
    as persistent 82 f.
    in a relative sense 90
    as a space of possible worlds *IV.7*;
    and substance *V.5-7*
    two-valued 45 f.
    unhomogeneous *V.7*; 203
    yes-and-no 46; *IV.4,5*; 107, 199, 201
  subjects see Subjects
  syntax see Syntax

Mathematics 111
  statements of 13, 216 f., 219
Mauthner 2 n.
Maxwell 27
Meaning 119, 140, 171 n. 2
  clue theory of 140, 196
  and denominatum 121 f., 138–40 (cf.
    196 f.)
  of logical connectives *VIII.1*
  of modal components 168 f.
  of names 120–2, 130, 138–40, 172 f.
  Name Theory of *VII. 1*; 137–40, 193
  and reference 121
  and sense see Sense
  and 'thing meant', 139 f., 154 n.
  of 'true' and 'false' see True
  and use 138–40
Metaphors, syntactical *X.10*
Metaphysics
  and semantics 194 f.; *X.11*
  Wittgensteinian (cf. Logical atomism
    2, 133, 143, 186, 194; *XI*
  Wittgenstein's view on 2, 225
Modal
  component 161
  games *IX.5,8*
  import 169, 175, 210 f.
  operators *IX.2*; 170
Mode of speech, formal and material
  (Carnap) 183 f.
Monism 79
Mood
  and descriptive content *IX*
  'descriptive' 178
  imperative 157 f., 163 f., 169
  indicative 150; *IX*; 211 (cf. assertion)
  interrogative 157 f., 163 f., 169
  logical *X. 9*
  'negative' *IX.8*
  of obligatoriness 162
  semantical 161, 175 f.
    and grammatical 168, 175 f.
  semantics of 157 f.; *IX.5,8*
Mystical 23, 222–5


Names (cf. Denominatum) 63, 65, 68;
  *VII.1,2,7*; 144 f., 155, 173, 187, 193,
  199, 202 f., 211
  bearer of (cf. Meaning and 'thing
    meant') 122
  categories of 131, 136; *VII.7*; 187, 193
  and signs for complexes 65, 120,
    124 f., 200
  composition of 125
  and 'definite descriptions', 64 f., 135,
    139, 142
  as deputizing signs 130; *VII.7*; 201
  as elements of sentence-tokens *VII.4*;
    *VII.6* (cf. *X.4*)

Names (*Continued*)
  fictitious 142
  function of 122, 128, 136 f., 193
  logic of see Logic
  and pictures 135 f., 193
  predicative *VII.7*; 173 f., 202 f.
  and primitive signs 65, 122–4
  proper names 196
  and sentences 118–20, 122; *VII.3,4,8*;
    184 f.
  simpleness of 125
Name Theory of Linguistic Meaning 119,
  140 f.
Nature, logical 21, 36
*Naturnotwendiges Zeichen* 199
Necessity 59 f.
  logical 74
Negation 147–50, 165; *IX.7,8*
Negative see Positive
Neustic 157, 161
Newton 27
Nonsense (nonsensicality) 2, 6, 22, 78,
  182–5, 192; *X.7,8*; 213; *XI.4*


Object of naming 121
Objects (individual things) 23 f., 61; *V.1*;
  147, 206
  (logically) atomic see 'Things'
  category of 20–2, 213
  and predicates, complementarity of
    27 f., 62, 131 (cf. 20, 68, 138)
  instantaneous 83, 84 n.
  linguistic 187
  persistent 82 f.
  reality of 119, 138 f.
  relevant 34, 131 (cf. 26, 94)
  syntactical 195 f., 199, 206 f.
Ontological statements, 182 (cf. *X.10*)
  as 'disguised' statements on language
    6 n., 183–8, 198, 206, 213
*Ort* (position), 55


Particulars 21 n. 3
Perfect language 137, 155, 189–92, 194,
  196 f. (cf. 200)
Peter of Spain 21 n.
Philosophical statements, *X.3,8*; 211–13,
  226
Philosophy
  as an activity *X.8*; 224-6
  practical 218
  theoretical 217 f.
Phrastic 157, 161
Picture
  adequate, see Picture, logical
  in colour 101, 108
  as a fact 97 f.
  false see true

Picture (*Continued*)
fictitious 89; *VI. 11*; 142, 205
impossible 103 f., 201
interpretable and uninterpretable, 104, 107
isomorphic see Representation
logical or (logically) adequate, 6
101 f.; *VI.8*; 114, 117, 179–81, 211–3
mental 113, 116
metaphorical 213
naturalistic *VI.9*; 113, 116, 137
as an object 97, 137
spatial 101, 108
true and false 96, 98, 140 f., 166 (cf. 89)
true *a priori* 104 f.
Wittgenstein's concept of *VI,5*; 105–7, 179–81 (cf. 143 f., 146 f.)
Picture-field 98, 104, 129, 166, 190, *and passim*
'Picture Theory of Language', descriptional and ontological *X.1*; 182, 194, 200 (cf. 137 n.)
Picture Theory of Sentence meaning *I.4*; 120, 133, 143 f., 155 f., 158, 161, 200; *X.10*
not implying logical atomism 123, 125, 155 (cf. 194, 200 f., 203)
as a theory of (semantical) elementary sentences 12, *VII*; 147 f.
in an extended sense, as a theory of compound sentences, 143 f., 146; *VIII.2,3*; 156, 165, 178
not implying that names are pictures, 136 f.
and ontological picture theory *X.1*; 193 f., 200
as a theory of sentence-radicals *IX.3*
Positive and negative in a state of affairs, possible world, picture, or picture-field 53, 149 f., 155, 166
Positivism 213 f., 223
Predicates (qualities and relations; cf. Objects), 19–22
(logically) atomic see 'Things'
category of 21, 61 f., 213
always directed 139, 172 f.
external (material) and internal, 36, 68 f., 72, 76; *V.8*; 118 n., 182, 207
logical, of sentence-tokens (cf. Predicates, syntactical) 134–7, 149, 155, 187
names of 12, 136–8, 155, 173, 200 f.
reality of 138 f. (cf. 119, 213)
second order 80; *X.10* (cf. 118 n.)
syntactical 195, 199, 206 f.
notation for 195
in themselves 27, 68
Present 11, 99, 118, 129, 141, 151 n., 155, 161, 165 f., 179 n.
Probability 13

Property see Predicates
Pseudo-concepts and -statements 184 f., 206, 219

Quality = one-place predicate 22, see Predicates
Quantification *VIII.4*

Ramsey 136 n., 192, 219 n.
Realism 119 (cf. 138 f.), 213, 222
Reality
piece of, and world 51
structure of see Structure
Reason, theoretical and practical 215–8
Reenpää 45 n.
Relation many-place predicate 24, see Predicates
Relativity, theory of, 83 n. 2, 86
Represent 98 f., 140 f., 151 n., 166, 179 n.
Representation (cf. Key, Picture) 89, 91
of a fact 89, 94–6
form of see Form
isomorphic *VI.4*; 118
Representing relation 98
Rhees 221 n. 2
Rules, conventional 191, 194 f., 202 f. (cf. 209)
logical 149, 151 f., 175, 195; *X.5.9*
Russell 21 f., 29, 64 f., 68, 119 f., 135, 136 n., 139, 141, 145, 162 n., 170, 189 f., 192, 206, 221
Ryle 112, 212 n. 2

*Sache* ('thing'), 61
*Sachlage* (=state of affairs, 33) 30, 32 f.; *III.4*; 53, 90
*Sachverhalt* (=atomic state of affairs, 33), 6, 8 f., 12; *III*; 61, 89 f.
*and Sachlage* 30, 32–5
*and Tatsache* 29; *III.1*
*Satz* (sentence), 6 n., 12
*Satzradikal* (sentence-radical), 159 n.
*Satzzeichen* (sentence-token), 9 n., 55, 129
Say
what can be said and what can be shown *X.2*; 183, 222 f.
Schopenhauer 87, 214–7, 223
Science as a fact 185
Sense, a kind of meaning peculiar to sentence 118, 120 f.; *VIII.3*; 171 n. 2
and denominatum 120
as descriptive content 12, 120, 130, 155, 157
vs. descriptive content, 157–8, 161, 165, 175
and direction *IX.7* (cf. 43)
and reference 121

Sentences
 bi-polarity of 171, 173 (cf. 43)
 complete analysis of see Analysis
 and arrows 118; *IX.7*
 compound 12, 126; *VIII*; 161, 166
 depicting, see also Language, depicting
  144, 156, 161, 210
 elementary 12, 31, 33 f., 37, 49, 63, 65,
  125 f., 143 f., 155 f., 200 f.; *X.6*
 and semantical elementary sentences
  126, 144, 205
  function of *X.6*
 epistemological basic 206
 false see False
 as facts see Sentence-token
 fictitious *VII.9* (cf. 205)
 logical see Logic
 logical basic 204, 206
 meaning of see Sense, Picture Theory
  sentence meaning, problem of, *VII.3*
 meaningful 6, 65, 117, 143 f., 178, 182,
  218, 220
  general form of 6; *VIII.6*
 and names see Names
  vs. enumerations of names 128, 130
 as pictures see Picture Theory
 semantical elementary 126 f., 156, 196,
  203 *and passim*
 semantical primitive 203 f.
 syntactical elementary 195 f.
Sentence-radical 159, 175
 direction of 172, 174
 and modal component *IX.1*
 notation for 162–4
 as a picture *IX.3*; 175
 semantics of *IX.3,4*
Sentence-token 9 n., 55, 129
 as a fact 130–20; *VII.6*; 185, 193
 and sentence 129, 135 f.
 syntactically correct analysis of *VII6*;
  191–5
Show 99, 130, 136, 141, 148, 151, 158,
  160 f., 220, 222 f.
 and exhibit 178 f.
 and say see Say
 externally vs. internally 179–81, 198–
  203
Shwayder 31 n. 2
Signs, symbols, expressions
 deputizing *VII.7*; *VIII.1*; 170
 logical see Logical
 primitive and defined 65, 122–5
 simple 65, 125, 155
 symbols (expressions) in Wittgenstein's sense 68, 79, 133 n., 188 f.
 unsaturated 138 n., 193
Signification (symbolizing), way of 188
Signify
 directly vs. indirectly 65, 122–4, 200,
  205

*Sinn* (sense, direction) 121; *IX.7*
Solipsism 221 f.
*Spielraum* (range) of a state of affairs 57
Spinoza 214 n.
State of affairs
 atomic 12, 33; *III,3–5*
  and atomic facts 29, 31 f., 35
  existent and non-existent 12, 30–2,
   35 f.; *III.5*
  in a relative sense 53
  and elementary sentences see Sentences
 independent vs. logically connected
  see Logical independence
 inner structure of 61–3, 132 f.
 system of all 49 and *passim*
  priority of 50, 52, 65
  and substance *V. 3–7*
 elementary 90, 126, 186
 in general (cf. World, possible) 30,
  33; *III.4*; 53, 67
  vs. atomic states of affairs 30; *III.2*;
   34 f., 37
  vs. facts 30, 32; *III.4*
 (merely) possible 53, 99, 114–6,
  127, 202
 range of 57
 and (piece of) reality 35, 51, 53
 in relation to an articulate field 33,
  90
Stenius 19 n., 132 n., 139 n.
Structure
 categorial, of a system of elements 92,
  100
  identity in, between an isomorphic
   picture and its prototype 92,
   100 f., 130 f., 180
 of 'language' 188, 194–6
 of 'reality' (as 'shown' by 'language')
  180, 188, 193–8
 and content 80 f., 94; *VI.9,10*; 110
 descriptive 175
 external (of an articulate field) 71, 79,
  81, 90, 100, 166, 208 (cf. *II.4,5*)
  identity in, between isomorphic
   systems 93 f., 96, 103 n.
  as shown by a picture 95 f., 99;
   *VI.8,9*; 148, 166, 178–81
  of a sentence-token (cf. Syntax,
   logical), *VII.6*; 181
 internal (cf. Form, logical) 71, 79 f., 90
  vs. categorial structure 91 f., 101 f.,
   106–8 (cf. 71 f., 75)
  description of 71, 73–5, 78
  in an extended sense 182, 198
  identity in, between a logically
   adequate picture and its prototype 103; *VI.8*; 179–85 (cf. 91 f.)
  of 'language' 177, 181 f., 194 f.,
   198 f.

Structure, internal (*Continued*)—
    of 'reality' (as 'shown' by 'language'),
        177; *X.2*; 185 f., 188, 194; *X.5*;
        206, 208, 213, 219, 224
    'logical', in an unspecified sense *IV*;
        177, 189 (cf. *II.4,5*)
    pure, 110, 205
Subject, metaphysical see Ego
Subjects, logical, of a sentence-token (cf.
    Objects, syntactical) 134–9, 149, 187
Substance (cf. 'Things'), *V*; 90, 112, 116
    apriority of (cf. Framework; Logical
        space; States of affairs, atomic) 66;
        *V.10*; 219
    Aristotelian category of 21 f., 66 n. 2
    common to all possible worlds 66, 80;
        *V.10*; 116, 219
    internal structure of see Structure
    logical form of see Form
    and logical space *V.5–7*
    as persistent *V.9*
    and the system of all atomic states of
        affairs *V.3–7*
    = the totality of all 'things' 66, 71, 74,
        84, 155
Substitution, possible 207
Superstition 59 f.
Supposition 162 n.
Symbols see Signs
'Syntactical statements' (Carnap) 183
Syntax, logical 133, 183; *X.4*; 207 f., 212
    (cf. 78)
    in a narrow and in a wide sense 197
    as a logically correct syntax of a
        language 133 f., 191–4, 207
    as the syntax of a logically perfect
        language 189–91
    and formal logic 197
    rules of 184, 191, 194 f., 197
Synthetic propositions *a priori* 214; *XI.1*
    (cf. *IV.9*; 104 f.)


*Tatsache* (=fact) 6, 22, 29; *III.1,4*; 48
Tautology 57; *X.9*
    two senses of 76, 201 f., 219
That-clauses 164
Thing in itself (cf. *Ding an sich*) 23, 27, 68
Things, individual see Objects
'Things' in Wittgenstein's sense 61, 223
    *and passim*
    categories of *V.1,5*; 132 f.
    as elements of the world (cf. Substance)
        *V.8*; 84, 116, 155 (cf. *II.4,5*; *VI.2*)
    (logical) form of see Form, logical
    independence and non-independence
        of (cf. Complementarity) *V.4*; 138 n.
    persistence of *V.9*

'Things' (*Continued*)
    simpleness (logical atomicity) of *V.2*;
        76; *VI.2*; *VII.2*; 143, 200
Thinkable 116, 202, 218 f.
Thinking, thought 6; *VI.13*; 202, 218–20
Transcendent, Transcendental 216–8,
    221–4
'True' and 'False', meaning of 53 n., 145,
    150, 165–7
Truth
    correspondence theory of 167
    modal and descriptive *IX.4–6*
Truth-conditions, tautological 76
Truth-functions 5, 11, 56 f., 146; *VIII.3*;
    155 f., 166
Truth-grounds 151 f.
Truth-possibilities 76 n., 150–2
Truth-values 6, 150, 159, 166
Types, theory of 21–2, 68; *X.7*


*Unaussprechlich* (inexpressible, ineffable)
    223
Universals 21 n. 3
*Unsinnig* (nonsensical, anti-sensical) 22
Urmson 137, 213, 221 nn. 2, 3


Variables *X.7*
*Verbindung* (connection, combination)
    61 n., 119 n.
*Verkettung* (concatenation) 63
*vertreten* (deputize) 97, 201
*vorstellen* (depict) 88, 98, 140


*Wahrheitsfunktion* (truth-function) 5
*Wahrnehmung* (Kant) 215
Waismann 42 n., 57 n. 2, 155 n., 219 n.
Weiler 2 n.
*Welt* (world) 22; *IV.6*
What and How 224
*Wirklichkeit* (reality, piece of reality) 35,
    51
Wisdom 131 n.
Words 129
World
    as a fact *II*; 84 f., 97
        vs. world as a thing 22, 27 f.
    and piece of reality *IV.6*
Worlds, possible 38, 40, 43–5; *IV.7*; 54,
    66, 84, 155, 217
von Wright 13 n., 162, 163 n., 214 n.


*Zeichen* (sign) 188
*Zeigen* (show) 178 f.

## (ii) Passages from Wittgenstein's Writings

*Tractatus:*

| | |
|---|---|
| *1.* | 1, 5–7, 9, 18, 22, 26, 28 |
| *1.1* | 7, 9, 15, 18, 22, 26, 28, 31, 35, 61 |
| *1.11* | 35, 48–50 |
| *1.12* | 9, 31, 43, 48–51 |
| *1.13* | 14 f., 42, 48–50 |
| *1.2* | 7, 18, 26, 28, 35 |
| *1.21* | 34 |
| *2.* | 5 f., 8, 10, 29, 31, 35 f., 48, 50, 70 |
| *2.01* | 8 f., 61-3, 119 n. |
| *2.011* | 64 |
| *2.012* | 67 |
| *2.0121* | 67, 77 |
| *2.0122* | 68 |
| *2.01231* | 68, 118 n. |
| *2.0124* | 66 f., 84 |
| *2.013* | 15, 67 |
| *2.0131* | 15, 77 |
| *2.014* | 73 |
| *2.0141* | 67, 72, 133 n. |
| *2.02* | 8 f., 64 |
| *2.0201* | 64–6 |
| *2.021* | 66 |
| *2.0211* | 66 |
| *2.0212* | 89, 116 |
| *2.022* | 84 |
| *2.023* | 84 |
| *2.0231* | 36, 66, 68, 79 |
| *2.0233* | 67 n., 81 n. |
| *2.024* | 66. 80 f. |
| *2.025* | 79 |
| *2.0251* | 77 |
| *2.0271* | 82 |
| *2.0272* | 63 |
| *2.03* | 8 f., 63, 133 |
| *2.031* | 98 |
| *2.034* | 31 |
| *2.04* | 8 f., 31, 51 |
| *2.05* | 8 f., 31, 51 |
| *2.06* | 9, 32, 35, 36 n., 51 |
| *2.061* | 34, 58 |
| *2.062* | 34, 58 |
| *2.063* | 35, 51 f. |
| *2.1* | 7–9, 88 f., 117 |

*Tractatus:*

| | |
|---|---|
| *2.11* | 15, 53, 88 f., 91 |
| *2.12* | 88 f., 117 |
| *2.13* | 97 |
| *2.131* | 97, 130 |
| *2.14* | 97 f. |
| *2.141* | 97 f. |
| *2.15* | 98 f. |
| *2.151* | 99, 102, 104 |
| *2.1513* | 97 f. |
| *2.1514* | 97 f. |
| *2.17* | 89, 99 f. |
| *2.171* | 101, *cf.* 108 |
| *2.172* | 179 |
| *2.18* | 106 |
| *2.181* | 101 |
| *2.182* | 101 f., 106 |
| *2.19* | 101 |
| *2.2* | 7 f., 101 |
| *2.201* | 99 |
| *2.203* | 32, 99, 114 |
| *2.21* | 89, 96 |
| *2.22* | 99 |
| *2.221* | 99 |
| *2.222* | 96 |
| *2.223* | 97 |
| *2.224* | 103–5 |
| *2.225* | 103–5 |
| *3.* | 5 f., 10 f., 112, 117 |
| *3.001* | 114, 116 |
| *3.01* | 9 f. |
| *3.02* | 10, 114, 116 |
| *3.03* | 10, 114, 116 |
| *3.04* | 10 |
| *3.05* | 10 |
| *3.1* | 9 f., 117 |
| *3.11* | 32, 128 f. |
| *3.12* | 128 f. |
| *3.13* | 79, 109 n., 129 |
| *3.14* | 128 f., 133 f. |
| *3.141* | 129 |
| *3.142* | 128 |
| *3.143* | 193 |
| *3.1431* | 137 n. |
| *3.1432* | 126, 132 |
| *3.144* | 118, 120, 128, 171, 173 |
| *3.2* | 9, 129 |
| *3.201* | 121, 129 |

*Tractatus:*

| | |
|---|---|
| *3.202* | 121, 125, 129 |
| *3.203* | 120 f., 129, 147 |
| *3.21* | 130 |
| *3.22* | 63, 130, 135 |
| *3.24* | 65 |
| *3.25* | 65, 122, 155 |
| *3.26* | 65, 122 |
| *3.261* | 65, 121–3 |
| *3.3* | 9, 118, 128 |
| *3.31* | 68, 79, 133 n., 188 |
| *3.317* | 133 n., 190 |
| *3.32* | 188 |
| *3.321* | 121, 188 |
| *3.323* | 189 |
| *3.324* | 189 |
| *3.325* | 189 f., 192 |
| *3.327* | 190 |
| *3.328* | 46 |
| *3.33* | 190 |
| *3.331* | 190, 207 |
| *3.332* | 207 |
| *3.333* | 207 |
| *3.3411* | 125 |
| *3.3441* | 125 |
| *3.4* | 9, 15, 55 |
| *3.41* | 55 |
| *3.411* | 55 |
| *3.42* | 15, 56, 115 n. |
| *3.5* | 9 |
| *4.* | 5 f., 8 n., 10–12, 117 |
| *4.002* | 153, 200 |
| *4.003* | 208, 222 |
| *4.0031* | 2 n., 226 |
| *4.01* | 11, 117, 143 |
| *4.011* | 117 |
| *4.012* | 132 |
| *4.014* | 118 |
| *4.0141* | 118 |
| *4.015* | 118 |
| *4.016* | 11, 137 n. |
| *4.02* | 11, 127 |
| *4.022* | 130, 148, 160 f., 166, 178 |
| *4.024* | 127, 130 |
| *4.026* | 127 |
| *4.027* | **127** |
| *4.03* | **127, 137** |

*Tractatus:*

| | |
|---|---|
| 4.031 | 141, 158 |
| 4.0311 | 137 |
| 4.0312 | 144 f. |
| 4.04 | 92 n., 113 n. |
| 4.0412 | 92 n. |
| 4.061 | 148 n. |
| 4.062 | 173 |
| 4.0621 | 148 |
| 4.063 | 145 |
| 4.064 | 148, 171 f. |
| 4.0641 | 56, 148 n. |
| 4.1 | 11 f. |
| 4.111 | 226 |
| 4.112 | 209 |
| 4.113 | 218 |
| 4.114 | 218 |
| 4.115 | 218 |
| 4.12 | 178 f. |
| 4.121 | 178 f. |
| 4.1211 | 190 |
| 4.1212 | 178 |
| 4.122 | 69 n., 118 n., 182 |
| 4.123 | 72, 76 f. |
| 4.124 | 207 |
| 4.1272 | 206 |
| 4.2 | 12 |
| 4.21 | 33, 143 |
| 4.211 | 34, 58 |
| 4.22 | 63, 119 n. |
| 4.221 | 63, 65, 69, 119 n., 125, 128 |
| 4.2211 | 31, 63, 65 |
| 4.24 | 55, 126 |
| 4.242 | 154 |
| 4.25 | 31 |
| 4.3 | 76, 150 |
| 4.441 | 145 |
| 4.442 | 170 |
| 4.46 | 76 |
| 4.461 | 210 |
| 4.463 | 15, 57 f. |
| 5. | 5 f., 8 n., 11–13, 55, 56 n., 143, 146 |
| 5.1 | 12 f. |
| 5.101 | 57 n., 151 |
| 5.134 | 58 f. |
| 5.135 | 58 f. |
| 5.136 | 59 |
| 5.1361 | 59 f. |
| 5.1362 | 222 n. |

*Tractatus:*

| | |
|---|---|
| 5.15 | 13 |
| 5.156 | 13 |
| 5.2341 | 171 f. |
| 5.4 | 145 |
| 5.42 | 123 n., 145 |
| 5.43 | 210 |
| 5.473 | 192 f. |
| 5.4732 | 193 |
| 5.47321 | 46 |
| 5.4733 | 192 f. |
| 5.475 | 92 n. |
| 5.5151 | 147, 172 n., 173 n. |
| 5.521 | 153 |
| 5.523 | 153 |
| 5.524 | 154 |
| 5.53 | 155 |
| 5.5301 | 154 |
| 5.5302 | 155 |
| 5.5423 | 26 |
| 5.55 | 85 |
| 5.551 | 85 |
| 5.552 | 86, 224 |
| 5.5541 | 86 |
| 5.5542 | 86 |
| 5.5562 | 85 |
| 5.5562 | 85 |
| 5.5563 | 85, 192 |
| 5.557 | 86 |
| 5.5571 | 85 |
| 5.6 | 221 |
| 5.62 | 221 |
| 5.631 | 221 |
| 5.632 | 221 |
| 5.633 | 221 |
| 5.6331 | 221 |
| 5.64 | 222 |
| 6. | 5 f., 12 f., 143, 156 |
| 6.1 | 13, 76 |
| 6.12 | 201 |
| 6.1202 | 201 |
| 6.124 | 197, 199, 201 |
| 6.13 | 218 |
| 6.2 | 13, 219 |
| 6.21 | 219 |
| 6.233 | 219 |
| 6.3 | 13, 219 |
| 6.31 | 219 |
| 6.32 | 219 |
| 6.321 | 219 |
| 6.3211 | 219 |

*Tractatus:*

| | |
|---|---|
| 6.36 | 220 |
| 6.361 | 220 |
| 6.362 | 220 |
| 6.36311 | 59 f. |
| 6.37 | 59 f. |
| 6.3751 | 42, 47 |
| 6.4 | 13, 222 n. |
| 6.421 | 222 |
| 6.423 | 222 |
| 6.4312 | 223 |
| 6.432 | 222, 224 |
| 6.4321 | 223 |
| 6.44 | 224 |
| 6.45 | 223 |
| 6.5 | 14, 222 |
| 6.52 | 225 |
| 6.521 | 225 |
| 6.522 | 222 . |
| 6.53 | 225 |
| 6.54 | 2, 17, 209, 224 |
| 7. | 1, 5 f., 13, 225 |

Preface

| | |
|---|---|
| | 1–3, 5, 13, 16, 220 |

Log. Form

| | |
|---|---|
| | 42, 47 n., 76 n. |

*Phil. Inv.*

| | |
|---|---|
| | 16 |
| § 1 | 118 |
| § 22 | 158–72 |
| § 23 | 175 |
| § 24 | 158 |
| § 40 | 122 |
| § 43 | 138 |
| § 46 | 62 n., 84 |
| § 48 | 62 n. |
| § 55 | 66 n. |
| § 57 | 139 n. |
| § 58 | 139 n. |
| § 133 | 226 |
| § 522 | 109 n. |

Notes on Logic

| | |
|---|---|
| | 132 n., 158 n., 165 n., 170 n., 171 n. |

*Blue Book*

| | |
|---|---|
| | 139 n. |

Notes dictated to Moore

| | |
|---|---|
| | 132 n., 136 n. |